Behind the
Red Curtain

a Memoir

Hồng-Mỹ Basrai

Los Nietos Press

Downey California 2020

Cover Art: Havannah Tran
Excerpt from "There Are Things to be Said" used with permission of
    Bob Arnold, literary executor for Cid Corman

Published in the United States by Los Nietos Press
Downey, CA 90240
www.LosNietosPress.com
LosNietosPress@gmail.com

Library of Congress Control Number: 2020900145

First Edition
ISBN-13: 978-0-9984036-9-4 (hardcover)
ISBN-13: 978-0-9984036-6-3 (paperback)

2 3 4 5 6 7 8 9 10 11 12 13 14 15

This book was written with the following people in mind:

My beloved parents, Lê Đăng Khoa & Hoàng Lệ Quân

My husband Shabbir Basrai who, through his patience and love, helped rebuild my confidence. And my beautiful children, Jauhar, Diya, & Tanisha

My eight siblings who challenged me to reach for the impossible

And all the people aspiring for freedom

Contents

Behind the Red Curtain

Prologue

In 1975, after thirty years of ideological conflict, South Vietnam finally succumbed to the communists of the North.

America pulled out its last soldiers and government officers.

The rich and well connected were flown out of the country to better skies.

Many destitute people with nothing to lose were able to escape not only a country in turmoil but also a condemned life without opportunity.

Amidst the chaos and confusion, many other families were still scrambling to gather resources, delaying their departures in the belief that Saigon would be saved, and they would not have to leave everything behind. Even if they had to leave, they reasoned, there was still time. And the departures would be orderly, well-coordinated, and safe.

Part 1

1975-1978

1.

1975: Year of the Cat

March returned to Saigon with the colors of spring and my thirteenth birthday. For some time, after hiding beneath my skin like two seeds under the brown soil, my breasts had budded. The small button roses were now visible through the thin white cotton of my uniform shirt, a dull pain under fingers.

Soon, it would be impossible to hide the evidence of my transformation behind the large pockets of my school shirt, and parading around braless would be inappropriate. I would have to tell her. My courage evaporated at the mere prospect of mentioning "breasts" to my mother, much less asking her to buy me—*how absurd!*—the hard, pointy contraption women wore underneath their blouses. Lowering her reading glasses down the bridge of her nose, she would refocus her brown, piercing eyes and scan my chest with interest. She would ask intrusive questions, want to see *them*. She would surely discuss *them, vú,* over dinner, calling them as they were and not just hinting, and I would have to endure my brother's and sisters' mockery. *She has vú . . . . She has big vú.* No! I would rather die.

Let me devote myself to better contemplations—my birthday, for example.

March 26, also the Fields for Farmers national holiday—*Ngày Người Cày Có Ruộng*—was fast approaching. Already, banners and flags were flapping in the streets of Saigon. But who cared about the

Land Grant Act? What bounced up and down my mind were my birthday invitation cards and gifts. I thought, I should pour my preoccupation into Dad's ears. Around this time each year, I had to sweet-talk him, but: "Ask and thou shall receive." I had succeeded a couple of times. Besides, to my advantage, none of my eight siblings cared as much about their birthdays. To them, a year more or less was just the same. Chị Mai—my parents' firstborn, hotheaded, as full of bravado as I of shyness—who was a horoscope cycle older than me and therefore also a tiger, had her first *boum* at age eighteen. But that didn't count. The grand affair we celebrated wasn't just a birthday but, in Mom's plain terms, her debutante ball.

That day, strings of triangular flags had garlanded our courtyard. The minuscule kites with their noses upturned and loose tails waving happily were advertisement materials for Esso, where Dad worked. A cardboard Esso man, his droplet-shaped head wearing a smile, stood guard by the main gate in all his endearing cardboard charm. It would be hard to ask for a fancier party.

With the last of my five older siblings departed to study abroad, I had ascended the rank to finally become the oldest child at home. This year, I had serious reasons to celebrate elaborately. Cake, decorations, gifts, candles, balloons—I desired them all. Maybe I should also ask for a new dress. And leather pumps. One such pair, with satin lace at the ankles like Cinderella's glass slippers, was displayed at Bata, the best shoe store in downtown Saigon.

I had thought of many possibilities, dreams of gifts and fun. Alas! I should have asked a more relevant question like, What would 1975 bring to me as a year? I had thought of changes—of growing pains, relationship with boys, responsibilities, but I was too young to think of the unthinkable—of dark, malevolent storms brewing over the fate of my country.

As the calendar pages peeled off, a somber mood descended on the population. I saw tension on the faces of the adults. The news was grim; pictures of slain, mutilated soldiers and civilians flashed daily on the television. In black and white the red did not show, but you knew it was blood because it stained the torn shirts on lifeless bodies splayed in odd angles. Faces up with eyes wide open. Faces down on limbless corpses. Babies crying over dead mothers. Families fleeing on foot shouldering their belongings, children in baskets at two ends of carrying poles, in the background always the mourning tune of "The Exodus Song."

The sounds of the war did not stop with the television shut off, but droned on the radio day and night and reverberated in the people's conversations. The thirty-year civil war between North and South had finally reached the doorsteps of Saigon with all its horror.

At school, we drilled for emergency evacuation in preparation for bombing raids—what to do if we were caught in an upstairs classroom, where to assemble when the siren sounded, who would be assisting our science teacher, Ms. Thanh-Cảnh, that year burdened with pregnancy. Truthfully speaking, it was an exciting time for us. We were glad of the disruption in our routines. Instead of fear, doomsday appealed to us in all its romantic tragedy. We hurried to exchange *Cahier de Souvenirs* and collect farewell notes from friends in a frenzy before the school term wrapped up.

What we experienced wasn't clearly defined, veiled over with childish hope of a happy ending like in books or movies. Our national conflict was at a climax, but everything would resolve. It always did. Oliver Twist was back in the protective home of Mr. Brownlow. The Von Trapp family reached the Switzerland border, singing.

The swift collapse of the republic in the last two months must be all fabrication, dramatized by the media for effect. The first waves of evacuees from various parts of the South caused confusion and then, for the first time, panic in people like my parents, people who had been too busy raising their families, too naïve in politics, uninformed, trusting their government and the might of America. Still, they continued to be in denial. Saigon would never fail, could not. America was on our side, and America was undefeatable. This faith, this unshakable belief, was so firmly planted in these Vietnamese minds that there was no place for truth. Had they only opened their eyes, they would have seen plainly that we had been long abandoned; our last lines of defense stood no chance against the fast-advancing enemy. From the beginning, this contest for lands had been between two superpowers. One persevered. The other had lost interest.

Looking back thirty years later, we realized our parents had sadly missed the cues. Nixon had shaken China's hand. South Vietnam was only a token piece, and was no longer needed on the world map. In a way, their faith and hope were as childish as my own at thirteen.

Then, I thought, it was just another public hysteria, like in an epidemic that passed through some years ago. Every time one of us came down with a fever, we were quarantined for days under Mom's anxious eyes. But nothing had ever happened. Those who succumbed were not family members or friends and, in the end, there were no lasting consequences. The same pessimism had returned, surreal, a little more urgent, much scarier—the preparation to save lives, even the reality of packing our bags—but at worst, it would be like another Tết Mậu Thân (Tết Offensive). Grandma would bring home sandbags and have a bomb shelter built under her staircase. We might do the same, or run over to her place. I remembered the scene of that New Year clearly. Dad was away on a business voyage to Hong Kong, and that night, the explosions from the Việt-Cộng's attack had lit up the night sky like a firework. Michelle was still a tiny baby strapped to Mom's belly when we ran to Grandma for shelter, terrified.

My apprehension was quickly dismissed. Let the adults fear. Let them plan for doomsday, so we all would fly away from Vietnam. I secretly wished the war would worsen. What else would I hope for, at barely thirteen, but to exchange backward Vietnam for a more glamorous country: Belgium? France, with Paris, the City of Light? We would definitely go, I told my friends with airs. How lucky, they all said. Most of my friends were Southerners. Their families had no idea about the communists. Having fled communism from the North once, my parents knew better. We had to leave. I thanked my stars for this once-in-a-lifetime opportunity to go abroad so early on. A realized dream.

My older brothers and sisters had to work hard all twelve years of school. To study abroad they had to pass the Baccalaureate with high Mentions. I was so fortunate that fate was doing me the favor of speeding things up.

* * *

Summer vacation started in mid-April, two months ahead of the school schedule. Oh joy! I would have all the time in the world to pack for the four of us. Paris would be our destination, Dad had said. "So pack appropriately," Mom added, dumping the thick woolen wares she had ordered from Aunt Giáp, whose family made machine-knitted sweaters for a living.

In a way, having a mother who was not too fussy over the details of our lives suited me well in a time like this. I preferred to have complete control over the arrangement of our valises. Free from the demand of school, I enjoyed my task thoroughly. But I soon found out that packing to move away wasn't as simple as I had first imagined. Folding and refolding our clothes, I had trouble fitting in everything we wanted to bring with us—and that meant everything, since we would not be coming back. Cold-climate essentials like the assortment of colorful turtleneck sweaters—so bulky they wouldn't stay flat—plus knit caps, gloves, and woolen socks quickly filled all the available space. But what to do with our valuable keepsakes? My diaries and book collection? My mother's portrait that hung large in the living room? Would it be left behind for strangers to do whatever with? I thought about mentioning things like that to Mom, but I guessed she wouldn't have time nor the temperament to deal with such details in this time of turmoil. And our beloved dog, Pijou—where would he go? With regret I decided to leave my books at home and let my brother Patrick bring his plastic pistol. No, not his long sword. My ten-year-old second-youngest sister, Anne, would not let me take away her precious doll. "Yes, bring it," I said to her.

"And our *banh đũa*?" Little Michelle, my youngest sister, reminded me about the ball-and-stick game we favored. "Of course," I said. Twelve chopsticks and a tennis ball could be inserted almost anywhere. "Are we not coming back? Forever and ever?" asked Michelle, again wanting my attention. "For ever and ever," I confirmed with a twinge, suddenly stricken by the finality of my tone.

I would not see this room again, where we had all grown up from babyhood. There was the humongous pegboard Dad had mounted one day on the wall for us to hang our drawings on, filled with our handmade art and my favorite quotations. Inside our dresser hid a stuffed monkey, Dad's gift to me. I had cherished my toy until the day I brought it to my favorite cousins to show it off, and their mom, Aunt Mục, had exclaimed, "Who in their right mind would bring home a bad-luck thing like that?"

April 27th. Done with packing and nothing else to do, I sought my maids' companionship in our kitchen. Situated at the back of our villa, it abutted our neighbor's house, from which we could clearly hear women talking, their laughter, and a sewing machine rattling, and where, if we had wanted to, when the fluorescent-tube light shone bright against the night sky, we could easily spy into their upper room, standing on the large roofed balcony off Mom's bedroom. Our kitchen was mopped twice a day, and sunlight bounced off its red tile floor.

"Don't stand there in the crosswind; you'll get sick" was our maids' constant nagging when I bounced down into their world. They were right. On windy days, you were buffeted like a sail in a storm. Around the house, the shutters of doors and windows banged violently, sending the maids first to one side, then to the other, in a frenzy to close them.

A small brick patio linked the Bùi Thị Xuân Street side of the kitchen to the maids' chamber. On the Trương Minh Ký Street side, through a screen door, also double-shuttered against the elements, a small concrete pad led to what we used to call "the laundry room," then years later, "Ancient Grandma's house." This building, with its own kitchen and bathroom, had been added for our maternal great-grandma, or Ancient Grandma. She moved in one day and lived glued to her bed, a morbid presence. Deranged, hateful, she shuffled like a shadow about her bed guarding her box of money—fake coins, just to satisfy her need to count it—an old habit she never grew out of. We were terrible to her, her craziness, her shouting "Thief!" at anyone passing by. We often threw water through her window and aggravated her for mere pleasure.

After Ancient Grandma's death, her house was turned into our game room. Dad put in a large foosball table, and all of the kids in our Lê clan spent many happy hours gathered there in matches of twos or fours—rodding, trapping, pinning, slamming a rubber ball from one end of the table to the other, trying to score goals in whatever manner—even spinning, though it was against the rules. It was a place where sheer madness was allowed; hooting, howling, roaring accompanied the rushing of a ball down the wooden slot as someone made a victorious goal. The younger children, too short to reach the rods, played nearby, running back and forth between their own circle and the larger circle of foosball players and spectators.

Our family shrank as my older brothers and sisters, one by one, left to go abroad. The game room, no longer of use, slowly deteriorated into junk storage, where an unused baby crib sat amidst broken furniture and old photo frames.

But our kitchen took on the central role in our life.

To this place, where our noses were always greeted with a whiff of fresh-cooked food, a girl of thirteen often came seeking solace in her helpers and their answers to her zillion questions on hot, lonely afternoons. She would half-reveal to them her teen secrets, matters she did not feel comfortable opening up about to her own parents or even to her friends: the longing for romantic love, the first attraction to boys, beauty tips, family gossip .... That girl, who began looking at her reflection in the mirror with critical self-evaluation, who would rather not pick up the black telephone receiver to dial her closest girlfriend to say, "I caught him looking at me, and it felt like lightning when our eyes met," whose body manifested troubling desire for a stronger love—that girl was me, sprouting breasts and hair in all possible places of my one-meter-fifty, forty-kilogram body.

I chose the grownup points of view and advice of my three maids instead. A bit older than myself, they were my friends and older sisters at home. They were country girls growing up in the South, personally referred to my mom. They lived with my family and rarely took holidays, saving their vacations for the long Lunar New Year breaks. Loyal and loving, they would deny their lives' comfort for us; our priorities were their own. All three had learned to read and write, an exception to the norm—most country folks were illiterate. Chị Sáu, who was bright and the most effective helper, became a sort of assistant to my mother, splitting her duties between our home and my mom's pharmacy, where she functioned as a clerk, working at the cash register, and rearranging the medicine cabinets. She was even allowed to dispense common remedies, including aspirin and most-prescribed drugs.

Chị Bảy, our main cook, who spoke with a heavy Quảng-Ngãi accent, was sweet-natured and easily teased. She wasn't as bossy as Chị Sáu.

Chị Dệ, oldest and ugliest, her sad face pockmarked, looked after the babies of the family, Anne and Michelle, born a year apart. For three meals a day she ran, bowl in hand, after my two little sisters and even Patrick to spoon-feed them while they played. Engrossed in their games, the kids soon stuffed their cheeks with the hated nourishment that was forced into their mouths.

From day one, Mom had instructed her young hires to address us as "Missy" and "Mister." However friendly our relationship was, not once did we stray from this distinction. A pampered doll I might be sometimes, but at all times the maids were to submit to my will and power. At thirteen, I knew my boundaries, too, having been taught to be considerate and compassionate with all alike. It was to these sweet sisters that I ran for my first feminine lessons: what to expect at menstruation, what is normal and not, what pad to use, is it true that after a girl gets her period she can get pregnant sitting on a chair a guy has sat on . . . . I drank in their wisdom as well as age-old myths. I had, fortunately, somebody besides my own mother to whisper to, because I'd rather die bleeding than mention my periods to her.

Mom and Dad had full-time jobs. An engineer, Dad worked from seven to four-thirty Monday through Friday as Esso's marketing and business director. Mom was a pharmacist with her own drugstore.

And that made me the only girl in all my classes to have a mother working full time and, sadly, unavailable to cater to my girlish needs. By the time I entered sixth grade in 1973, she had also ventured into manufacturing animal feed. The business started out as a mad idea from Uncle Chấn, her brother. He noticed that breweries' discards were dumped daily by the truckload. And what were they? Barley, wheat, or corn—stuff that cattle would eat, perhaps. Why not? These could be used to substitute expensive grains that had to be purchased, while the breweries' waste could be obtained free. At first, the brother and sister set up a small production line to make sample products, which they began giving out to cattle farms around Saigon. Mom also wanted to try the new products on her own livestock. A hole was cut into a wall of our above-ground swimming pool and a wooden door installed and, voila, in the place of a pool we had a pigsty and two pink piglets raised on Mom's new brand of farm food.

Within months, the mere business idea had morphed into a lucrative opportunity. On top of managing her pharmacy, my bounce-back-doll mother also ran a manufacturing production plant in Bình Tây. It took guts. It took faith. It also took boundless courage and energy, but Mom possessed all of these. Her first litter of five children was studying in three countries: Belgium, France, and the USA. The expense associated with their education was astronomical, even for two young professionals. She couldn't say no to extra money. It was imperative to launch full steam into money-making. Her strategy? She unloaded her motherly duties at home to the three housekeepers. The schools would teach us all the necessary skills. In the long run, she reasoned, money would help propel the family into a better future.

Meanwhile, we had cages of hatchlings in the game room, chickens running in the yard, and snorting pigs instead of water in our pool. Our household staff doubled to include, besides the maid whom we called Chị Phấn, a boy of sixteen named Kỉa and two chauffeurs: Bác Dậu, who was an older, jovial man thrice married, and Chú Tuấn, a handsome young man.

The introduction of livestock and men into the household

completely changed the dynamic of our family. Throughout the day we had lots of people in and out of our gates, cars pulling in and taking off, loading up and dropping off stinky bags of wet *hèm*, the animal food my mother produced from fermented barley. Often, Chị Phấn, hired to mind the animals, was seen chasing pigs with a broom through the living room and shouting to both pigs and dogs, who joined in the game of pursuit, barking furiously.

Soon enough, under my very eyes, were scenes of men chasing maids in a new game we had never witnessed: the love pursuit. Romance blossomed between the young Chú Tuấn and Chị Sáu. In Chị Bảy's eyes, her bedmate's new love was an act of infidelity, and occasionally, in fits of bitter jealousy, she dumped all of Chị Sáu's belongings in the yard for the pigs to trample on.

Nonetheless, missives, through my facilitation, flew back and forth between the two lovers. His were written in a flowery script and an even more flowery language, hers with my suggestions to add a flair of literature. Chị Sáu read each letter hungrily, then, as I begged and threatened to cut off my messenger service, the private sentimental declarations were shared with me. I devoured them, word by word. They often went like this:

My love, eternal apple of my eyes
My hand was trembling at the mention of your name. My heart beat wildly at the sight of your lovely silhouette. I stared into the night, unable to fall asleep, longing for your beautiful appearance . . .

I was in love heaven!

My parents were knee deep in their careers' most productive years and hardly looked up to watch for the signs of national turmoil. My mother wasn't a reader; she was a woman of action—a maker and a doer. But my father, who loved to read and who read the daily news on his way to work, should have spent a fraction of his time following world news. Both should have paid more attention to the rumors to know that even President Thiệu was cashing in his last chips. South Vietnam was about to be wiped off the map. The future of the Lê Đăng family, the future that Mom and Dad had been painstakingly building together, brick by brick, child after child, would be altered completely in merely 48 hours. In hindsight, I see this as clearly as I had seen our kitchen that morning of April 28, 1975, already chaotic, already different from the day before.

Our maids, driven almost to insanity, labored against time to cook and pack. Steamed rice was smashed, shaped into buns, and loaded into bags. In a large pot, heavily salted pork stewed in fish sauce was waiting. The last bag of our journey West was ready. Now, we could talk. But what else worried them? Why the lines on their foreheads? Why those lost eyes staring at me dumbly, faces blood-strained? I was too young to understand, too excited about leaving. How could I have any notions of what life under communism would be like, would have in store for all of us, for them? Our maids and people like them were our country's poorest who relied on the richer population for employment and some measure of safety, to survive. Unlike my parents, they had nothing stashed away. They had us, their surrogate family, their protector and provider. Without an employer, they would be jobless in a city of thousands of jobless maids. Not knowing that I would be, in this time of sorrow, an extra burden, and having nowhere else to go to calm my nerves, I intruded.

"I've come to say goodbye," I began, in my awkward teenager's way, the farewell I lately dreamed of, and then suddenly, moved by the meaning of my very words, I burst into tears. As if on cue, the three maids started sobbing. They wailed louder as each one joined in.

"Take care of yourself," Chị Sáu said, sobbing and dabbing. "I'll remember my princess . . . always!"

My pent-up emotion now appeased by the release of tears, my thoughts already far into the days to come, I saw myself in that distant land where people ate chocolate and apples daily, where little girls wore coats to school and walked in the white snow. I saw myself a princess, truly in a princess' kingdom, where there would be no mosquitoes, no cockroaches or rats, where dogs and cats wore collars and slept on rugs. I realized how lucky I was, compared to my helpers just a few years older but born under worse stars. I felt guilty for my melodramatic tears. No, I wasn't at all sad for leaving my home, my dog, my land, my country, my whole universe for that matter. To recompense them, I offered a bright promise: "I'll send you good things from over there."

Two ear-splitting blasts jolted us. Explosions shook the ground. *Boom. Boom.* My mother's footsteps scraped down the stairs, her voice panicky, "Children . . . ." The attack sounded much too close; we should not have lingered. Just a few blocks from our home, in the direction of the international airport Tân Sơn Nhất, dark, thick smoke rose into the sky. Sirens blared, stopped and blared again, unrelenting. The chauffeurs scrambled to get our belongings into the cars. Car trunk lids slammed down.

"Where's Dad?" Mom kept asking. "We have to leave. It's getting too dangerous."

But Dad was away at work. The ground attack was growing worse while we waited for him, Mom pacing, on edge. She hollered at the maids to hurry. They had done all they could, and there was nothing else to do but wait for our departure. The panic in Mom's voice prompted me to quickly round up Patrick, Anne, and Michelle. Just in time! Our Red Gate swung open, our Mazda veered in from the dirt road, and Dad jumped out with his Samsonite briefcase.

"Let's go!" he said at once.

"Why so late?" from my seat in the back of the Mazda I heard Mom ask as they hurried to join us.

"I wanted my last paycheck. But apparently the administration has left."

Through the car window, Grandma's house looked mournful with all her windows and doors sealed off. Aunt Diệp, Dad's unmarried youngest sister, and Grandma lived there, separated from us only by a courtyard. At Grandma's urging, Diệp had taken off with her friends a few weeks ago.

"You have no choice," Grandma had told her when she cried and wanted to stay back. "You're young, unmarried. Việt-Cộng will take you to give to their amputees as wife. I wouldn't take the risk for you to . . . to . . . ."

Grandma had cried, too. "In any case, your brother will take good care of me. Hasn't he always?"

My pretty aunt departed with a small bag. Without proper paperwork, she fled to the airport to catch her chance of leaving Vietnam with the mob. The area had been bombed heavily since, and she had not returned. At Dad's request, another of his sisters had come to scoop up Grandma. Until a week ago, Dad had thought he could secure a visa for his eighty-year-old mother. He had plenty of good connections who had promised to intervene to get all of us out in time. But one after another had fled without his knowledge. And Esso? He had his company's affidavits and travel documents for our family in that black attaché, but none had been provided for Grandma.

And now we were leaving without saying goodbye.

The servants were given their last payments as well as bonuses. Mom lingered on details such as what would be distributed to whom and when, especially the handling of her livestock, which included our quarrelsome old turkey, a haughty rooster, and his hens.

"Kill them for meat when time comes," I heard her say.

With Dad sitting next to Bác Dậu and Mom crowding in the back seat with us, the Mazda slowly grinded up the dirt road, leading the car procession. Behind it followed our local-branded La Dalat—its white frame all banged up—and our blue Ford minivan. We passed our maids, who lined up for a last goodbye, sobbing into their handkerchiefs. Pijou whined. I turned my head to see him in a thin veil of dust, white with brown-spotted fur and drooped tail. The neighborhood kids hung on to the line of cars, chanting: "The engineer is leaving. The engineer is escaping."

The cars slowly moved through the obstacles of the small alleys, cavorting over countless potholes. From the alley of Bùi Thị Xuân we turned left at Thoại Ngọc Hầu, heading toward the international airport. We hadn't gone far when our procession halted behind long lines of cars. The way to the airport had been barricaded with checkpoints guarded by armed men.

We inched along. Many cars had to U-turn. Fifteen minutes. Then half an hour. We could smell the smoke. Our car shook at each detonation. No one said a word. We waited. After an interminable time, a patrolman approached. Under the green metal helmet, his evil looking face, with dark smokers' lips, was marked by a large scar across one cheek.

"Why are you here?" he asked.

Clicking open his briefcase, Dad took out the thick folder of documents. "I have the required clearances to the airport," he said in his usual authoritative voice. He hated policemen, and I prayed he wouldn't lose patience like the time a cop had stopped us on our way to my school.

Shoving the stack of papers back, the man smirked, then said, "These are useless. You have to turn around. We had strict orders to not let anyone through. Nobody, even your white bosses." Then just like that, he walked away, slinging his rifle menacingly over his shoulder.

I was shocked. How indecent! Was he not there to assist us, to give us directions on what to do? Mom turned to look at Dad. Bác Dậu waited for his order. We all held our breath, waiting to hear the next words from his mouth. A shadow of hopelessness crossed his smooth forehead. Dad, always optimistic, who believed in miracles, was now left to his own wits, without a plan, without the intervention of God in a perturbed world, left holding a briefcase full of important but useless documents.

The first thing he did, after a long, searching silence, was to make the sign of the cross and lead us in reciting three Hail Mary's. Bác Dậu shifted uncomfortably as nearby explosions rattled the car windows. The bombs whistled, their piercing octaves tearing at the hushed lines of automobiles filled with large families. Dad said finally: "Let us head to Uncle Chấn!"

There was no traffic on Công Lý, only debris. We sped toward Nguyễn Huỳnh Đức Street, to my mother's brother's home. Why go to him? I didn't understand but was glad that we did not return home to a life I already considered our past.

2.

Past and Present

The canopy of tamarind trees formed a roof above our heads as Uncle Chấn's gates closed behind our cars. We were transported back into the calm serenity of his home as if awakened from a bad dream, still confused from the vivid sounds and sights of the mayhem we had left behind. My two sisters, deep asleep, were carried inside.

Uncle Chấn and his wife Danielle rushed out, intoning in unison, "Hello, brother and sister Khoa," but this ordinary greeting did not match the concerned expression on their faces. Mom grasped Aunt Danielle's hand and there were tears and panic in her eyes. I followed them into the cool interior of my grandparents' former home. The same ceiling fans spinning lazily, the soft alcove lights, the tiled floors that had echoed Grandma's footsteps—nothing had altered since I was here last. Grandma's portrait witnessed our solemn arrival from the large mahogany sideboard. Grandpa had migrated to France a few years after her death and, since then, in their place was the young family of Uncle Chấn—his pregnant wife, a toddler daughter, and Mai-Xuân, his nineteen-year-old Eurasian daughter from a previous love.

Aunt Danielle gently pushed Mom down onto their plush sofa and ordered the maids to bring us some iced water and fruits.

"Tell us," she said to my mother who, in her high-pitched, urgent voice, began recounting to them the events of the last few hours.

Following my old habits, and knowing Mom would soon chase me away from listening in to their "adult" conversation, I bounced upstairs, and as I reached the top landing my uncle's words trailed after me, "The South boundaries are shrinking by the hour. Nothing except a miracle would save us."

Mai-Xuân was on the telephone in the dark hallway. She gestured to me to go to her room, as I often did. I found her large bed crowded with my siblings in various sleeping positions and slipped under the cool blanket with them, waiting for her. My eyes traveled the familiar walls, my mind still occupied by the calm features of Grandma depicted by her portrait. How I wished I could see her again.

Why my father chose to seek the counsel of this uncle was beyond my comprehension. Because we met the Lê clan more often and had many cousins our age, we bonded better with Dad's side. In contrast, except for grandparents Hoàng, whom we visited occasionally and had learned to love, the rest of the Hoàngs, the majestic Hoàngs, were basically nonexistent to us, their story of a bygone era remote in time and space.

Lying there in the dark to await a new day, possibly a new fate, I kept thinking of Grandma, my *bà ngoại*. When I was small, I used to stay over at their house on Phùng Khắc Khoan Street. She would come to my bed in the middle of the night to send me to the bathroom. By then, she had lost her eyesight. Once an impatient, proud individual, she was left vulnerable and lonely in her large home. When I visited, she and I often took walks in her garden and stopped to say hello to all the flowers. Leaning on my guiding arm, she listened to my vivid description of our little world, smiling and warning me of the hidden danger inside those blooms.

"Listen, child! Admire them, but do not bring them to your nose. They carry bugs that can make you sick, perhaps blind."

Poor Grandma! God did not spare her. The philandering Hoàng men had contributed a fair share of trouble to the family and filled her cup with bitter seeds they freely gathered. Uncle Chấn, the third born, had pocketsful of such seeds. Like his brothers studying in Paris, he often entangled himself with girls. Unlike them, he was not careful enough to get out unscathed. A brief fling with a Parisian girl had resulted in a child.

Ashamed, Chẩn decided to keep his daughter's existence secret from his parents back home. But the family's eyes and ears were all over Paris. A blunder of that magnitude was hard to cover up. All pretended to be unaware of the painful fact that a tiny infant member of the family was growing up inside an orphanage in Strasbourg, France. Then, guilty, Uncle Chẩn and his brothers took turns visiting the crowded orphanage. They couldn't ignore the little girl, especially the conscience-pricked father.

A stolen morning here, a half-afternoon there over the years, and the bond between the Oriental father and his Eurasian daughter grew stronger. They looked so much alike. She wore his dark and thick hair that was bobbed to simplify the task of combing. Her angular jaw gave her the masculine toughness of her father's profile. Those same almond-shaped eyes mirrored her father's gaze, although much more solemn. Chẩn's heart warmed each time he called his daughter with a name the little girl could hardly pronounce, Mai-Xuân. The foreign sound lit up the orphan's thin face. Bloomed such, the girl's face could be compared to the yellow *mai* flower she was named after, which would bloom each spring in her father's land.

But Fate was cruel to her. Not many years had gone by to strengthen the tie between them when Uncle Chẩn received the order to return home. It was time for him to fulfill his filial duties. Like most Vietnamese families, Grandparents Hoàng had always thought their eldest son, Pierre Chẩn, would be responsible for their caretaking in old age. But years ago, Pierre had severed ties with the family. It had been unfortunate that he had decided to marry a French girl. It was premature of him to bring her home before properly preparing his parents for the shock of their life. Grandma Hoàng's response was to slap her daughter-in-law's marble-like face.

Chẩn returned to Vietnam, and the years passed quickly. Mai-

Xuân was ten years old when the family in Vietnam finally learned of her existence. Although indignant, Grandma reacted differently. She had learned a dear lesson. Having lost a son to societal pressure and her unchecked temper, Grandma did not hesitate to answer her heart's call. Without further questions, she sent for her granddaughter and brought her into the family fold in Vietnam.

My mind was still traveling the elastic path between past and present when from the foot of Mai-Xuân's bed, I heard the soft calling of Grandma as in the old time, "Hồng-Mỹ, wake up! Bathroom time."

I awoke.

It wasn't Grandma, but Patrick tugging at my leg.

"Wake up! Time to go."

3.

Last Dragonflies

It was the morning of April 29th, 1975. The adults had stayed up all night to come up with a new plan for fleeing Vietnam, and it was time for our family to depart.

"You cannot leave Danielle in her condition," Mom told her brother. (Aunt Danielle was pregnant at the time.) "Your daughter and your wife are French nationals. There is no reason to fear."

Aunt Danielle, a French citizen? This was new to me. But everything else had also turned upside down—all things unknown to me had become known only in the last 24 hours. My uncle paced the living room in a nervous state, now glancing at the wall clock, now tuning the radio for more news. It crackled until BBC picked up. Then it was my turn to be frustrated, because I could hear the urgent tone of the anchorman and see the pallor on the adults' faces. However, I could not make out the meanings of the foreign words. Often, the rising pitch of the siren pierced through the whole city, "*Ooooooooooo . . .* ," like the howling of a dog, wailing on as if it would never end. Yet, when the sound ended, it did so abruptly, as though the dog's throat had been slashed with its nose still pointing at the sky. With each "*Ooooooooooo . . .* ," Mom would plead with Dad, "Hurry," until finally, they seemed to reach a breaking point. No more thinking. No more debating.

Dad stood up. "Let's go."

Mom reached for the bag of provisions and called for us. Stopping by our car, she held my uncle's hand for a moment. Their fingers enlaced—Mom's light skin shone against my uncle's darkness, his hairiness contrasted with her smoothness, their hazel eyes solemn.

"Peace and health be with you," she breathed.

"I will stay back." He nodded.

We again clambered into the backseat of the red Mazda.

Dad came out with his briefcase, the only item necessary for this change of plan. We left all our belongings behind. I understood that our family would head to the American embassy, located a few streets away. On top of the embassy building was a heliport; inside were the American ambassador, Graham Martin, and his key personnel still holding out hope for a last-minute reversal of fortune. We would join them.

Dad's way to say a heartbreaking goodbye was to attempt a light joke. Slapping my uncle hard on his shoulder, he said, "If you don't see us back by tomorrow night, come check for us. If we're dead, give us a proper burial." Of course, he had made sure that Mom was not within earshot. This untimely pleasantry would have surely upset her and caused them to quarrel.

The other cars and our luggage were sent back home with the chauffeurs, and Dad drove the Mazda to the Esso Building on Thống Nhất Street, which we reached within fifteen minutes. As Dad locked the car, a man approached to propose money for it. He had guessed correctly our intention to leave the country. Dad was not interested, but the man insisted on a deal.

"We aren't leaving," Dad said, irritably shaking the man off. "Leave us."

We hastened toward our destination on foot. In a few blocks we reached the mass of people on the streets. The normally impeccable blocks on which sat the government headquarters and foreign buildings were littered with debris and rubbish—food scraps, discarded luggage, clothing, empty cigarette boxes, papers.... Tramping through these, people ran this way, that way, eyes searching—where to run to? Hollering, panicking. Lost children, thieves, the sound of bombs. Mayhem.

Rising above the frantic scene was a majestic building, a formidable boxy fortress enveloped in white concrete lattice: the vast compound of the U.S. embassy. Above the barbed-wired walls, soldiers in green helmets and military camouflage stood guard, rifles in hand. The tall, iron gate was shut tight. Also locked was a smaller side door that occasionally opened to let in certain people, who hurriedly pushed through while a group of soldiers fought to bar the crowd. Outside the walls and gates, we were but six animate objects tossed in a cauldron teeming with people.

People, young and old, with angry, mean faces, shoved and elbowed toward the prime location by the wall, closest to the forbidden gate. Frantic parents bawled out the names of their children. From all directions, the calls of "*Cu ơi!*" for the straying boys echoed.

I kept a vigilant eye on Patrick. Time and again he loosened from my grip, if only to pick up a pebble off the ground, which he flitted with his finger as he would a marble to divert himself. We inched forward with our parents—Mom with Anne's hand in hers and Dad shouldering little Michelle—I dragging Patrick first like a dog, then like a rag doll, then a burdensome appendage, my brother clearly tired and I beyond exhaustion. For most of the morning we were the crowd and the crowd was us, ebbing and flowing like a foaming tides to the sea wall that was the embassy, to cross into another world where "those who have done good, to the resurrection of life, and those who have done evil, to the resurrection of judgment ... and he will separate them one from another as a shepherd separates the sheep from the goats, and he will place the sheep at his right hand, but the goats at the left.... And they will go away into eternal punishment, but the righteous into eternal life" (John 5:29).

We were the sea and the sinking objects inside it.

The day lengthened. The fight for survival had worn people out;

they were no longer on their feet tussling for territory but spread out on the pavement, some dozing, others snacking to regain their strength. The crowd was at the same time patient and aggressive. Like glue, they adhered themselves to the ground. Like air, they quickly filled the gaps left by the people who either had given up the wait to return home or, finally, were allowed in through that side door. The latter group were people with political connections or with the backup of large fortunes. But we would get there, thought the ones like us who were left still fighting for our lives. This remote possibility was enough to keep my parents hoping and persevering amidst the swelling mass.

By noon, the small breeze brought in the odor of urine. The little boys did not wander off anymore. The little girls' hair hung undone, the hoarse wailing of babies sounded like cat screams, and the men started to curse everyone present and absent. The government was "a son of a bitch," and anyone encroaching on sacred territory in this desperate quest for life was lambasted with words so dirty, words I often caught in the alleys around our home uttered by drunkards or deranged people, with explicit meanings I only understood fully thirty years later. Brawls broke out in what little space each party claimed.

While we were thus buried in the anonymity of the mass, the sound of Mom's name rose above the brouhaha. Mom looked frantically about for that hailing, for it might mean help in this sea of devouring sharks. At closer range, it became distinct. There she was, Aunt Khang, cupping her mouth with the name of her cousin, "Quân, Quân! Over here."

Mom swam toward her across the human sea. The two briefly conferred. They separated, Mom swimming back with great difficulty to us, while Aunt Khang hastily departed in the opposite direction. In bits and pieces my mother relayed the urgent message to Dad.

"Go to Bến Chương Dương," she told him. "They're ferrying people by the shipload to the sea to be airlifted."

He listened to her, hanging his head over hunched shoulders, his favorite ear pointing toward her while the other, with its thick lobe, was pointed in my direction, as if it was trying to remove itself from the debate, doubtful of the new option.

In the end, the left ear won and Dad refused to budge from our current position. He would not waste any more precious time running to and fro, for who exactly knew which way to freedom, who was right and who not, while the odds were already fast stacking against us?

For many more hours, we doggedly kept our station. Time and again, in bursts of desperation, Dad got up to approach the embassy's gate to no avail. The human mass, packed in layers immovable in front of that gate, had become an effective barrier against him or anyone trying to cut through. Normally docile and accommodating, the grievous and abandoned Vietnamese people had turned savage, easily provoked to violence if slightly challenged to yield their ground. Young men now attempted to climb the barbed-wired fence, only to be thrown back by soldiers guarding it.

The sun descended, and the heat rising from the asphalt all afternoon like hot steam started to dissipate. Following the example of the streetwise people, we climbed atop the roof of a car to rest, lest we would be trampled in the event of a stampede toward the gate. Overhead, noisy choppers came and went, their blades whipping the air like the blades of a giant blender. Suddenly, from the far horizon appeared a double-helix Chinook, looming larger every minute through the trees, pulverizing leaves and twigs, sucking up clouds of dust like the vortex of a tornado. At that same time, inside the gates of the embassy, where an enormous tamarind once stood, a massive evacuation was conducted. The American ambassador, Graham Martin, had referred to the majestic tamarind as the symbol of American might when he objected to felling it. We didn't know about this important detail then, but that night only a stump was left of that almighty symbol. Unbeknownst to the Vietnamese populace, the ants had won an elephant. Washington had long ago given up South Vietnam to Russian-backed Việt-Cộng in exchange for a more profitable diplomacy with China. The death certificate of Saigon had been signed, and the brave resistance of our soldiers in the last hours of the city was a mere abortive effort against the advancing enemy.

For weeks, while my parents and those ignorant like them were carrying on as if the late attacks were just another Tết Mậu Thân, the American radio had been playing "White Christmas," the coded signal for the abandonment of Saigon. While "Lady Ace 09 is in the air with Code Two"—the ambassador flying away safely in the last helicopter, in his arms the folded Stars and Stripes—my parents and countless other innocents continued to fight for their families. It must have been about 4 a.m. when I heard a great commotion and a shout: "The gate's open!"

The gate was down. Jubilantly, like ignorant fools, our parents dragged us through the crowd, using their elbows as weapons, lunging and squeezing through—pulling their long tail of kids like a great serpent in the "dragon and serpent climbing up the sky" game. The objective of this game was to not let anyone cut through.

Once inside the sovereign building, we climbed a narrow flight of stairs, higher and higher. At a landing, I heard a soft fizz, then my eyes burned.

"Tear gas," a voice cried. Confusion ensued. Would they shoot us next? Where are we? I sputtered, my eyes stinging. Mopping my face, I kept ascending. There was no stopping now. I was pushed from behind, and in turn I pressed forward, obeying the force of momentum. When I thought I could no longer bear the pain in my watery, swollen-shut eyes, I felt a whiff of fresh air.

And a cheer. "We broke through."

I was pushed into an open terrace. Looking around, I saw my family and, above, a starry night. Hope smiled at me, at us. Mom was beaming with joy. Dad said, "Thank God almighty!"

The fatigue of the day's struggle lifted. I felt new energy. Everybody sat down and looked upward in silence, eyes scanning the heavens, like praying together. There was cooperation again, a mutual agreement to behave, as if through the process of ascending higher toward the heavens, the wolves from below had achieved higher karmas, had shed fur, dropped fangs, and transformed into nobler beings with conscience. The departure would be orderly.

Among us was one American civilian. He, like the mass, searched among the stars for the "dragonflies," as helicopters were dubbed. There were but a few—single, purring, descending black dots that left noisily and hurriedly, in a commotion of throttling. Then again, another one approached. Again, all necks craned. All eyes shone. Arms waved. Blades yielded again to a dot, then naught.

A terrible truth settled like a weight on the hearts of the multitude. You learn to detect hopelessness on people's faces. When one more dot appeared from afar and the crowd grew agitated, the white man stood up. He talked to us, the crowd which he did not wish to belong to but now included him, though clearly alien to him. I did not understand his words—they were harsher than the soft French that I knew—but I could easily guess from his gestures.

"Sit," his arms said, pushing down the air around him. "Be quiet," he touched his index finger to his lips.

A man rose and translated the brief talk into Vietnamese: "Show the pilot you are peaceful. He might not risk his life and plane otherwise."

The crowd acquiesced. Silence blanketed us in the drape of Death. Even the babies stopped stirring. In that suspended position, we waited. Waiting, we perceived the sound of choppers above us but could no longer see them. We were waiting still when dawn rose over the horizon. No flying object was seen in the lighted sky. But foolishly, dumbly, we continued to sit in our stillness, waiting. The white man got on his feet and left. One by one, the people around us did the same, swallowed by the opening that the previous night had been a door to heaven, that this morning was the mouth of a devilish cave, gaping wide, eating.

There was no more hope. I felt it.

My ears picked up Dad's saddest announcement. "Let's go now, children. Let's leave, Quân."

This was the second time in less than three days I had witnessed him giving up. I could not understand. How could he leave this place, so close to the other world, to the flying objects like delivering angels, after so much struggle? Doesn't he desire freedom? Life?

I had placed my full confidence in him to lead us out of danger. He had never failed me before. Why this premature surrender? I felt angry, betrayed. Then I became angry at myself for thinking ill thoughts against my father. How could he know? Did God know? Did God allow this to happen?

"Our Father, who art in heaven...," I prayed. I prayed automatically, like a zombie, without faith. I believed Dad now; we could no longer be saved. The clock stopped ticking. Alas, we would be alive when the morning sun was being replaced by sickle and hammer, bathed in blood.

We wound down the same flight of stairs that took us up last night. The daylight revealed to us the many doors we hadn't seen going up, when we fumbled blindly toward a false hope. Beyond those doors nothing had been left unturned. Office chairs were toppled like wooden horses kicked by spoiled children. Drawers fallen out of the cavities of desks, their contents spilled like vomit from a sick patient. Papers littering the floor. From below, mobs of looters continuously pushed up, ransacking in their feverish search for goods or whatever was left of the previous plundering. Women and children ran left and right for bounties, whooping as if picking for treasures on the beach.

The same chaos was seen on the streets. It was as if a storm had blown by. The whole city's contents were on its boulevards. We walked amidst floor fans, blades silent inside their metal cages; ceiling fans, yanked right off some rooms; book cabinets; toilet bowls; sinks. Here sprawled books; there lay binders with the pages torn off, the loose papers fluttering up with the soft breeze like white birds. Someone's refrigerator waited patiently for a random owner under the late morning sun, sharing its surprised fate with countless pieces of furniture.

Our initial shock subsided, we walked on, muted, beyond caring, anxious to retrace our way back to the Mazda. Worse things might await us if we didn't hurry. The thick woolen dress I wore felt as heavy as lead. I perspired underneath it, and buckets of sweat poured down from my temples and forehead, stinging my eyes. In the glaring sunlight, convoys of tanks rolled in on Highway One, flags billowing, bearing soldiers in green fatigues. Innocently, for a brief moment, I took them for our own brave soldiers, heading back to defend our capital. Shame on me for not knowing the difference. No, they were not our soldiers, but the enemy's. Our army was the uniforms there on the ground, in hurriedly, recklessly discarded shreds. Those blood-soaked, mud-stained greens! The color of forest and bravery. The embodiment of discipline and patriotic duties. The throbs of many girls' hearts. The mourning of numerous Southern families. Now lying there in rags. Abandoned. Shame. Shame. Shame.

The enemy's army was advancing into the heart of the Southland to claim their victory. We had lost the war.

At the corner of Thống Nhất, relieved, we found our crimson Mazda waiting patiently. "EO3592" beamed its license plate like a sign held up by an old friend to greet his long-lost pal at the airport. Dad pulled out his set of keys, and we boarded uncomplainingly. A guard ran out from his shack. He might have recognized Dad as one of Esso's employees for, concerned, he said, "Why are you still here? Don't you know the war is over? The president is on the news announcing our defeat."

Dad quickly turned on the radio. Over the waves droned the monotonous voice of the country's new president, Dương Văn Minh, in office less than forty-eight hours after the defection of Mr. Nguyễn Văn Thiệu, who had abandoned the country and evacuated with his money, family, and close staff.

I hear it still, so distinctively: "Compatriots! I declare the war over. I order all of you to put down your weapons and join our liberators in the process of reconciliation. I repeat! The war is over!"

Dad cut off the radio, and both our parents sobbed. Their ravaged faces suddenly looked aged. Wiping off their tears, they stared into the sun-clad boulevard, seemingly lost. Our car rolled through streets devoid of life, passing under leafy tamarinds, and brought us away from downtown. Soon, we reached Aunt Sự's home. There were two cars packed with her family members, including Grandma, and other people I didn't recognize. It was as if they had been waiting for us, for as soon as she spotted our car, my aunt ran out to attach two small flags to each of our side mirrors, the Red Cross flag and the tricolor flag of France.

Perhaps believing that a hospital would be the last place to be bombed, we sped toward Saint Grall, one of Saigon's few good hospitals. I remember us staying in one large, whitewashed room of the hospital. After a few days, we returned to our home.

The old quarrelsome turkey had been slaughtered for meat while we were absent, but all was as before. Our three servants decided to stay with us. The chauffeurs had already gone their separate ways, their service no longer required nor possible. They understood as well as we did that from that day forward, a wealthy lifestyle with car ownership and private household employment was a thing of the past. No one would like to be associated with a family like ours, with people dressing as we did, speaking as we did, having a past like ours, and living in a home like ours.

We expected persecution, but most South Vietnamese thought they would be safe.

4.

An Odd Life

We adjusted to new routines. Meals consisted of rice and pork stew intended for our travel lest it would spoil. We ate it at lunch in the stuffy heat and then at dinner under the shadows cast by kerosene lamps and candles. Outside, Saigon, deprived of electricity, was plunged into complete darkness.

Home seemed no longer a safe harbor but a place of penitence. Each day came with fear of the lurking unknown, ready to strike, whether it was in the daytime under the glaring heat or at night in the cooler air, while we were sleeping, clung together in Mom's bedroom on one large bamboo mat, or awake, inside the covering of our mosquito net or huddling together and seeking security in one another's company. At any time, the police could burst in through our gate to take away Dad, or all of us. I began to rehearse confessing my sins against the state, to say them in a way that would lessen my punishment. We knew then how mice felt inside their holes, waiting for the hungry cat to go away. Or would it get us?

Until now, only our mother had slept in the master bedroom. None of us, including Dad, liked to sleep without the air conditioner, the bed netted, and the windows and doors always tightly shuttered. Moreover, to us kids, it was a place associated with confinement, sickness, and work. In the afternoon, beware, loud kids! One shriek, an abandoned laugh, and the unruly would be forced to take a nap with Mom.

Oh, the dark room! And Mom reclining with her head on a hard tin box, a strange practice passed down from her mother, "to keep my head cool." Besides the still darkness and the cookie-box pillow, another instance of Mom's strangeness was her need for her back to be thumped by one of us to fall asleep. When we protested and said we weren't at all sleepy, she would say, "Come lie down next to me. Thump my back until I drift off then you can go." But no matter how hard we fought against sleep, by lying down in that room with her, in the dark stillness, facing her broad back and thumping it rhythmically—*poom, poom, poom*—the drowsiness would completely claim us, too, until the entire afternoon was forever gone, wasted. We were also brought into this torture chamber when Mom's hand detected fever on our foreheads, which to her was the first sign of influenza, chicken pox, mumps, or any typical childhood illness. So here in her dungeon we would stay, isolated under her watch, while the rest of the merry world went on without us.

Yet, by and by, in those sad months of summer 1975, I accustomed myself to this room, her room, and learned to love it like the rest of our home. With no place to go in the endless summer, I sat for hours atop her balcony looking out to my neighborhood below and, for the first time, discovered the view beyond my home and the life of my neighborhood. My eyes often followed the narrow alley outside our Green Gate to the main street, Trương Minh Ký, where buses lumbered by, leaving their trail of black smoke.

In the alley, which was too narrow for car traffic, the poor kept encroaching into the available space by pushing their belongings to their front porches. One day it was a broken chair, a washing basin, a laundry line. Soon a rickety gate was propped up against some bricks crudely cemented together. Opposite these dark, dingy, tin-roofed hovels where the street kids and their families lived was their contrast: our parish church's vast grounds, with its elementary school and rows of doors and windows. The church property was defined and protected by a concrete wall taller than an adult's head.

Years ago, Dad had bought a vacant lot in this Tân Sa Châu neighborhood to build a home that would replicate another spacious house at 46 Belier Street, Hanoi. He had fond memories of that house, the first one the Lê brothers bought together at the peak of their success, entertaining foreigners with the family band at Le Coq d'Or. He hired a French architect to incorporate the many features he had loved. Nosing around my parent's closet one day, I had found the original blueprint of our home. It was like finding a rare picture of my parents when they were little. Together with Dad, we studied the details of our home; some I had grown up with—the gracious arched doorway outside our living room's double French door, Mom's balcony with its louver doors and scrolled rails—and some I discovered existed only on this print. Folding the precious document, Dad sighed.

"If not for an old feud with our parish church," he said, "our Green Gate would have been our main entrance. It's too bad." He proceeded to tell me an outrageous tale of warring between the parish priest and our family. "The old fart wanted his church to dominate our neighborhood," recounted my father, to my great surprise. "When our home was completed, he wasn't at all pleased to see our rooftop soared above his church's steeple."

In his Sunday sermons, the old priest kept instigating. "My brothers and sisters, will you allow a mere human's home to grow bigger and taller than God's property?" In the end, the Green Gate had to be abandoned and, to my father's utter disappointment, another gate had to be added to the Bùi Thị Xuân side of our home for our cars to come in and out of. Located on the opposite side of our villa, this gate—dubbed the Red Gate—opened onto a pockmarked dirt road and the most ramshackle part of our neighborhood. Ever since, a barrier had gone up in my father's heart against these "vindictive ecclesiastics" next door.

Thirteen years hence, by a twist of fate, since we could not use our cars anymore, we began using the Green Gate more often, for it led us directly to the bus station and other public transportation. The territory on the other side belonged to the unruly street kids in our neighborhood, whose entertainment was to terrorize us, "the engineer" side, each time we set foot outside. The scrawled words

"Fat-butt Engineer," aimed years ago at my sister Madeleine, often seen riding her Honda moped through the alley, were still there on the exterior wall of the Green Gate, taunting us.

The kids did not stop at graffiti. They defecated on the front of our gate and littered it with whatever they could find: broken bottles, trash, cigarette butts. Before, traveling inside our car, we would ignore these kids. Dad often advised us, "Why lose your energy over small matters? Do you argue with excrement on the road? Then why bother with these delinquents who don't know any better?"

Sitting in Mom's room, I often wondered how my family would cope with our neighbors in the new situation. Would the old resentment escalate into hatred? With the political reversal, our malefactors were now heroes of the state, with weapons in hand.

"The smallest worm will turn, being trodden on."

The strident voice of a female revolutionary woke us each morning, hammering our heads with phrases such as "the greatness of the Party, its immense generosity toward the followers of the old regime . . ." and "forgiveness of crimes committed by Americans and their allies . . . ." They sent chills down our backs.

Our parents had told us countless times the reasons they had forsaken their birthplace, cutting away the root of ancestors by abandoning their well-established life in the North and fleeing the communist League for the Independence of Vietnam, called the Vietminh. Our neighborhood, Tân Sa Châu, new Sa Châu, was built by Catholic refugees from the old Sa Châu. They had crossed the Bến Hải River in 1954 to move south. Relatives on both sides of Mom's and Dad's families had left hastily, bringing with them whatever they could in order to rebuild. Decisions of what to take and what to leave behind were made arbitrarily. People brought with them necessities, but also keepsakes and mementos.

Grandparents Lê carried their ceiling fan south with them because it had been blessed by a bishop. It escaped communism but not my dad's hands, a fact that Grandma Lê never ceased to remind us. Grandma was seriously sore each time she saw her antique fan with its beautifully carved blades spinning gracefully from the tall ceiling of our living room.

"Your dad said it's going to be installed there only temporarily while our home is being constructed. It has been thirty years. He never had any intention of giving it back, saying removing it would destroy the look of your living room."

Her recurring complaints helped make sense of her meticulous habit of marking her initials on all her belongings. Whatever could not be initialized would be personalized with a red dot.

Religious and political affiliation had brought my ancestors south, while patriotic idealism had kept many Vietnamese nationalists north under the leadership of Hồ Chí Minh. "We almost lost Uncle Chấn to Vietminh," admitted my mother when Dad spoke to us about the allure of communism in the intellectual circle. My mother's brother had disappeared from home one day, a motivated youth ready to die for his country, only to "crawl back a wretched, skin-clad skeleton" to the gate of his family compound, miraculously escaping starvation and the Vietminh's persecution for leaving its movement.

We were all wide-eyed at hearing this story. Right away, Patrick shoved Michelle down, pointing his finger-gun at her and screaming, "Traitor." The game was on. Michelle, crawled away, then leaped to her feet and thrust an invisible sword to his gut, shouting, "Die, die. I am the hero."

Upon hearing the word "hero," Mom let out her trademark, "Huh!" Heroism had no place in her life. Dad's love of music and literature was enough for her. Into her "Nonsense!" dustbin she swept my romanticized notions of poverty, as in "Blessed are the poor, for they shall inherit the earth;" of love, regarding which she said, "Wait until you starve to see if love can make your tummy full;" or of heroism, for which she responded "Huh!" disdainfully.

To her, "Music and poetry are useless when you have not a penny sticking to your pants." She scolded when we devoted too much time to playing our instruments or, in my case, reading. It seemed that as a mother of nine, and having fought for too long to stay ahead, she did not want her children to struggle economically.

She wanted to instill in us practical clarity: pursue a profitable career, marry among an affluent society, and settle in luxurious comfort.

I knew Mom, and her realistic, sometimes crude remarks about life never surprised me. But Dad's words shook me when he talked about communism. "It was like stomach worms," he said to us often. "Once inside you and developed, they had ways to invisibly suck away your lifeblood. Some would slither into your brain and heart, turning your thoughts against God and family members, claiming your heart's goodness and turning you into a monstrous foot soldier, ready to kill on order."

"Children," he went on to say, "communism is not fully understood by many patriots. Those who follow it did it at first to liberate Vietnam from the French. They didn't know it was just an exchange of sovereigns, until communism reversed North Vietnam into the Stone Age."

In that time span, the South continued to prosper with political money from America. Indulging in luxury, it forgot why the country was divided, and why France had failed to secure a stronghold on its former colony, while the communists remained faithful to their idealism. The tortoise steadfastly gained its ground while the arrogant hare slept peacefully, and lo, one morning, awoke to the victorious trumpeting of his slow and awkward enemy.

That conversation with my father had long escaped my memory until the history lesson caught up with us. The refugees from the North now relived their old nightmares. Where could they run? The nautical borders were sealed tight. The people looked desperately skyward and wished they were birds and not humans. They searched inward for answers for their misfortune. "*Bất quá tam*," they lamented: *No more than three times*. But this was their third encounter with the communists. Perhaps they were truly doomed.

Our parents looked grim but coped as best they could. To avoid all risks, Dad quarantined himself at home. A false accusation might send him into the hands of the state police followed by imprisonment. Anybody in this poor neighborhood, knowing his tie to Esso, could denounce him as a former supporter of the Old Regime and an avid American spy. He preferred to be a bird in a cage, kept safely away from the sharp claws of the hungry cat. Mom represented our family at all mandatory community meetings to be informed of the "new procedures," learn of the Party's greatness and immense generosity, and give thanks and glory to Uncle Hồ. I was her chosen companion in all these boring daily meetings, in case something might happen. I, her oldest child and a girl, was perfect; she might not want to risk Patrick, a boy.

The meetings were held at the airport hangars. People, mostly the neighborhood women, came with their conical hats and gossip. The hats served well as seat mats, protecting their pants. They sat in rows and queues, a loud mob. Southern ladies traditionally donned their *bà ba*, light shirts with open-neck collars. Even without her Western attire, and in the black *bà ba* and black cotton pants, Mom couldn't achieve a peasant look. Although her short hair had lost its last perm and was intentionally neglected, she stood apart from the women around her. Her skin was too shiny and fair without makeup, her clothes unsuitable to her mannerisms, her hair too short and brown, lacking a chignon at the nape of the neck. The combination made her a strange bird with exotic plumage—except for her pointy hat. This was the only part of the costume deemed successful because it covered her hair and hid part of her face. As soon as the hat was placed on her head, Mom was one of the crowd, a country woman, albeit one with an ample bodice. Her proud posture, the hat could not hide.

At once, the womenfolk loudly greeted Mom: "Hello Madam, the Pharmacist."

She smiled diplomatically. "I am now just like all of you. We are living the new socialist system. Don't call me so. Just call me Mrs. Khoa."

They chorused their disapproval. Her title was her name. They could not reform their tongues, they said. "It wouldn't feel right."

* * *

Grandma Lê returned to her house and, just like before, all the shutters were thrown opened. From my room opposite her home, I could see Grandma in her living room fingering the black beads of her rosary. She had been waiting for her youngest daughter Diệp's return because no news of her had ever reached us. What had become of her? Had she perished during the evacuation, trampled to death in the mass exodus? Had she been blown apart by a bomb or kicked out of an overloaded helicopter by the crew—or flown to another sky, another life?

For a few more months Chị Ba, Grandmother's maid, had stayed on to provide her with the same care she had given in the past dozen years. At sunset each day, like clockwork, Chị Ba would close off Grandma's home. But since Aunt Diệp's absence, Grandma would demand, "Check the front door, will you? Someone's knocking. It could be Diệp."

"Old bat gone cuckoo," Chị Ba reported, annoyed by her employer's comportment.

Uneducated and deeply superstitious, Chị Ba suspected that the spirit of my aunt, surely having departed from this world in a painful, unresolved death, and having not been offered a proper rite of passage, was haunting the house. To appease the ghost, she sprinkled the house with holy water collected from the church.

The effect of the international embargo was immediately felt, especially in big cities like Saigon. Its dwindling fuel reserve was quickly nationalized and controlled. Electricity was cut. Without electricity, the pumping of water soon ceased. Saigonese learned to live with random utility outages. Country folks suffered even more. Rice was rationed. For over thousand years, the valiant "dragon sons, fairy descendants" had defied Chinese invaders to cling to their identities and mother tongue. But it was one thing to be trampled under foreign feet and another to be strangled by your own fellow countrymen. The people of the South were stunned by their Northern brothers' ill treatment of them. They hunkered down and bit the bullet.

Bicycles replaced cars and motorcycles. The city, fortunately, occupied only 809 square miles. And jobless, Saigonese had all the free time in the world to bike from one end of the city to the other for various purposes. But not everyone could afford a bike. As a high school teacher, Uncle Huỳnh's state-funded salary could not afford his family enough food, let alone a new bike. Dad offered him our Mobilette, once owned by my brother Khải. A Mobilette was a bike with a small motor that the rider started by pedaling fast. Without the fuel to run the motor, this heavy bike would be a burdensome means of transportation. But Uncle Huỳnh rode this mule dutifully, bending low and straining to pedal the distance between his home and school, then to Grandma's to keep her company. She waited for his daily arrival. The sun barely dipped, the clock chimed three, the cuckoo jumped out at a quarter after, at which the dogs would bark, the maid would run out, and the gate would screech open. From her window Grandmother could see her oldest son appear, tiredly pushing the Mobilette, his briefcase tied in the backseat, in his hand a small bag. He would collapse from exhaustion on her sofa after handing her whatever little he brought for her in the bag—some food treats, or the dog meat she craved but could not get from us. After napping a couple of hours, they conversed. Then he would ride home on whatever energy he had regained.

One afternoon, after his needed nap, Uncle Huỳnh woke and went up to Aunt Diệp's room on the second floor. Watching, I abandoned my game and followed him up. I wanted to visit my aunt's room, too. He emptied out the contents of all the bookshelves and extracted her diaries and poetry notebooks from her desk drawers. He stuffed her clothes into sacks and carried them downstairs, together with armfuls of books, photo albums, and magazines of all sorts, and out into the courtyard. By the mighty fig tree he built a big fire. Into this leaping monster he threw the vestiges of my aunt's whole existence.

"No, Uncle!" I cried out. "May I have them?"

He waved me away, telling me, the bawling girl, to shush or scoot elsewhere, for he had business to take care of. I dried my tears and lingered around the pile of books, eyeing the diaries longingly. While my uncle was busy feeding the fire, I scraped out one leather-bound notebook and read hungrily, devouring groups of sentences, my eyes racing across my aunt's handwriting against time. Desperately, I scanned through the details of my aunt's days, the years and the names, the family's anecdotes, but I did not have enough time to finish half of the precious writing when my uncle looked up and discovered what I was doing.

"Toss it in at once," he ordered me in a pained voice, and so I did. And the writing, the Lê clan's story, became only great smoke.

Our maids brought out many more books and family albums from our home. Gently but firmly, my uncle explained to me that what he did was necessary to save lives, our own and the lives of other family members still in Vietnam. Pointing to the snapshot of the extended Lê family taken in 1972 upon sister Mai's engagement, he asked me, "Who are no longer with us?"

Aunt Kim's family had left. Aunt Diệp was missing.

"What is Uncle Linh's wearing?" Uncle Huỳnh's finger traced the picture.

"He's in military uniform," I said.

"Is it wise for us to keep things like these?"

I kept silent. He threw the piles of albums into the bonfire. The fig tree watched as we collaborated the murder of our family's past. The leaping, dancing fire stuck out its tongue, and the pile of albums imploded. The skeleton of our past writhed in agony, its pearly flesh changing to a sickly brown, then ashy, then gray dust. I couldn't resist the urge to reach in. My treasure. The singed volumes of my aunt's poetry, momentarily retrieved, were tossed right back in. One volume of poetry had landed binder down and, with a great roar, the heaving beast leaped to assault it.

Oh! Gentle verses. One by one the words curled into smoke.

> *You left, my lean profile erased*
> *forgotten, were our days together by that old river*
> *Your promise of a future together,*
> *where was it tossed?*
> *How could you forget the round of my shoulder*

whose velvety eyes now gaze at yours,
now star-crossed?

The photographs of my family undulated then finally were consumed, but the poor books resisted. The servants had to pry apart the pages with a branch. The monster's tongue lapped them up, word by word, into its hungry belly. My father's *Paris Match* magazines, documents of all sorts, birth certificates, proofs of baptism—everything was only ash now; our passports and visas—our last hope—existed no more.

My uncle's eyes were again red as during the times he took liquor. But he kept a vigilant watch on the fire, nursing its strength with the family's archives. We sat there together, mute, until the twilight sun burned its last orange rays, our eyes stinging from the smoke and the heavy sadness of destruction.

Together, we witnessed the incineration of my aunt's personal poems from as far back as the '50s, the carefully penned records of my paternal Grandpa's last months, where day by day and hour by hour the progression of his sickness was written down, what had been said, who had visited, how Grandpa had looked. No one would ever get to read what my aunt had written in the hope of passing the memory down to the next generation. It took a whole day to eliminate the evidence of a life and erase the glorious past of my family.

After that day, we became like devout ascetic monks willing to exchange worldly goods for a blessed life. Hastily, we reversed our opulent life, shedding all signs and symbols of capitalism to gain the acceptance of the terrible god that was the Communist Party. One evening, Dad whispered into our ears that he needed help pushing all the cars into the street. All of us gathered silently in the yard. Through the Red Gate, still without uttering a word, we slowly pushed the cars out one by one. It was like the scene in "The Sound of Music" in which Captain von Trapp and his family push their car on the way to the convent. The only difference was we did not have to go far, only to the next intersection, where our small alley met the main street. We left our cars with their keys in the ignition and walked back home, feeling almost glad of the separation.

Within a year, the tin roof of the garage was sold for money. Uncle Huỳnh came to pick up Dad's stereo. Somebody else took brother Daniel's many guitars. When all that could be given or sold away was sold and given, we were left with the bulky living room set, our beds, and the piano. It sat quietly in a corner of the living room to remind us of Dad's unrealized wish for all his children to learn to play the piano well.

During this period, my diversion was to wander the swap meets held at any street corner. Here I gawked with curiosity at the abundance of items available at low prices. One could select a variety of things: military tools, fans, furniture. These looted objects were now displayed for sale, with or without price tags, in working condition or broken. While people like us were trying to get rid of our stuff and reduce our encumbrance, poor folks were delighted at finding affordable goods, from clothing, shoes, and silverware to household appliances. Fans and typewriters were possessed for the first time in many people's lives. Mom gave me the money generously to purchase little gadgets.

She told me, "Soon this money will be useless."

I picked up a green canvas bag for school use. It used to be a military gas-mask bag.

5.

Upside Down

The two-way street, once named Thoại Ngọc Hầu, stretched on much farther than my child's mind could remember and my child's feet could ever measure. The Thoại Ngọc Hầu Street I recalled was that portion of the tar road on which sat my mom's pharmacy, connecting faraway Ông Tạ to the international airport, Tân Sơn Nhất. Before the fall of Saigon it was always loud and dusty, choked with lines of cars—foot-pedaled and motored—as well as man-powered cyclos, taxis, motorcycles; in short, all manner of transportation passed our pharmacy as if on a conveyor belt.

Along this street were tailors, dry cleaners, doctors' offices, printing companies, jewelry stores—all sorts—and Chợ Ông Tạ, an open-air marketplace a twenty-minute walk from home, where you could buy anything in the world if you had the money. For my maidservant, everything in the world meant groceries: a kilogram of fish, half a piece of pork, lard by the block, vegetables, the quantity two bags could hold and her hands could carry. Sometimes she let me tag along, and it was an exhilarating experience as well as intimidating. I found the crowded place dirty and loud. Flies buzzed the meat stalls. Fish swam crowdedly in too-shallow tubs; dead fish were displayed on ice with eyes wide open and gills slit, with heads, without heads . . . .

I was about fourteen when I made my first purchase. It was an exquisite pair of wooden clogs, about two inches high, with an embroidered front strap. They were in screaming fashion that year, affordable but not so cheap as to be common, carved to hug the arch of the feet, the wood lacquered, and the nails to hold the strap had a bold, beaded face, colored to blend in with the design.

Later, allowed to venture on my own anywhere my bike could take me, I still never went farther than Ông Tạ, being a shy, cautious girl. Most of my errands took me in the opposite direction, toward the airport and downtown, to my school. I regret that I never visited the famous temple of a Catholic missionary Pierre Joseph Georges Pigneau de Béhaine, or Lăng Cha Cả, farther north.

At 34 Thoại Ngọc Hầu Street stood our humble pharmacy. "Pharmacy Tân Sa Châu," proclaimed the store sign in large lettering and, beneath, my mother's name in a smaller font. This monument to my mother's pride and our livelihood squeezed itself in between two loft-style buildings typical of Saigon's commercial districts, where Saigonese lived above their businesses. On the left of our pharmacy stood a small convenience store and, on the right, a noodle house so narrow the owner ended up placing a kitchen cart with its huge pot of broth right on the sidewalk. Around the steaming cart, hungry customers with chopsticks sat perched on little stools, their faces buried in the flavorful steam rising up from the bowls placed in front of them. Crowded around were beggars, bony starved children with their hands extended and eyes fastened expectantly, now on the strands of yellow noodles hanging between the bowl and the customer's mouth, now on the piece of meat that briefly rested between the teeth, and then, oh, utter disappointment! The precious morsel had traveled safely to disappear inside the sweaty face. Below roamed an emaciated mongrel, also waiting for his luck.

An ongoing procession of street hawkers traveled this maze during most parts of the day, passing by our pharmacy, bringing products right to our doorstep. Often their baskets outsized their little bodies, and all that one saw were white conical hats in between bouncing baskets, weaving in and out of streets and alleys. There were cooks with mobile kitchens, catering snacks and hot food to the customers' mouths; grocery peddlers selling vegetables and meat; fishmongers carrying their stinky loads; itinerant tinsmiths; shoe repairers; knife and scissor sharpeners who could be heard clicking their scissors and singing, "Sharpening knives and anything that cuts."

All over town, these flat-footed ballerinas danced to the needs of Saigon, balancing their livelihood on bamboo poles. We met them with their baskets at the fringe of the market. They competed with the kiosk merchants to feed the working crowds and shoppers. At school recess, they sat around the school gates to satisfy the hungry students.

They often stopped in front of the pharmacy to entice us with street food, yummy snacks that no one could reproduce in their home kitchens. Mom loved the convenience of buying groceries at her door. The pharmacy was our window to the world. As a family business, it had served as our training ground toward a responsible adulthood. Mom put us through an enforced internship there for many practical reasons. She needed us to keep an extra pair of eyes in the pharmacy during her needed nap at home. My two older brothers Khải and Daniel (Khả), both Boy Scouts with a taste for adventure, were sent to sleep in the pharmacy to guard it at night. They returned home with tales of ghosts, mice, and rats, but no human intruders. When it was my turn to work, years later, I found a stash of *Playboy* magazines to testify to their presence. Primarily, my mother sought to mold us into savvy businesspeople who could make a living out of our wits, unlike the Lê on my dad's side.

Eloquent and musically talented, any of my Lê uncles would gladly seize his opportunity at the microphone to fill in the role of master of ceremony or musician. Any one of them could easily give lengthy speeches and quote literature, recite poetry, or sing and play music with any instrument available to him. Once a Lê stood up, he would surely make his audience cry at a solemn occasion, or laugh at a merrier affair, and be applauded, his speech, or jokes, or performance forever remembered.

Born into a family with no artistic talents, Mom recognized her in-laws' gifts but, innately pragmatic, she never let her admiration of their arts turn into its adoption. She often cited the Vietnamese proverb, "Eat enough first to ensure oneself enough strength to shoulder one's religion." What finally mattered to a family was bringing home good incomes.

Under my mother's plan, any of her children old enough for simple arithmetic was old enough to be placed on a high stool behind the pharmacy counter. Once propped there, the future businessperson would do whatever his common sense dictated to assist in the business. Following the family's rite of passage, beginning in sixth grade, I was the little boss that Chị Sáu punctiliously roused from my nap each afternoon, despite my waves of angry protests, and marched like a prisoner through a maze of alleys to the back door of the pharmacy, ready to reopen for the post-siesta hours.

I continued my disrupted nap on a lounge chair in a corner of the store, enduring the attacks of bloodthirsty mosquitoes. But once the first customer showed up, my drowsiness quickly lifted, and I began to function. Perched at the cash register asking for payment and giving out receipts, I was our pharmacy's vital organ. If I wasn't needed at the cash register, then I could help cleaning up the counters, putting away the medications that were newly delivered or taken out for dispensation. Each pharmacy had its own method to display and store medicines. What seemed like helter-skelter to outsiders obeyed a certain internal logic, whether the order was alphabetical, by frequency of usage, or by type of illness. Through my mother's hands-on method, I learned the trade like a toddler learning to speak: by doing.

The local poor visited Mom for their usual pills and free medical advice. They trusted their pharmacist with mild cases of hypertension, influenza, or chronic headache that did not justify the cost of a doctor's visit. Over the years, talking, listening to her neighbors' medical symptoms, and filling their prescriptions, my mother, who was our family's most trusted doctor, was also her clients' reliable medical advisor. When sick, we, her own brood, did not have the option to refuse her pills, which were cut and crushed into bitter powder. But that these neighbors had willingly chosen her over a medical doctor was a fact she proudly cited every time we objected to being given the same pills that were used to treat her livestock. There was never a need for a vet either, or their pharmaceutical supplies. Mom, our doctor and the neighborhood's, was also our animals' doc. Expired medicines, deemed not fit for human consumption, were set aside to cure her sick animals— weaker doses for chickens and more powerful ones for pigs.

Mom crossed the yard to Grandma's home daily to check on her stock of medicine and resupply her. All the shots that Grandma required daily were administered by a trusted male nurse who came to the house regularly, bringing his mild manners and a black bag that, when opened, displayed an array of thin vials and menacing needles—then the room would be filled with the scent of rubbing alcohol.

Because her clientele was mostly poor, Mom served them thriftily and sensibly. She never pushed her patients to purchase more medicine than they could afford, although it was more profitable to sell prescriptive medicine by the bottle. To economize for her poor neighbors, Mom would take a pill or two from her container and supplement with free samples. Although a rather generous, charitable pharmacist, she never completely followed her heart to abolish good business practices. She would ask for what was due her. Customers who abused her trust would never be able to buy on credit again.

We always wondered if, given the chance and time, our humble, dusty little pharmacy would one day grow into a large, modern, multi-register store. By that fateful last day of April 1975, three of my five older siblings had pursued a career in pharmacy in the hope that they would return to Vietnam to fulfill my mother's dream of something bigger. A pharmacy at a better location, with many cashiers bustling back and forth, or a pharmaceutical company?

Together as a team, they could surely manage anything, and our family name would have a place in the annals of Saigon's most known pharmaceutical contributors.

But my mother's dream died when the Revolutionary Army thundered down Thoại Ngọc Hầu Street. When it was all over, the carcass of a burned-up tank sat smoldering outside Tân Sơn Nhất International Airport. From our window to the world, we gazed out to the street, now emptied of cars, to find that life continued on its head.

After the so-called reunification of our country, Mom reopened her pharmacy with one simple goal: She would serve the neighborhood until her stock ran dry and then she would liquidate her business. Customers poured in from close and far to stock up for the future, breathing life and the illusion of prosperity into Mom's little store. The pharmacy employed two full-time staff, with Chị Sáu helping during the busiest hours.

In this period right after the event of the fall of Saigon, we had a lot of *bộ đội* as customers. Dressed in green army uniforms, helmets on heads, their bare feet strapped in black tire sandals, they were foot soldiers freshly resurrected from the Hồ Chí Minh Trail to roam the magnificent streets of the Pearl of the Orient. To tell the truth, they were rather handsome to my fourteen-year-old eyes—suntanned, muscular, frank, and naive like cows. The city life clearly intoxicated their souls. There were a million glittery things to see and touch. Simple objects delighted these soldiers who had grown up in the forests. They streamed in and out of our pharmacy looking at everything and buying little. Everything dazzled them, especially our two female clerks who were in their twenties and good-looking. The *bộ đội*'s speech amazed me. They were Northerners like us, yet they spoke with a peculiar accent, confounding the "l" with the "n" sounds, their speech harsh, their vocabularies ridiculous. We laughed at them. They laughed at us. It was a merry interaction at the pharmacy. They were friendly and keen to make friends. We were girls, and keen to collect male admirers. And Mom accepted the easy-going interaction. The enemies were our friends. That discovery surprised me, and confused me greatly.

One of the soldiers was very cheerful. He wasn't anybody's hopeful boyfriend, more like a big brother. He came into the pharmacy to visit and chitchat almost every afternoon. Then we didn't see him for a couple of weeks. When he returned, he wasn't as jovial. He asked what an antibiotic could be used for and left promptly, dragging his steps. Then one day, the truth. He had contracted syphilis from the girls on the street.

With quivering lips, he murmured to Mom, leaning close to her ear, "The doctor might have to cut it."

My curiosity got the better of me, and I strained to listen in.

"Who told you?" Mom asked.

"My friends. Quartered like an orange," he said, looking miserable and embarrassed at the same time, his eyes darting, ashamed.

"I . . . I may not be able to have children."

"Don't listen to them." Mom said. "You shouldn't have been careless, but it isn't the end of the world." She urged him to let a doctor examine him immediately.

"Bring back your prescription. You need antibiotic," she added.

As soon as he departed, the staff rolled on the floor laughing, repeating over and over, "Quarter it like an orange." I laughed, too, although clueless about the role of a male genital in all this business with the call girls.

Steadily, courtship resulted between our clerks and these soldiers. Even Chị Sáu, the least giddy among our employees, dated. This time, she seemed as much in love as the first time around with Chú Tuấn, even mentioning marrying. After her solider left with the promise to come back for her, she decided to pay him a surprise visit and traveled by train up north, to the territory no Southerner, much less a single maid, had ever set foot in. She returned disheartened but glad she had checked things out. The man she thought would marry her already had a wife.

After a few months, her pharmaceutical samples depleted, my mother had only words of advice and consolation to offer her sick, penniless clientele. Soon, her shelves of medicine also emptied. The druggist without chemicals was powerless, save for her vast knowledge of chemical properties commonly found in food, herbal products, and simple folk remedies. She proposed anything she thought would help relieve the fever, the incurable ache, the skin infection, the wracking cough. The locals respected her. And she felt thankful for their alliance, especially in this difficult time.

Often people stayed longer for the sake of conversation. Mom was very cautious in her talk. She'd nod and smile, adding, "You don't say!" to the badinage, yielding patiently to all the simple babble and paying respect to vented frustration. My mother twirled from client to client, taking care of everyone's medical needs but, at the same time absorbing the state of their collective mood like a weather vane at the change of winds. She would bring her reflections home to share with Dad. My parents started to speak privately, or stopped mid-sentence when one of us passed by. What was going on? We were not used to being left out of our parents' conversation.

I sensed what was not told. The enigmatic response Dad gave me— "I'd rather not tell you things you would not be able to keep to yourself"—was like a thunderclap to my ears. He never before withheld information from us. But the devil revealed to me, through obvious manifestations, whatever knowledge Dad kept to himself.

I witnessed the plague of changes. The firm ground under us was slipping away, pulling everyone underfoot. Even the people of my neighborhood, who had had experience dealing with communism, were caught off-guard. Before, in the North, they could flee ahead of the destroying current. They now had no choice but to be malleable when the hammer came down, to bend like grass in a ravaging storm.

The government dictated: "You are not to address anybody by rank or title. The society will be operating on the same level of comradeship."

We did not understand the new order. To be forced to address one's elders as "comrade" was very confusing. It was almost comical to hear Mom—the most adaptable member of our family—attempting to "comrade" our father.

"But this is serious," she protested at his order to cease and desist. "I need to practice this new form of greeting people."

Patrick brought Mom back to firm ground with "Comrade Mom! When is dinner?"

Comrade Mom was not at all amused. She gave him two burning slaps.

Maybe this was why our parents no longer included us in their confidences. They were afraid—afraid for the family, for us, for them—afraid of this new disregard for societal alliance, for the elderly, the learned, and the religious and social leaders.

The whole foundation on which our culture stood had buckled. In the Vietnamese Confucius society, each is ranked according to his or her sex, age, relation, and status. Now, forced to abandon this ranking system, the basic societal order that made a person a Vietnamese would be destroyed. A father would be nothing to his son. And a son who no longer addressed his father with respect would eventually be considered a bandit, sowing disgrace, "a worm that spoils a whole pot of soup."

No one knew who he should be, how he should behave. All he knew was that the old ways, the previous points of reference, were no longer valid. How terrible to have to rethink one's codes of conduct, starting a culture from scratch. I remembered this disorientation, this feeling of isolation, when I was transferred to a new high school and had to adapt to a set of new friends. Coming from an all-girl establishment and never having been around male classmates, how I trembled in the new classroom.

We were bracing for the next elimination. Even the most simple, uneducated Vietnamese knew about Karl Marx's anti-religion views: "Religion is the sigh of the oppressed creature, the heart of a heartless world, and the soul of soulless conditions. It is the opium of the people."

To avoid the visit of government officials to their homes, our people, known to be ancestor worshipers, stealthily stripped their family altars of elaborate ornaments to display only photographs of the dead relatives. Buddhists cleared away the heavy copper *lu*—a three-legged vase filled with rice in which incense sticks were planted—and various statuettes depicting Buddha in his many forms, the favorites being the Laughing Buddha with his unsuppressed happiness, the Blessing Buddha with his right hand upturned, and the Good Fortune Buddha on his bag of prosperity. Catholics like us took the crosses off our living-room walls and moved them into the bedrooms, where the Virgin Mary and Jesus were already hiding.

People felt that their accursed existences were being threatened from both worlds. On Earth, they were persecuted by the Red Army. From above and below the Earth, in their different worlds, the neglected spirits of their ancestors and other loved ones would come back to haunt, either stirred to anger and revenge or saddened by their abandonment.

Everyone was trying to appease the spirits with private offerings, murmuring prayers in the depth and darkness of solitude, or silently counting the beads of a rosary. Imagine our shock when we received the order to display the portrait of Hồ Chí Minh in a central location of our homes. The old women came in droves to the pharmacy to commiserate with one another about this new farce. How puzzling to witness the communist government condemning idol worship and the veneration of God, only to mandate the worship of an old man long dead. Nonetheless, everyone complied without questioning. That or be thrown into jail.

I had my own way to rebel.

In our house, Hồ, our arch-enemy, was relinquished to the highest shelf of our entertainment center. Out of sight, therefore out of mind. The statuettes of two black cats stared him down. May he rot in hell.

In addition to the display of Hồ's portrait, we were mandated to hang a banner saying "Uncle Hồ lives always among his people" at the pharmacy. Coming in and out, people would shake their heads in disapproval of the sign, until someone came up with a marvelous idea. Toying with the Vietnamese syntax to deliberately omit a hyphen, the word wizard twisted the praise into an insult: "Uncle Hồ lives always inside our pants."

The proletariat look of crumply, dark clothes heavily patched up was à la mode. In a short time, the dry-cleaning businesses were displaced by a procession of mobile tanners, chanting intermittently, "Tanning shirt, tanning pants, tanning all your life *heeere*." Steaming vats balanced at the ends of their bamboo poles as they bobbed with their quick steps.

I watched a tanner at work with a small batch of our clothes. Into the boiling, black dye the woman dipped our colorful cottons. She stewed them as if they were beef shanks intended for *phở*, stirring occasionally. It wouldn't have looked out of place if she were to taste them, smacking her lips afterward. She worked effectively, with quick movements, transferring the blackened shirts to the second vat, "to cure them," she explained when I asked. It was the most economical way to reinvent one's wardrobe, and thus reinvent one's identity. Before, one could be a pharmacist, an engineer, a city girl. Now, a peasant woman, a field worker, a poor child. Dark like the earth, colorless as anonymity. Faceless animals fading into their surroundings for survival. Black clothing set off my mother's light skin and made her look sick, ghostlike. The sun could not bake her into a browner shade.

It was the end of private employment. Men not sent to the re-education camps were home jobless; women, if not in public meetings, spent their time like little ants in lines, for rationed rice, rationed coal, rationed oil—every basic supply.

Charcoal replaced propane in the kitchen. It was hard at first to live like cave dwellers. No more switches. No more tanks. The cooking fire was patiently stoked with tinder and bits of paper, with face bent low, mouth blowing, hands fanning, eyes watering. Our kitchen walls blackened in no time without the help of the tanners. Indeed, black clothing suited our new lifestyle well. Mom wore it everywhere. She could sit straight on the dirt floor with the other womenfolk when attending meetings.

The co-ops replaced the rations of rice with unrefined bulgur, rejected corn and wheat meant for cattle stock. Having nothing else, we ate it, for hunger did not have the luxury of choice. A full stomach, a feeling of fullness, was the ultimate fulfillment. We felt full for a long time, battling constipation. With patience and time humans could conquer anything, I realized. Fire. Then flour. We improvised on whatever basics we obtained from the bare co-ops. From indigestible grains to flour. From flour to homemade noodles and cassava cakes.

We reinvented life. A new language was born, codified to safeguard vital communication. Following the Southern custom, we substituted names with numbers to protect people's identities. Khoa, my grandparents Lê's fifth son, became Fifth Uncle, "*Ông Năm.*" Ông Năm could be anyone. You could walk down the street and there would be Ông Năm the shoe repairer, Ông Năm the one-legged war veteran begging at the corner. Ông Năm was no one in particular. Ông Năm was safe, one ant in a million, as long as he was smart enough to crawl away from crushing feet. They tried. The fathers, the mothers, the girls, the boys, children, adults. Oh, how they tried. Some succeeded. They lived in a blackened anonymity. Some died. They died in anonymity, like ants.

Shadows followed us at night as we moved with our lanterns from room to room. They were there to remind us that walls had eyes and ears. Keep mum. Be watchful. Lie. Act. Cheat. Live. Put your mask on and dance to the tune of death, but hang on to life. Repeat after them, shouting propaganda if you must. It's only your mouth talking. Not you. Your tongue praising Hồ Chí Minh. Not you. Forgive me, mothers and fathers, for the accusations vomited from the foul cavity of my face. Believe me, sons and daughters. What comes out of me is devoid of meaning at heart. It is done, in spite of me, in order to live, to beat the system, to beat them with their own sticks.

We live, is what counts.

6.

Head Full of Lice

School Year 1975–1976

September 1975 came but there was no talk of school. A daily downpour turned our courtyard into a swift river. It was a perfect season to launch paper boats and watch our creations sail out from their safe harbor at our front porch to the fig tree, where a gurgling maelstrom drowned them. No matter how perfectly we made them—with roofs, sail rigs, oars, and sailors—they went down with other debris into the sewer.

The rain lessened in October, when "It's dark before we get to smile"— *"Tháng mười chưa cười đã tối."* School resumed eventually, and we returned to teachers and friends with both regret and gladness.

We also returned with our heads lice-swarmed, the white eggs like confetti on our hair—a gift from that hellish night waiting for a helicopter lift. Instead of being scooped up by angels, our heads were adorned with our first public shame as we descended further into despair.

Monkeys and apes we had become, spending our days combing each other's manes with our fingers, searching for lice to pick. Our servants taught us to use the special comb with thin, dense teeth and gather the lice on a white piece of paper, then kill them one by one with our thumbnails. It was satisfying to listen to the explosion of the tiny bodies. When all else failed, we washed our heads with a liquid pesticide—the same kind sprayed to eliminate mosquitoes—and rubbed the corpses out with a towel. This method worked well, but somehow we contracted lice again within weeks. The three young kids had short hair and were quickly lice-free. My hair was down to my waist, so it took me longer to get rid of the eggs. Then the younger ones got lice from me. And the cycle repeated. Mom proposed to shave our hair off.

"Over my dead body," I told her.

I would surely perish of shame if my friends found out. Covering my infestation in a neat ponytail, I went to school properly corseted that school year but, ironically, bringing with me a greater secret than budding breasts that could not be hidden behind large pockets. What to do?

This would be my third year at the Franco-Chino-Vietnamese Collège Fraternité—Bác-Ái Học-Viện. Up until sixth grade my academic life was spent in a Roman Catholic, all-girl establishment, in classes run by nuns wearing full convent garb. Daily catechism and devotional in the school chapel were part of my formal education. Why was I the only child in the family to attend a religious institution? I never knew for sure! Equally mysterious was Dad's decision to switch me, at the end of fifth grade, after all those years, to Collège Fraternité, where four of my siblings were enrolled.

"The nuns are making you work too hard," he had objected when catching me fighting the mosquitoes late at night through tons of homework. Then on countless occasions: "Fraternité is a progressive school. I have a lot of respect for Mr. Brun."

After the 1968 education reform, when Vietnamese teaching only was mandated, Fraternité, besides Colette and Marie Curie, which were de facto international schools for foreign children, was the last place where parents could still find a French education for their children. Mr. Brun, a Frenchman and Fraternité's director, continued to promote his French immersion program as before. When the inspector from the education department came for his impromptu visit, the teachers would be signaled to switch to Vietnamese textbooks.

I strongly suspected that the truth behind my transferal lay in Dad's evaluation of my academic ability. My grades had been far from sublime. At the rate I was going, retention would be bound to happen if I didn't transfer out from under the nuns' harsh, antiquated methods.

I started sixth grade full of misgivings, never having had boys in my class. In my eyes, they were turbulent beings, constantly in motion and collision. Standing in lines, to my great discomfort they would now and then shove one another into the girls, causing screams of distress. Shoe prints covered the lower part of the classroom walls. Deep carvings marred the surface of desks. Offensive drawings of anatomy parts and obscenities covered the bathroom stalls. Worse, that year, being new, I was stuck in the back with all the bigger boys. The one sitting next to me was particularly gigantic. Cung Phùng Vĩ Thành—even his name brought to mind the vision of a massive citadel.

I remember him clearly—large grin with big teeth, black mane, thighs like two tree trunks below the loosely worn blue shorts, stomach bulging over the waistline. My terror was in my face, I was sure, for he kept baring his horse-like teeth at me.

I jumped each time this banyan tree of a boy moved.

"They love to put lizards into the back of skirts," warned Chị Tuyến, the daughter of my parents' friend, when I asked about her experience at the school. She might have been pulling my leg, for the only animals that ever materialized from the hands of my giant friend were the ones carved onto erasers. He had three or four boxfuls of the homemade stamps, erasers embossed with comic-book figures: the Smurfs, Obelix, Asterix, Tintin and Snowy, you name them. My fear of him quickly yielded to adoration for his artistic talent. The feeling of friendship must have been mutual, because he began to offer me his less-treasured stamps and taught me how to make my own.

By seventh grade I had become one of them, Fraternians, and the subject of male adoration. After a tumultuous summer and a long break from school, I returned to school excited, a grown eighth grader. Patrick and I had pedaled the long way from home in Gia-Định to our school in Chợ Lớn. The normally twenty-minute car ride cost us an hour biking. But we were thrilled, fledging birds finally with wings to explore. While Dad locked himself at home and Mom was swung like a yoyo by the local authority, the bikes gave us an unexpected independence from our parents. We had argued until our voices grew hoarse to convince Chị Sáu we could take care of Anne. And so we did, taking turns carrying her. The pig, she was so heavy! Eight-year-old Michelle, however, was too young to ride with us and was left uneducated at home.

Our brakes squealed in unison as Patrick and I entered Nguyễn Trãi Boulevard, shocked. Normally choked with fume-spewing cars, the portion of the boulevard in front of our school was jam-packed with bicycles of all makes and colors. Pushing my bike through the crowd of white-and-blue uniforms, I was happy to locate most of my friends. We weren't the only ones staying back in Vietnam, then. It was a great solace!

From afar, I recognized a boy named H. L. Ya, a Don Juan smile plastered on his white face. The creep! One day last year, at recess, right in the middle of the football field, he had declared in the witness of all our friends, "I'm in love with you," hugging the *cartable* that he was supposed to keep for me while we girls were busy playing hopscotch.

His bold move had opened the floodgate to a torrent of copycats. All of a sudden, the boys in our class were free to admit their crushes left and right. Unsuspected mute worshipers like P. D. Phúc, the bespectacled mature boy who hardly threw a glance in our direction, shamelessly loosened his tongue to our class president, Françette; Hiệp to the smiley Ngọc-Thúy; Phong to Phi-Loan. Passion spread unchecked, like fire through a dry field of grass, until it licked the pants bottom of Maurice—class clown, prank master, joker. Audacious boy for picking on Rose Mỹ-Hồng! His subject of adoration was famous for having a viperous tongue, deadly poisonous. In anger, her eyes cut like steel.

He came straight to her. "Will you be my girlfriend?"

She responded quickly with a loud smack to his monkey face, to our shock and the delight of his clan. He stepped back, his hand nursing his branded cheek.

"That is the loudest *yes* I've heard, sweet Rose."

The boys all clapped and hollered with delight.

Open courtship was a new game to be won by the guys. Even during an intense soccer match, a boy on the sideline with no ball to chase after would launch a "Dear love! Will you marry me?" at any one of us girls, whenever we happened to cross the field. The boldest among us would toss back, "Not in a million years."

"How about next year?" another would bait, not yielding.

Now, Ya pushed his bike toward me. Ever since that first day of declaration, a daring boy, full of male confidence, he had been pursuing me, lurking around the places I frequented, the source of my embarrassment. His family owned Givrall, one of the best bakeries in Saigon, catering to the elite and five-star restaurants.

"Hello, there!" he said, and I, mortified, breathed out a soft, courteous "Hey," hoping that the mutual greeting would simply end there.

"I'm glad we didn't lose you to France," he said.

It was with great relief that I saw the opening of our school gate.

"I've got to hurry," I said, leaving him quickly to bring my bike inside the roped-off dirt lot. "Leave bike at your own risk" was written on a piece of cardboard stapled to a wooden pole. Roped lots like this for bike parking had sprung up all over our city, some guarded and issuing tickets, some not. You locked your bike and hoped that it would be still standing there waiting for you.

Innovation on the fly was a Vietnamese quality.

Inside the school, big changes had been made. The sign reading *Fraternité* had been removed. I would be attending eighth grade, not

Quatrième as under the old French system. Academic subjects were reduced to make time for learning about the Party and Uncle Hồ, and to sing the new revolutionary songs, like:

> *Last night I dreamed of Uncle Hồ*
> *His beard was long, his hair was white*
> *Elated, I sang with him . . .*

Over time, the kids of Saigon changed the lyrics to suit their reality:

> *In my dream last night I found a purse*
> *In the purse was twelve hundred bucks*
> *Elated, I showed it to Uncle Hồ*
> *Smiling, he asked for half*

The changing face of our daily life soon turned into a game to us—the trickier, the more exciting. We believed that our parents would be there, mightier than any danger, to protect us from harm. We began to take greater risk without consulting the adults at home and take our life into our own hands. After the first week, our taste of freedom dulled away. Biking Anne to school became an ordeal. Like a bag of rice, her body would slump on one side and drag my bike. Securing her with one hand would mean leaving the front of my skirt at the mercy of the blowing wind. *Do I risk exposing myself or drop my sister?*

Then, a bright idea!

Patrick and I would let Anne hop on the bus that stopped outside our alley. Biking along, we would follow her until the last bus stop in front of Petrus Ký School. There, she would emerge safe and sound to rejoin us on the back seat of my bike for a short ride to school. Voila!

Our parents, too, adapted. Filling out our school forms, without hesitation Dad would write under "occupation": "blue-collar worker." After a second contemplation, under "place of occupation" he scribbled in "The Flying Horse." The Flying Horse? The name was Dad's improvisation upon Esso's old logo. A horse, a laboring member of the field, would surely kindle the Party's sympathy. Would Esso be pleased with this improvement upon its brand? For the time being, Dad had bigger concerns.

Often, returning from school, we found him quietly playing solitary Chinese chess, a guidebook for beginners in his hand. The chessboard and his book were printed on cheap, thin paper. Recently bought, the paper was already yellowed and creased from usage. The chess pieces were identical round pieces of soft wood. Carved-on Chinese characters indicated which was king, queen, castles, knight, or pawn. He played the blue team, then green, against the book, learning. "The pieces move according to their ranks, their relative positions, and the will of the player," he explained.

My father spent months learning the strategic moves, training himself. Looking back, I now see that we had all been engaged in a game of chess. We were mere wooden pieces moved by the invisible hand of fate—lucky pawn sometimes checking a badly positioned king. Then again, each of us was a beginning player learning the moves, persevering through all losses, adapting, getting smarter, training in the hope of emerging as winner one day.

7.

National Grace: A Dream Shattered

At twenty-nine, my mother's youngest sister, Aunt Bích, had wedded Mr. Nguyễn Gia Kiểng, a graduate of L'École Centrale de Paris. She was from a well-to-do family, he from a humble background. It was an elite, Western education that had brought their social platforms on the same level. Uncle Kiểng had had none of the necessary ingredients for a successful life that his young, pretty wife had: family wealth, an educated mother's vision and ambition, a smoothly paved upbringing. He, born into poverty to illiterate parents, had only one gift: intelligence, and perhaps luck. At the end of high school, he had earned a government scholarship. It was only natural that he would make it his mission in life to return to the motherland as soon as he had earned his college diploma, to help poor Vietnamese improve their lives.

He successfully convinced his westernized wife to forgo their good life in France and resettle in Saigon. They repatriated in 1973 and re-established their careers in no time. He began working for Việt Nam Thương-Tiến, a commercial bank; she was a full-time medical doctor at the newly constructed Vì Dân Hospital. They lived in a nice-sized home in a coveted complex owned by the bank.

My cousin Caroline Nguyễn Hoàng Quốc-Phái was born in early 1975. Her name, meaning National Grace, was unconventional. I could imagine the exalted state of her patriotic father when he proudly printed each curve and diacritical accent of his firstborn's name on her birth certificate for the world to see. National Grace was destined to be the futuristic daughter of Vietnam: well educated yet traditional, prosperous but non-exploitive, and free from domination—be it by men, foreign culture, social expectation, or self-deprecation.

Ironically, the fall of Saigon followed the birth of Caroline Quốc-Phái within weeks. The table was turned. Merely a year before, the couple Bích–Kiểng had been an illustrative example for young and aspiring intellects to emulate. Overnight, the same couple could be persecuted for their political and social associations, their existence in Vietnam turned precarious for countless reasons. Uncle Kiểng's anti-communist view was well known in intellectual circles. In fact, his ambition to live in Vietnam was partly inspired by a desire to redirect the course of history, to steer the deeply troubled South away from the Việt-Cộng. Aunt Bích had lived too long in France for the new anti-Western regime to tolerate her. This deep concern for their immediate safety precipitated drastic action. So, Caroline, barely a month old, was left in the hands of our cousin Mai-Xuân, while her parents, together with Uncle Chấn, hastened southward to escape by boat.

It was a logical plan. As French, Mai-Xuân would be immune from harassment by the new government. As soon as plans for foreigners to repatriate were established, she would be safely on her way, carrying in her hands Caroline and a fake birth certificate. The baby would be reunited with her birth parents in France. The separation would be weeks, at worst months.

The reality turned out to be more complicated. Bạc Liêu's police immediately captured Uncle Chấn and the young parents, Kiểng and Bích. At home, the relationship between our cousin and her stepmother Danielle deteriorated. One day, Mai-Xuân came to us crying and insisted that we take her and Caroline into our home.

Mutual tolerance between the belligerent stepdaughter and her father's wife was no longer possible. Aunt Danielle concurred that the situation had gotten out of hand, and reconciliation would not be possible.

Their quarrel followed the classic theme of Cinderella. From age ten to eighteen, Mai Xuân had been Uncle Chấn's only child and love. Suddenly, at eighteen, another woman walked into their lives and stole her place to become her father's companion, sharing his bed where Mai-Xuân usually slept, and giving her orders and contradicting her in every way.

My parents agreed to move Mai-Xuân and baby Caroline in with us. Caroline slept in the family crib last used by Michelle, in the downstairs bedroom. We were delighted to have a baby in the house, and Mai-Xuân was a fun cousin to be with. She was slender and stylishly dressed, her French-accented Vietnamese endearing to our ears. Under our parents' easygoing lifestyle, Mai-Xuân tasted her freedom again and once again was her own boss. Because of our help with babysitting, she was now free to go out with friends.

One evening, home from an excursion downtown, she relayed to us a funny story, which described her independent spirit and her pride of being Vietnamese. That day, a policeman had stopped her.

"What are you?" he had asked her.

"*Người Ta!*" she had said, unaware of the ambiguity in the Vietnamese language. She had used a homophone, "*Ta,*" a Northern expression to say, "I'm our people," as opposed to "*Tây,*" meaning Western or French.

To the Southern policeman, this French kid was being insolent for replying, "Me? I'm a person." How dared she? Mai-Xuân did not understand why he had given her a hard time, until we, laughing, explained to her the nuances of her very correct language usage.

That incident, however, did not deter our twenty-one-year-old cousin from enjoying her daily excursion downtown. Every day she left Caroline and her prepared bottles to me. Caroline grew fast, putting on chubbiness and growing her first tooth. She was pretty. She smiled easily, showing off two large dimples, an angel on earth. I slipped into the role of surrogate mother, giving her the bottles religiously, then playing with her and putting her to sleep.

One day, after her afternoon bottle, Caroline felt asleep in my arms. I decided to put her down to nap with us on our bed. I drifted off to be awakened by Mom's howling. Something had gone terribly wrong. She bent to blow into Caroline's mouth. The baby was limp, unresponsive. Mom tried and tried, mixing her tears with the baby's saliva. Finally, she gave up. Oh God, Caroline had died.

A small coffin was brought home. Caroline, my Caroline, was laid inside in a white dress, looking as peaceful and happy as always. We sat with her coffin on a hired Lambretta, which sputtered to the local cemetery on Thoại Ngọc Hầu. Caroline was laid to rest under a hastily dug, promptly covered mound of dirt. Her life had been short, shorter than the life of a monarch butterfly. Conceived in love, Caroline died, with Saigon, in the turmoil of a revolution, away from her beloved parents. She, a princess born in aristocracy, had gone home in a wooden coffin barely primed, buried in anonymity like a fallen peasant girl.

She lived on inside me. Many times, I ponder the meaning of her name and her short life. Born to be our national grace, a supposedly beautiful gift from her parents to an envisioned prosperous and free Vietnam, Quốc-Phái died a senseless death as a consequence of her parents' patriotic aspiration. Her name, briefly recorded and swiftly destroyed, was only one along with thousands of precious archives purged to save many Vietnamese from the communist persecution. The tragic loss of Caroline's life paled against the loss of a whole country, of countless family separations, of her own parents' life turmoil with their freedom losses.

In a corner of my conscience, there existed a black spot, blacker than the dark lumps of dirt thrown down to little Quốc-Phái. Who was to blame? Was her death partly my responsibility? Her parents'? My parents'? Was it her fate to die an infant, born at the wrong time in the wrong country? Or all of the above?

8.

The Tolling Bell Rang On

What did I know about the significance of our country's flag? It was purely by habit, on past Monday mornings, that I would gather with my whole school in front of the national flag and salute it, singing joyfully, "O People! The country nears its Freedom Day. Together we go forward to the open way . . . ."

I used to watch my country's flag billowing, puffing up like a Siberian tiger ready to pounce. When from atop high-rise buildings my scanning eyes recognized the familiar red-stripes-on-yellow symbol of my country painted on rooftops, or when leafing through the pages of a dictionary and finding under "Flag" the national colors of South Vietnam among the various countries' flags, an intimate association swelled inside me, constricting my heart with many feelings: pride, patriotism, dedication. It never occurred to me that there would come a time when that symbolic national identification would no longer exist for my children; when I, returning to the place where I was born, would never see the three-red-stripes-on-yellow-background flying high, replaced instead by a hideous, bloodstained piece of common cloth.

What did one know about the value of freedom, as long as one's life was secured in a cocoon of wealth and health?

Uncle Huỳnh's health steadily declined. He lingered about a

year, wasting away, until he could no longer rise from his bed. Dad said his brother was dying from exhaustion, as he was already frail from liver cirrhosis. Must I mention my uncle's drinking habit? To us, the Lês, this would be a trespass upon his honor, he who was to many a saint: a faithful husband, a devoted son, a self-effacing brother and, to us, a thoughtful uncle. Physically, he was a tall man with well-defined features. He bore a resemblance to his father, Mr. Lê Huy Diễm—square jaw, strong shoulders, long legs. It was said that he married dutifully but without passion for his older and somewhat haughty wife. She conceived many times, but the pregnancies never lasted, and the couple remained childless.

I was christened as Aunt Huỳnh's goddaughter, but while my relationship with her ended there, Uncle Huỳnh held a special place in my heart. His authority fascinated me, the way he carried himself with so much righteousness, his wisdom emanating on his gentle countenance. I remembered, as a child, talking with him.

He would ask me, "Do you think a rose is beautiful?"

"Yes, Uncle," I would say.

"Do you know roses have thorns?"

"Yes." I was confused.

"Do you think of the rose's beauty or its thorns?" he would ask, half-revealing life's secret to me, urging my thought.

Each time the big family gathered, Uncle Huỳnh would stand up for a long and emotional speech. We started the ceremony with the following simple song, composed by him:

> *My dear grandparents, we love you*
> *You belong to Big Uncle*
> *You belong to Small Uncle*
> *You belong to uncles' wives*
> *You belong to all my aunts*
> *You belong to me*
> *O, Great Cougar!*

We chorused happily, connected as one big Lê, with the same

grandfather and the same grandmother who belonged to all of us. Such a strong revelation of bloodline through utterly simple lyrics.

When he grew too weak to call out for his wife from his bed, she gave him a bell. Each time he was forced to use it, he excused himself. On his last day, Grandma was by his side. He looked at her with tears streaming and begged for her forgiveness: "Mother! I am a treacherous son to leave you early. Please forgive me for not staying to care for you and bury you on the day you die. Mother, forgive me!"

Then he expired.

He had paid his price for freedom: the freedom to preserve his dignity under a merciless and ignorant government that deprived its citizens of food, fuel, and medicine. The sorrow in his heart from a loveless marriage had already rendered my uncle a melancholy soul. The further lack of children had robbed him of the joy of fatherhood and driven him to attach himself to the bottle. But it was the exhaustion in his body that ultimately caused his spirit to be broken and destroyed his will to fight on, to survive.

Within months of my uncle's death, more bad news tumbled home from different corners of the country. All three members of Mom's family, Uncle Chấn, Uncle Kiểng, and Aunt Bích, were still serving time in a high-security jail in Bạc Liêu, one of the most pro-communist localities of the South. The people in that part of the country loathed city dwellers for their easy wealth and luxurious lifestyle. It was now their time for revenge, time to punish the capitalists and followers of Western culture. Mom was told that her brother and brother-in-law were forced to enter the jail's waste tank to clean it with their hands. My aunt, barely recovered from her recent Caesarean section, had developed an infection while serving her term of forced labor. She might not survive to return home.

On the Lê side, two uncles and a cousin were held indefinitely in different concentration camps, sharing their fates with thousands of other military personnel. These people, encouraged by the new government to self-register for a short-term re-education program, had presented themselves at designated centers in Saigon with only a small bag for overnight stay. Prompted by the state promise of general clemency, these men had left their homes with a simple "Don't forget to line up for rice today" tossed casually at their wives. With their nets slack and waiting, the local police branches had only to wait for their school of fish to swim in, mouths gulping the sweet morning air, gathering, increasing in number. The nets were quickly pulled in. They were loaded onto waiting trucks "to be transported to a re-education center for some simple formalities, to have their names crossed out from a master list so that they would not be again bothered."

That was the last they were heard of. All had been transferred to the faraway undisclosed concentration camps, some as far as North Vietnam. The state never fulfilled its promise of clemency. A year after they left home, their families still did not know their exact whereabouts. Dark presentiments settled over the city.

9.

Chameleon

There was a unique bond between my childhood home and me. In 1962, both were brought into the world. I was born at Hospital Grall and transferred directly home to the master bedroom of the house in Tân Sa Châu, the only room that was completely finished. The rest of this new home we called Tân Sa Châu was still under construction while I suckled peacefully in my mother's arms.

I knew my home intimately, had traced my feet on each crack in the floor and sought in every nook a place to hide in a "Five, Ten" game. The best place to watch the sunset was from the open window of the second-floor landing. I used to stand there with my hair still wet from my afternoon shower. The sky was stained a mixture of turmeric yellow and saffron orange, then deepened into a lollipop red as the sun sank away, yielding to half shadows.

We were often up in the terrace during kite-flying season. The year that my brother Daniel actively participated was the best of all years. The terrace was littered with newspapers, scissors, and liquid glue. Rolls of nylon strings lay tangled with bamboo sticks. My brother's eyes intensely scanned the sky, his feet moving swiftly, his right hand pulling on a string, guiding his kite up and away from the neighbors' kites, each of a different design made simply of old newspaper, their tails long and fluttering.

"Watch out, brother Daniel," Patrick cried out, but too late. Our kite had been clipped by another kite's string and plummeted, only to be caught by tree branches, irretrievable. Brother Daniel was eight years older than Patrick, so he must have been fifteen that year, Patrick eight, and I ten.

Then the years rolled by and our older brothers and sisters left home and left their rooms to us, the four musketeers, our parents' "second litter."

We grew up no less rambunctious. Outside Mom's bedroom, we used to climb across from rooftops to landings, daring the devil himself while the servants and Grandma looked on in terror, Grandma exclaiming, "Jesus-Maria! My God."

With all the changes taking place around us, our home was an intact haven, a calm harbor to anchor our indecisive lives. Mom returned each day from the pharmacy and the mandatory meetings to seek refuge in her familiar master suite. Exhausted, she quickly got rid of her cumbersome peasant disguise and slipped into her loose cotton pajamas, dropping her body onto the large bed like a farmer letting go of his heavy sack of rice. Lying there on her side in the dark, head resting on her tin box, she closed her eyes and attempted to unburden herself.

Easily anxious, my mother had become a bundle of raw nerves. Many times, unable to calm herself the natural way, she popped Valium. If I could not find the tiny white pills she demanded, her tired voice would tell me, "Just give me a pill, any pill you can find."

Our parents took their afternoon naps together, during which time the master suite was locked for intimacy, something we never suspected existed between them. They included us so completely into their lives that if we had learned there were moments that they were exclusively for each other, we would surely have been scandalized.

This sleeping arrangement suited both our parents in many ways. My mother preferred her bed chamber dark, hot, and quiet, while my father could not tolerate a stuffy room, insulated from light, cool air, and music. After the departure of his two older daughters, Dad moved into sister Mai's bedroom. Here he could run the air conditioner all day without his wife's complaint. He even kept the unit on at night. This room was remodeled to suit his taste. In this office-bedroom—his world within my mother's reign—he had a custom-made countertop mounted along one wall to serve as writing space. Above this long desk, shelves and cabinets were installed for books, propped up spine to spine in no particular order. Dad treated his friends-in-print the same way he cared for us: keeping them within reach in a relaxing atmosphere. The way our father dealt with us and with the world must have derived from the same natural source that enabled plants to cling happily to their soil, birds to lift into the sky, or fish to breathe inside a body of water. He was never to his family an authoritative figure, but a respected friend.

He was to me more than a friend, for he shared with me many passions. Dad's propensities for literature, music, and poetry made him my best friend. He did not write stories or poems, but his letters were marvelous pieces of creative writing—factual, yet lively and poetic. Like me, Dad had a liking for cupboards and storage units. He spared no expense to realize his fantasies, when he could afford them, and throughout the years would bring home at intervals: now a dresser, now a cupboard, sometimes mis-matched, other times a whole matching set for a bedroom or the living room. Sometimes he would go to the extreme to have custom-made shelves and countertops installed, not because there was a particular need for more display or storage space, but just to be surrounded by it.

In recent years, Dad had modernized our home and retrofitted it with modular air-conditioning units, added double-glass panes to all the windows, installed wooden wainscoting to the ground-floor walls, and repainted the exterior a dazzling red.

Ah! My home. Its beautification process, made affordable by the sweat of my parents' brows and years of frugality, was suspended midway, never to be completed. So the bank of bedroom windows looking out coquettishly remained bare and cold, missing their layers of draperies—a Cinderella half-transformed. So, when aching for my home, I remember not only its perfect architecture—the elegance of its austere aloofness, with its louvers shut for privacy—but also its imperfections: its interior barrenness, the wet and slippery floor during the monsoon seasons, the overflown sewage, the clogged toilets. My childhood home comes back to me in its true form—a dream half-woven, a first love made fierce in a child's breast. Time could not destroy it.

My home and I were born together and grew into the world together. While her beauty was enhanced by my parents' money, my appearance was mine to fashion according to my primitive aesthetic sense. I had long hair, and was constantly experimenting with different hairdos: braided and adorned with colorful ribbons, tied in a single ponytail, then in double-tails, curled, or straight and shiny. I had no jewelry, since my mother was herself oblivious to its appeal— she did not even wear her wedding ring—and makeup was inaccessible, the thought of it almost shameful.

Inwardly, the maturing process rendered me an independent teenager who needed her own space. To have some degree of freedom for myself, I moved into my brother Daniel's room on the third floor. It had not been used since he departed for France, just a few months prior to sister Madeleine. There, living by myself on a separate floor of the house, higher than the trees outside my window, I perched among the birds, with an immense sky above. It was much quieter up, away from the maids, my younger siblings, and the noisy dogs.

The room's two large windows let in plenty of air in the hot afternoon. From one window, I could see Grandma's kitchen, her unscreened door shut tight since her helper had quit. We used to come to Chị Ba, her maid, to check out her leftovers—bits of fish stew, a bowl of Salyut leaf soup, or sometimes simply rice, eaten with roasted and crushed sesame seeds mixed with salt. Our visit to Grandma's storage room was also motivated by her bunch of dwarf bananas—fists with fat, yellow fingers—hung to ripen in darkness until their skins thinned out, their white meat tasting as sweet as candies.

From one window, my eyes could sweep from Grandma's kitchen door to her bedroom on the first floor. Her balcony jutted into the magnolia foliage at a perfect height for us to pick its fragrant blossoms, our favorite sport. The treetop caressed the terrace's landing above, offering us another possibility to pluck the flowers, which we collected in large amounts for Grandpa's altar. From the vantage point of my other window, I could observe the daily activities of the church school and spy into the dark recesses of my neighbors' home. The alley was partially shielded by the soaring church roof, its height elevated with the years, hoping to surpass our home. The old priest never let go of his ancient grudge against our family; he nursed it inside his heart like a badly scarred wound that had become part of his identity. We knew the old man for his ill temper. Many times, he chased us off when we approached his private quarter in search of a straying ball or coconuts that had dropped on the wrong side of the wall at harvest.

"Away, Satan!" He would bolt out from his private chamber and thrust his rosary in the air at us.

Many of my afternoons were spent sitting at my desk—the only proper desk in the whole house, with three drawers on its right side, in which I meticulously placed my pens, containers of knick-knacks, a small sewing box, and diaries of all sorts. I watched flocks of birds pass across the large frame of my window, while Francoise Hardy crooned on the audio system *"Nous serons toujours comme des amoureux...."* Dreamily singing along, I almost forgot that the old time had vanished, that this sentimental French song was now banished. My heart was full of longing.

At night, I often woke to find the outline of the many trees immobile against the sky. At times, a small wind stirred the leaves; in the eerie light of a faint moon and the twinkling stars, they looked more like dancing skeletons. For a while, I stubbornly braved loneliness and an increased fear of ghosts, until my retirement to the cherished third floor felt more like a banishment to a torture chamber. But my pragmatism got the upper hand. I relinquished my independence with gladness and suggested my little brother, Patrick, move in next door, into brother Khải's old room. He would be separated from me by only a plywood wall.

This wall was erected after my two older brothers had grown out of the nursery room. In one old black-and-white snapshot, I was shown with a wooden tennis racket held against my wrinkled nose, smiling against the background of a spacious room separated by a net at the dividing line that was now a wall. Facing each other in two teams, my brothers and sisters played indoor tennis. Perhaps the large room was cut in half because my brother Khải, with his quieter and pious nature, had demanded a place of his own separated from the more turbulent Daniel. I always remember Khải, as a boy, attired like a priest in a white sheet, fervently doling out holy communion, while Daniel's idea of a game was to rouge his lips, powder his cheeks, squeeze himself into his sister's bra and dress, and walk around the house in high heels, dangling a purse. A dozen years later, here I was, an adolescent girl in a boy's room stripped of his belongings yet retaining his musky grown boy's odor, longing for the old togetherness.

Patrick was my junior by two years, as typical a boy as I was a girl. Although Patrick preferred to practice kicking a soccer ball with Anne and Michelle taking turn at being the goalie while I composed poetry in my room, there were many games we four played harmoniously together. When we played house, everyone enjoyed the setting-up phase—we gathered materials found around the yard to construct our home and piled bricks into kitchen, bedrooms, living room—a miniature version of our actual home. While I was busy transferring hot coals from the kitchen to our toy stove, Anne and Michelle were absorbed in their task, chalking streets on the courtyard concrete. Laying his tricycle on its side and, with both hands steering one wheel as if he was steering a car, Patrick could be, in an instant, a daredevil robber, burning his tires through the street maze rigged with multiple obstacles, closely pursued by Policeman

Michelle, and in the next, a gentle father reading his newspaper, puffing on a paper cigar, while dutiful daughter Anne set up the family dinner. Tiny plastic bowls and plates were our make-believe tableware. Our table was rich with food, rice mixed with cookies, and platefuls of other concoctions, mostly inedible—mixtures of mud and leaves, shredded papers, and even dead crickets.

The third floor became our isolated world once Patrick moved up with me. I dragged Mr. Esso Man out from the junk box under the staircase where he was last abandoned, and up to the third-floor landing, where he again stood guard as he once did at Chị Mai's inaugural ball many years ago. My imagination at work, I rigged him into an alarm system, stringing a steel wire between his saluting hand and the scrolled metal of the stair's handrail. Any time someone squeezed past my Esso Man, the wire jiggled the attached handbell. I, property owner and proud inventor, would jump out from my room to catch the surprised visitor and give a long lecture on trespassing. "Can't you read the sign?" I would point to a small handwritten note taped on Esso Man's greeting hand, "Do not pass." All the detective stories I had read heavily influenced me that year. At night, before falling asleep, Patrick and I communicated by sending Morse code back and forth, tapping the signals on the wooden wall separating our bedrooms.

After staying in brother Daniel's room for a few months, the novelty of the living arrangement lost its appeal. I was again on a hunt for different living quarters. In my imagination, a miniature room took shape, similar to the cabin-size room of one of my school friends. Without consulting my parents, I called our faithful carpenter and ordered one of our twin beds shortened, so it could fit into the tiny storage room on our third floor. This room did not even have a proper window. It was about the size of a bathroom, about six by eight feet. I cleaned it up, moved the bed in, brought over my favorite desk, and hung up a lightbulb. There I lived, feeling like a character in a fairy tale. My parents did not object. I had complete freedom of my home—to rearrange it according to my fancies, experimenting with the flair of a budding interior designer. It was like playing house with life-size toys.

Once, with the help of my maids, I brought the double wardrobe from the third floor down to the landing of the second floor and turned it upside down to be transformed into a large desk. I hung a large chalkboard up and converted the landing into an open classroom where I held daily lessons, acted as a schoolteacher, and forced my younger siblings to become my obedient students. I had the whole house at my fingertips and the kids under my grip, doing whatever I wanted. Either my parents were too preoccupied with the new challenges of our lives to notice the chameleon interior of their house, or they intended to give their despotic daughter a blind eye, so that she could get her chance to be a leader.

Our parents were oblivious to our parallel lives. Dad stayed mostly in his comfortable room reading and playing solitary chess. Mom was constantly in and out of the house, shuffling between the pharmacy, the neighborhood meeting, the long lines for rations, and the visits to many relatives to exchange news. Our childhood fantasies shielded our world from the maelstrom that churned our parents, who juggled their roles as peasants, blue-collar workers, simple folks, enthusiastic citizens, until one day, Mom was yanked back to reality.

Returning from the pharmacy in agitation, she called in Chị Sáu and questioned her in a stern voice, "Have you been smuggling out the feminine napkins from the pharmacy?"

Chị Sáu's jaw dropped. "Why are you asking me that?"

Mom retorted, her voice getting higher, "You don't think I have noticed? Most of the boxes are empty in the middle."

Chị Sáu understood. With a soft voice full of mirth, she replied, "Madam! It was the work of your daughter, Hồng-Mỹ. She has needed those sanitary pads for a while now."

Mom looked stricken. "Hồng-Mỹ has started her period?"

As soon as Mom learned the exciting news, she called me in for a lengthy interrogation. Head bent low, I admitted my thievery. Truthfully, my embarrassment was not for smuggling out the pharmacy products but in acknowledging the onset of my

menstruation. The failure to communicate this important
development of my life reflected my immaturity. Why was I bothered
by this natural course of time? I could not answer, except to say that
perhaps my awkwardness was stamped by my timidity, coupled by a
heightened sense of personal privacy that was often invaded by my
insensitive mother. I felt that something in Mom made me believe
that she would not know how to cope with the idea that her little
daughter was becoming a woman. All this—the breasts, the cycle,
boys—seemed to be one big life secret, hinting at something bigger
and terrifying to both of us. Sexuality. We would never approach that
can of worms. I was only trying to spare us both the trouble of facing
it.

After that embarrassing encounter with Mom, I thought my
trouble was over. I was doubly wrong. I forgot that Mom was born
without the tiniest fragment of tact. From that day on, each time
someone visited—a friend of hers, or an adult relative—she would
recount the incident about the stolen napkins and chuckle with her
group. Every time I walked past the living room, everyone's eyes were
on me. That was Mom, the reason I never shared any of my concerns
or secrets with her.

Not long after this incident, the local government appropriated
our courtyard for their weekly meeting. Each Wednesday, I prepared
to surrender the land around my home as Captain Nemo prepared his
Nautilus before submerging it away. I would draw the curtains in the
living room and shutter all the windows around the house.
Downnstairs, room by room, my finger would run through the
various light switches to flip the light off inside and turn on various
lighting in the courtyard. Such illuminated, the exterior of my home
shone in the night like a diamond in this sea of change. This
meticulous weekly habit let me take charge of what little I could. By
seven, the Red Gate would be opened and the locals poured in,
bringing with them their cone hats and loud talking. They sat on the
floor, on the low brick walls that surrounded Grandma's home, and
on doorsteps.

From upstairs, I looked out to find curious eyes wandering from window to window, looking up at the trees, taking in the landscape. Cowering inside thus, I endured the forced visit, feeling like I myself had been violated. How I raged silently! But I was powerless.

Then the meeting ended. The attendees left in droves, passing the gaping Red Gate. When it again closed and the tranquility returned under a silent, dark night, our yard would be littered with food scraps and cigarette butts.

10.

Paternal Grandma

Eventually, there would be no return to the happiness or sorrow of yesteryear. There would be no return to my childhood home standing proud and tall, its coat redder than the rising sun of the East, warmer than the pulsing blood in a young man's veins; no return to the sound of our church bells. Time trickles through life's cupped hands drop by drop until it is no more, leaving in its place a mere remembrance of distorted figures, of muted sound trying to vibrate seeming chords . . . but in vain.

In vain I seek the afternoons of my girlhood; the clucking hen, *pawk pawk pawk*, announcing the expulsion of her egg; the squeaky protest of a garden faucet's handle; my brother's howling, "Ow, ow," his face wincing as if in great pain when I hadn't put my hand on him; the tall and fruitful coconut tree by the western wall that separated our home from the church, the tips of its drooped palms scraping the tin roof of the chicken pen like a woman's fingernails. Under that tree was where Grandma's maid, Chị Ba, squatted, working the faucet to let out a gush of water, cleaning her crabs and shrimps until the basin was clear, then pouring the crustaceans in small batches into a soldier's helmet, she pounded rhythmically, grinding the contents into pulp for Grandma's soup.

Chị Ba was an older woman, a small, bent country woman with

eyes bleached gray by the sun, eyes that would never need reading glasses; with feet that had traveled many country roads and crossed many thresholds of life, with hands that had been intimate with the soil, killed countless chickens and fish for meat, chopped wood for fire, and closed the eyelids of dead people. Her ebony hair hid gray streaks underneath to match her years. Her face could fool children into thinking she was grim, but once we sat down and chatted with her, hard laughter escaped her belly and filled her eyes with tears.

Together in the same house, Chị Ba and our grandma formed a contrasting pair, with Chị Ba wearing only black and Grandma only white; one atheist, the other a devout Catholic. However, their tongues remembered the same things—speaking with a sharp accent that confused our Southern maids and favoring the taste of certain regional food, for they originated from the same part of the country, born in that same generation in which shiny, black-dyed teeth were considered attractive.

Grandma counted on her cuckoo clocks to tell time, on the church bell to remind her of the three daily Masses, and on Chị Ba for every domestic task.

We, too, sought out Chị Ba. After our naps, we often sidled up to her for small treats that she dispensed carefully from Grandma's kitchen, clucking intermittently, "That's about all I can spare. Run along now."

And we'd come back, after finishing the little morsels she distributed evenly among us, asking for "just one more piece, please." Sometimes we found her dozing off on her hindquarters, her head inside her arms. We had no mercy for her; we took great fun leaping up and landing just behind her with both our hands shoving her, screaming, "Hoo!" and bursting into laughter when she startled up, her eyes still full of sleep.

Then to appease her, we offered to pluck her gray hair. What pleasure it gave Chị Ba! Our little fingers traveled her scalp, separating her black strands and spotting the silver thread, crept to it slowly, slowly picking it out when she moaned, "Ah! Ooh!"

We gave her each silver hair to count. And were happy when she smiled broadly, praising us, "Your eyes are so bright."

Chị Ba stayed with Grandma all year long, leaving only for a week every few years. It never occurred to us to question why her life was such that she did not have a family and a place of her own to go back to.

Chị Ba was there, as naturally as that coconut tree in the yard.

One afternoon I came to Chị Ba alone. I sat close, entertained by her energetic movements as she struck the metallic helmet, rotating it on its round base to patiently redistribute the squishy content with skill, looking for a desirous pinkish smoothness, which I could only judge by its rising scent. After a while, bored by her labor, I suggested to her, "Tell me a ghost story!"

Chị Ba was never without a new ghost tale. Since the world of spirits thrived in undeveloped, rural areas where no sound of motors could be heard nor city lights pierced the nights, she had explained to us, ghosts roamed her village, and walking alone in the dark, anyone could run into these see-through apparitions. "Ya heard of the one who dragged herself nightly in the dormitory of a high school?" she began, focused hard on her task and shifting now and then to let blood circulate through her squatted legs.

"Tell me," I implored, pushing closer. The wind lifted, scooping up leaves and dust into a swirling spiral; in the center were dancing phantoms. Swarms of dragonflies swooped around the garden, joining the leaves and dust in an aerial choreograph.

"That lady committed suicide cuz she did not pass her exams to graduate. She hangs herself with her own long hair above the school balcony."

"Nobody prevented her?"

"Nobody saw. It was during a holiday. She stayed back to study."

How vivid in my mind was the image of a thin and white-faced girl, eyes with dark circles from late-night study. There she was, suspended by her long hair, hair that was shiny and velvety, having been combed daily with the conscience of a well-raised, well-educated girl. That feminine luster haunts my mind until today, each time I walk down a dark hallway all alone. I hear her distinctly, dragging herself under the weight of her academic burden, a silent specter, her hair hugging her calves.

As the clock chimed three, I left Chị Ba and gathered my siblings to join Grandma in her midday prayer. *Bà nội* was small and frail, dignified in her white cotton pajamas. She lit the candles on Grandpa's altar and fumbled in her pocket for her black rosary.

"Hail, Holy Queen, Mother of mercy, our life, our sweetness, and our hope. To thee do we cry, poor banished children of Eve . . . ."

Afterward, she handed the devoted kids their awaited rewards: sweet sugar lumps, a bowl of cold rice and soup, sometimes a deliciously ripe banana. We lingered for more sweets and bothered Grandma with silly questions, asking her why her skin was so wrinkled and thin. And did she pay any attention to that old man who came daily, leaning on his cane, to pay her a visit? We asked her if she loved Dad more than Mom, and why she needed to iron her underwear. Grandma, at times exasperated, looked up to heaven, smoothed her pants with her two hands and lamented, "Jesus-Maria, my God!"

We loved to climb Grandma's many trees, especially the fruitless mango by her front entrance. When Grandma caught us dangling on her mango branches like monkeys, she would rush out with her white paper fan and try to hit our legs, wailing, "Jesus-Maria, my God! If your mother sees this . . . ."

Grandma's favorite dish was dog meat. Every now and then, she would smack her lips when she saw our mutt, Pijou, frolicking in the yard. If I was nearby, she would call out to ask me how old our pet was, then sigh, "What a waste of God's gift to let that meat toughen."

We were filled with horror each time Uncle Huỳnh supplied his dear mother her delicacy, brought to her in a tin box. Grandma would ask Chị Ba to store the box in the refrigerator and consumed the white meat little by little. How horrid of Grandma to remark aloud to us how tender the meat was. Seeing the look on our faces, she grinned to appease us, flashing her black squamosa-seed teeth. Instead of toothpaste, she kept her black teeth healthy by chewing daily on betel-leaf rolls of tobacco, areca nut, and pink lime, spitting out the blood-colored juice in a copper pot hidden nearby.

Each morning, she sat with her hair hanging on one side of her shoulders and combed through the thinning, peppery threads, gathering them up into one long tail that she wrapped tightly into a black velvet cloth; this she rolled around her crown, finally securing the neat hairdo with black bobby pins. Her breasts hung down and made two large lumps behind her lower pockets, one of which contained her black rosary.

Everything about Grandma was of another time remote from us. She was closer to God than to us. To us, she was chiefly the messenger to warn us of the penalties below if we failed to pray and attend daily Mass. She spent her day reading the Bible, praying, and attending all three Masses. She had no hobbies, never knitted or sewed, contributing absolutely nothing to this physical world, saving all her labor to secure a seat in heaven. Serene Grandma! The only person who managed to upset her was Chị Ba. And once, not long ago, we witnessed for the first time a terrible quarrel between her and one of our uncles, her second son.

Uncle Giáp, the opium smoker, came rarely to Grandma. Aunty Giáp made the filial visits instead, bringing her beaming smile, her moonshine face. That afternoon, he paid her a visit and talked with her about his financial difficulties, about bad luck and health problems. We knew the storm was brewing, for Grandma was very quiet, her face drawn, and both hands smoothing the pant fabric that covered her thighs. She stopped her gesture when Uncle Giáp blurted out finally, "You are to help me. All I need are your antiques."

Grandma's words came out slowly, like the beads of her rosary when she pulled the silver strand from her pocket. "And what will they become? Smoke for your pleasure?"

He almost jumped up at her. He was furious, "I have the right. I am your son. But no! You despise me. I've been on my own ever since I was growing up. Not an ounce of help from you."

"Ah! Not an ounce. So you've been sprouting up from a hole." Grandma panted.

Then, "Take it. Chị Ba! Let him have it!" She called for her maid.

Chị Ba took a key from a drawer inside her dining table, a very small drawer that Grandma seldom opened.

She slid open the glass cover of the large sideboard curio. Her hand went inside the case and lovingly took hold of a tiny tea kettle. The one that whistled when poured. I gasped.

"Yes, that's the one I want," Uncle Giáp urged. "And that other one. The Ming plate."

He grasped the porcelains from Chị Ba's hand. Grandma was shaking on her legs, livid.

"Out of my sight. Out."

Oh! Grandma. That was a hard road for her to travel.

Later that year, in front of that curio with the missing tea kettle and Ming plate, she sat down with paper and pen to write to Uncle Khôi and Uncle Linh, who were in a concentration camp somewhere. She wrote in broken syntax with feeble penmanship, spelling out each letter carefully, painfully painting each curvature, making all the words so huge. These letters would stay pressed inside her Bible until a time in the future when they could be addressed properly to the two unfortunate sons. God help them! For the time being, all she could do was wait and pray for Uncle Khôi's and Linh's safety. May God keep them in His love.

Then Chị Ba, too, was gone.

This time, she was gone for good. It was time for her to return to her old country, to her son's tomb—who we had heard was killed in action by the Republic of Vietnam's army—a death she vowed to avenge, swearing allegiance to the Việt-Cộng.

Our Chị Ba . . . a Việt-Cộng. What had she contributed to our enemy for the downfall of Saigon? Grandma could only look up to the cross with sorrowful eyes.

After her maid departed, I often worried about Grandma living alone. During the day, our servants took to Grandma her prepared meals. But at night, who would hear her call of distress in case of an emergency, when illness struck? I thought long but was unresolved until the urge to move again rapped at my restless soul. It was then that a perfect solution presented itself to me. I might have told

Grandma about my idea to move in with her or might have not. As I was accustomed to do just what I wished at the spur of a moment, I matter-of-factly cleaned up Aunt Diệp's bedroom and moved myself in. It was sensational, that feeling of being in a poet's room, touching her belongings, running my fingers over the marvelous woodblock with her pen name carved, Hồng Vũ Lan Nhi. I felt at once connected with my aunt's emotive world, grown up and passionate.

Grandma did not openly approve my decision, but she did not protest. I only came to spend the night just before she closed up for the evening, after taking my dinner at home. After catching Patrick and me sharing the bed one night, she clearly spelled out her condition: "I have told you. You are to stay here alone for the night, or don't come at all."

She looked at me severely, "And don't let me catch you two sleeping together in my house again. Girls and boys cannot share a bed."

But Grandma did not know me well then to command me something I could not obey. The ghouls and ghosts that Chị Ba had peopled in my imagination returned each night from dark corners and behind cupboards, hidden inside the white shirt Grandma hung to dry in the bathroom, spying out from among the many heads peering from the painting of The Last Supper by the stairway. Above it was a deer head with its glassy eyes and enormous antlers. Death himself could be seen floating and gliding in Grandma's white-clad body. I did not want to be alone in Grandma's dark hallway and stumble upon her—God forbid—rigid, lifeless body. Patrick I must have, so I relied on my ruses.

Each night, after Grandma had retired to her second-floor bedroom, Patrick would steal over to Grandma's front door and rap lightly, *tap-tap, tap-tap, tap tap*, in bursts of two fast, three slow taps. Recognizing the coded signal, I would go softly downstairs to let him in. He'd spend the night with me and wake early to leave in the morning, loving every minute of our shared secret. He had proven himself once more a faithful companion in our many adventures, from climbing balconies and scaling terraces to devising coded pseudonyms, to setting up a secret hideout in Mom's built-in closet, imitating the heroes of the *Le Club des Cinq* series.

Once, while Patrick was in Aunt Diệp's bathroom whose only window had been blocked solid by the elevated concrete wall of the neighbor's remodeled home, I locked him in, then forgot him entirely for several hours. When I suddenly remembered my prisoner in that airtight chamber, I hurried back in panic. A surge of relief ran through me when I found my crying brother, dripping wet from the water he had poured on his head to cool himself, somehow succeeding in saving his life. No one else besides us knew about this near-fatal incident. The seriousness of it did dawn on me, and my guilt and fear of this sort of immature prank stayed with me for the rest of my life. At the time, though, I made Patrik promise to keep his torture secret from the adults, "or I'll never, ever play with you again."

And he did.

We had other mysteries in the family. "Why did Grandma choose to have her home here, with us?" We often sought the adults' explanation, only to be further mystified.

"It was our tradition. Old parents live with their son," one aunt told me.

I was not satisfied. I knew the higher ranking of a paternal grandma in a Vietnamese family, *bà nội*, meaning the *inside grandmother*—compared with their counterpart, the maternal grandma, *bà ngoại*, the *outside grandmother*.

But Dad was not the family's patriarch, being only fifth in the lineage of sons.

I went to Dad and shook his shoulder for an answer. He explained to me, in a tone that made me doubt his seriousness, that Grandma knew who loved her best and who was best qualified to take care of her. Then he added, "Your mother is the most agreeable daughter-in-law."

With time, a consistent picture emerged in which Dad had always acted as leader to the larger Lê family. His oldest brother, Uncle Huỳnh, was his role model in devotion and sacrifice, but it was Dad who stirred the sky and earth to shake his family from the grip of the Great Depression. It was Dad who had thought of forming a band with his musically talented brothers. It was Dad who sent his most eloquent younger brother, Uncle Linh, to knock on the door of Le Coq d'Or, a nightclub catering to Westerners, to work out a deal for the band's nightly show. Uncle Huỳnh would rather manage on his meager teacher's salary than work for money as an entertainer.

Again, it was Dad and Uncle Linh who had orchestrated the complicated move that brought the family safely out of Phát Diệm, their birthplace, to Hanoi, then from there south to Saigon. So I wasn't surprised that his wish to have his parents live near us was honored by his family. He, the risk taker, the ambitious son, and not his older brothers, would be the one taking charge of their parents. The plot of land that he finally purchased for its sizable acreage was ideal, not because it was big enough to build a home for his wife and children, but because it was vast enough for two large homes, one reserved for his parents.

Only recently we had learned about Dad's unspoken motives for keeping his parents nearby. It was not enough that he fulfilled the wish of his heart to provide for his parents. Dad also wanted to cultivate the love of his parents in his children's hearts. It was not enough that we shared them with him by blood ties. He had to claim our genuine affection and bonding for his family, especially for our grandparents. Of course, putting his parents in proximity with his children was the best means to achieve our continuous close encounters. But that was only the first step. To guarantee absolute success, he added for our grandparents' direct access to our hearts through bribing.

Bribing? Yes, we discovered this only years later, when the question of whether our love for our grandparents was bought no longer mattered. I remember it well. I remember running home across the courtyard, all excited with my extra red envelope, breathlessly telling Dad, "Look what Grandma gave me. An extra twenty *đồng* for *lì xì*. She said I was good to her all year, and pious. Look, Dad." I pulled out the bills from the little red paper pocket to let him see my good-luck money.

"Aren't you lucky? Did she not give you some good-luck money already when everyone was here wishing her luck?"

"Yes. She did. She handed out the red envelopes to all of us. All my cousins and us got the same amount, five *đồng* each. Then, after everybody went home, Aunty Diệp came out and gathered us four back in. Then Grandma gave us more envelopes. 'Especially for my preferred grandchildren,' she said."

We visited our grandparents as often as possible to maintain their special affection. After Grandpa's death, we took turns accompanying Grandma to Mass, sharing her daily prayers, dropping often into her home for all sorts of things: extra snacks, seeking a corner to hide in her house when playing hide-and-seek, dashing in and out to use her bathroom.

Only much later we learned the truth. The special treatment that we had attributed to Grandparents' special love for us had come from Dad's hand, to buy them our affection. Our grandparents would not have had the extra money to give us even if they had wanted to. Even the money that they gave to the other kids in the large family, to all the big and small cousins, came from Dad.

Dad's confession reached us long after both our grandparents had passed to the other realms, long after our love for them had taken root firmly. By then, we were already too old to rebel. His wisdom had prevailed. Children's love, once given, was not easily taken back—a love that endures time, distance, and death. Once this special bond was secured, manipulatively or otherwise, once it was gifted, it was for a lifetime.

11.

A Farewell Letter

The previous close encounter with Vietminh in 1945 and their narrow escape from the land reform campaign that resulted in the massacre of over 13,000 land owners had branded Northerners like my parents with searing memories of persecution. Regular citizens were dragged out of their homes to the village square, pushed down to the ground in front of the People's Court, there to be publicly denounced for "crimes" committed against the people— sons testifying against fathers, neighbors facing one another in hatred, all accusing, all wanting blood.

The People's Court, Tòa án Nhân Dân, was a court not appointed by law but made up of temporal jurists from the illiterate populace. Rigged together like a scaffold, this court was ruled by vengeful people who had taken the law into their own hands. These people, destitute and now elected onto the bench of judges, were ready to condemn. Their conscience was blinded by an old, vivid hatred born of a lifetime of jealousy. Their venom had been stored for years waiting for the opportune moment.

The echoes of those words— "Denounce his crimes," "Admit it," "Enemy of the state," words the immigrated Northerners thought belonged to their past—now pulsated in the charged atmosphere of Saigon. They were not convinced by the government's assurance of a peaceful reconciliation and a smooth transition toward unification. They did not forget these words, the stark truth, taken from anti-communist propaganda: "Do not listen to what a communist says but look at what he does." With their pursuers now close at their heels and swords soon at their throats, my parents, unlike most unheeding native Southerners, were prepared for the worst: major economic lashing, mass retribution, and bloodbath.

My parents' realistic preparations after the fall of Saigon in 1975 were carefully planned. First and foremost, they purged their home of all evidence of their past life: wealth, political and social connections. Next, they wrote a farewell letter to their five children overseas to prepare them for the imminent communication cut-off. For how long, they could not say. They dared not admit the possibility of a permanent separation. Historically, families had been divided across political borders in many countries: East Germany barricaded from West by a wall; North Vietnam severed from South by a river; Taiwan saved from its motherland by a thin strait in the sea; and more. Despite these barriers, people continue to scale border walls or swim across rivers at the risk of being shot or drowned. Otherwise, clinging to their roots, people would perish, like millions of Chinese under Mao who starved during the Great Leap Forward.

Our parents sat us down with them when they drafted their extemporized living will to Chị Mai. When Dad was done writing, I was to read out loud the contents of the fateful letter. I broke out crying as I sounded these sad words:

> *Dear Mai, Marie, Khải, Daniel, and Madeleine,*
> *We are for the moment a divided family. Our country is going through an indecisive time, and we don't know what is coming next. We trust Uncle Hồ and our great Party to do the best for us. Meanwhile, Mai, you are to be in charge of your brothers' and sisters' future.*
> *We will think of you all daily and pray for our reunion. We promise you, children, to do everything possible to be again with you.*
> *If, by God's will, we fail—*

I could not finish. My tears choked me and I was afraid to look up and be confronted by my family's pain. It was as if this moment was our last. Shaken with grief, I read the last lines of the letter with only my eyes:

> *Farewell, children. May God keep you in his love,*
> *Dad, Mom, Hồng-Mỹ, Patrick, Anne, and little Michelle.*

From a corner of my eye I noticed Dad's shoulders shivering violently, and my ears caught a terrible sound, like a suppressed cough, emerging from his chest, spasmodically hurling into a moan, his suffering dying in his lungs.

"Sign it," said Dad in a voice that our priest would use when he said, "Amen," after "Brothers and sisters you are to go home in peace," to end the long Mass. I put down my signature as if I was executing a final will, as if the last that my family overseas would see of their thirteen-year-old sister would be only her name, pressed inside an envelope.

"Sign it, each of you," Dad continued to direct us, his voice now calm with acceptance. "This may be our last letter to your brothers and sisters." I gave the signed letter back to Dad to pass around. Warm, salty sorrow inundated my face. I gathered in my memory the sight of my two little sisters wrapped in Mom's arms, their heads hidden in the folds of her clothes, their legs twisted underneath them by an agony incomprehensible to them. The three of them wailed uncontrollably. Patrick was immersed in his new pain, his face contorted with a childish cry, lips quivering and fists digging circles helplessly into his eye sockets, howling, "*Huck, huck, huck,*" as if he had just been beaten.

Little Michelle added kissing lips to her signature. This done, there was but the last task for our parents before we embarked into our unknown future: the liquidation of their assets to convert their lifetime savings into gold.

It was not a surprise for my parents to wake up one morning to the loudspeaker announcement of a fiscal overhaul. Overnight, the government had issued new currency. In exchange for the obsolete *đồngs*, each household would be issued an equivalent amount of the new money, up to a maximum predetermined sum. We lined up all night to turn in our useless currency, holding for the last time these dear old friends who were to us the vehicles of wealth, the symbol of our status, the glorious exchange for our sweat and labor. And we received them, the new *đồngs*, small and colorful paper bills—hideous and foreign.

My mother had teary eyes, but not because she was sentimental enough to mourn the passing of our old monies. Overnight, the last of their cash had been wiped out. The maximum amount of cash we were allowed was a meager sum, not enough to run our household. Their coffer was empty, worth no more than the wood it was made of. My parents thought they were prepared, yet the blow was blinding. On what would we subsist?

I saw alternately the worries on my mother's face—her pale agony, her red, tear-filled eyes with streaks of hopelessness—and a surviving determination. She was lining up her capable soldiers: the malleable, the adaptable, the creative fighters. She would not be defeated. My resourceful mother scrambled to find innovative ways to amass a sustainable sum for her household. She counted the cash, stacked it in bundles all over her large bed, picking up a stash, putting it down, thinking, moving the equivalent amount in her head. Her eyes traveled to Dad but looked past him. She mumbled to herself, "We can at least triple our allotment." Dad walked toward her, intrigued by her statement. "How?" he asked desperately.

Mom looked deep into his eyes, trying to give him a hint of her thinking, reaching for the words. Suddenly, she seemed to realize my presence and directed her stern gaze to me: "Get out and close the door after you. You don't need to know more than what you can keep." I understood instantly. Our world had changed and, wanting to or not, our parents had decided to keep from us their new burdens. I stepped outside Mom's room. In a few minutes, she emerged from it alone, holding a bag in her hand, and went downstairs, calling for our trusted head servant, "Sáu, Sáu."

I followed her. From a corner of the dining room I spied Mom and the other maids, saw her counting out the old monies to them and, afterword, softly explaining what they needed to do. She had them each repeat her words, finally beseeching them, "Do this for your sake and mine. In this amount is your salary, our food money." In her hoarse voice was an anguish I had never detected: "This is all we've got."

Each of the maids went out to the street where the money-exchanging tables were set up and lined up for the new cash. Each of them brought back their share of the allotted amount and gave it back to Mom. Our monetary problem was temporary solved.

One by one, our parents' debtors came to pay back their loans with the old money. It was unforeseeable, they lamented, and this was the best they could do to repay fairly before the New Year arrived.

The monetary overhaul was only the first step in the unification of Vietnam, an indication of what was looming. Like our flag, our soldiers, our money, the people of the south soon would be eliminated to make way for a brand-new system. They, as well as we, would not be easily fooled. The re-education camps were set up to give the populace the illusion of redeemable life, to keep them hanging, hovering between earth and hell, but hopeful.

But less resilient people had taken their lives—military families, people of older traditions who would rather escape to the world beyond than linger on in this sinister life, devoid of freedom and personal space. Their individuality as members of a society was, to them, too sacred.

Those who were more optimistic braced for the coming onslaught with their own escape plans via an ocean crossing, which, in their minds would not be as fatalistic as committing suicide, but in practice would lead them straight into the chomping jaws of Death. Destruction came in all forms. It came draped in the illusive promise of a new, forgiving state. It dressed up as life with its monotonous routines, yet devoured each unsuspecting citizen's flesh through years of starvation, through illnesses without the help of medicine, through malnutrition. It wore the gown of the benevolent professor who fed schoolchildren distorted views of the world, day after day, stuffing their young brains with myths and half-truths, falsifying facts straight from the dark underground of the Hồ Chí Minh Trail. Then it came with its alluring calm, leading Vietnamese families into tiny boats, into the Pacific Ocean, into the arms of sea pirates.

My parents were optimistic and at the same time realistic. They knew the hidden dangers of their escape plans. Would they risk their lives and the lives of their four children? Could someone answer a question like this without a pang to his or her heart? Millions of Vietnamese, facing the ocean, heads heavy with such unanswerable questions, had tossed their illusions for a better tomorrow into the sea.

There was but one choice: to flee or die.

Dad was well organized. He pooled together resources and a group of trusted friends and met with them regularly over many weeks in the summer of 1976. To me it was like the adults were playing our detective games. They came rapping at the gate discreetly, waiting patiently for one of us or a maid to open it, never pounding or hollering to be heard.

We started to give them nicknames, even with Dad's approval. Uncle Thành, distinct from the average Vietnamese man with his pitch-black mustache, was Goaty. He was our daily guest, who came riding a small-boy's bicycle. At times, he seemed drunk, his eyes bloodshot and demeanor melancholic. Now and then he brought a few of his boys. Sometimes all five of them. They called him *Papa*. His wife called him by the same title, brightening his dark face with some inner pleasure. That was the only French word they could speak. Then Mr. and Mrs. Thuyết showed up, clinging to each other. We called them "The Lovers," amusing Dad greatly but infuriating Mom. Mrs. Duyệt, a middle-aged matron, was present from time to time. She came with a very old, very myopic lady that Dad introduced to us as our distant cousin. She was as dry as tree bark, a stark contrast to her pudgy friend. One seldom came without the other.

They convened intermittently in the bedroom downstairs, in groups of three, sometimes four, speaking softly. They discussed the weather, the availability of certain boats, some connections, and the fees. They charted the course of typhoons.

We were allowed to mingle during the social hour, but once Dad signaled Mom to close the door we were pushed out. I pretended to fall asleep and was scooped up and brought out to the living room's sofa.

Besides those adults who were strangers to us children, there were the Trầns—Aunt Khanh and her boys—who became good friends to us. With the toddler, Bảo, dangling by her side, Aunt Khanh discussed with Dad their plans for departure, while her boys played in the yard with us. Hoàng became Patrick's inseparable friend.

For a few weeks, the older and more aloof Luân and his younger, more attractive brother, Vũ, came to visit us daily. By the new regulation, they and I, being teenagers beyond fourteen, were required to participate in the mandatory summer fitness program. This was a first step for the Red Party to gain access into their youths' lives, bending these citizens of the future into slaves to serve one common ideal, directed by only one owner, the mighty Party. Because our new friends did not want their absence to be immediately noticed and reported, they opted to attend the program offered in our neighborhood. Another benefit was added by their frequent visits with us: It would make their planned departure from our home less noticeable.

We finished our summer fitness requirement in July 1976, and soon after the Trầns left early one morning from our home. They would have to leave behind their military father; to wait for his release from the reeducation camp was to languish an indeterminate time not knowing when he would return. It was a tormented decision that many Vietnamese had to make to save their children, especially sons.

Within three weeks, Dad received the pre-established codes indicating the Trầns' safe arrival in Thailand. It affected Dad most positively. For the first time since the loss of Saigon, he beamed with excitement, glad to have found the right connection for our family's escape.

12.

Hà Tiên

There are things to be said. No doubt.
And in one way or another
they will be said. But to whom tell

the silences? With whom share them
now? For a moment the sky is
empty and then there was a bird.

(From "There Are Things to be Said" by Cid Corman)

Migratory birds are programmed to move south annually. From birth, they are groomed to endure the hardship of their flight, to follow in formation, to shift with the winds and rest only at sundown. In contrast, migrating people fleeing war are thrown head first, unprepared, into the unknown, facing possible death.

It was time to face our challenges. We had to leave our home and seek freedom, like the birds seeking a more tolerable climate in order to survive. Like these migrating birds, we had to leave before the first frost set in, before the collapse of the food supply, before the real danger was even palpable. We had to depart when the sun was still warm, the trees green with leaves, and insects abundant. Already, the wind had changed direction. At the end of the 1975–1976 school year, our innocent world began to topple. We were informed that our school would not reopen for us but would be utilized by the state as a university. We would have to withdraw our school records and enroll with our home district. I was dumbstruck. What would I find in my school district, among people that I had never truly known? How should I fit in among local girls who donned their white traditional tunics and boys from blue-collar homes?

One August dawn, our family departed from home. The younger kids left with Mom on a hired cyclo to a bus station located in Bình-Đông, Chợ Lớn, about 45 minutes away from home. Half an hour later, Dad pedaled out, dumped his bike at a friend's home, and waved down a cyclo to the rendezvous place. I was the last person to leave home. Together with Mrs. Duyệt, we headed to where the others had gone.

We arrived at the bus depot at its busiest time of the day—it was the only bus depot connector for the six main cities of the South. We were at once assaulted by the strong odor of diesel fuel, of mud and human sweat, and peddled foods.

The ticket window was already closed—all tickets had been sold out to the black market, which now purveyed the coveted items in full swing. We were drowning in a cacophony of haggling shouts, bargaining charades, and grotesque cusses. A strange place, it was intimidating, chaotic, loud. I hung on tight to Mrs. Duyệt.

The hours ticked by quickly in the craze to secure our boarding passes, to be arranged so that all members of our group would be sitting on the same bus. Finally, when even the black-market tickets were unobtainable, Mrs. Duyệt and I were left ticketless. Dad made a radical decision. The group would leave by bus to the sea-village, Hà Tiên, as planned, but I would ride on a chauffeured motorcycle with Mrs. Duyệt. At the destination we would regroup at the house of a designated host. When it was time to depart, we would be taxied in small groups to the mothership waiting in the open sea. Without further debate, Dad left. I clung to the woman, practically a stranger, now the only adult acting as my protector.

Renting a motorbike with driver was a mode of transportation adopted overnight in the South in response to the shortage of public transportation. It was an alternate means to travel the distance that foot cyclists could not physically endure. Even so, it was rare for a motorcyclist to be asked to drive an eight-hour trip, carrying two urban women. But we had no other option, and the owner of the two-wheeler could not in good sense refuse the heaven-sent income fallen in his lap.

The man wore simple pants and shirt. He was hatless; his toes stuck out from a cheap pair of flip-flops. Although he was courteous and patient, I did not want to be the one hugging to his back. I timidly asked Mrs. Duyệt if she would not mind sitting in the middle behind the man. She agreed readily; she would be much more comfortable on the padded seat, while my place would be halfway between the seat and the metallic bike rack. As soon as the seating arrangement was set, we started. It must have been around nine in the morning.

Soon, we had left our familiar cityscape and were hat to hat on the black tarred highway, carried by the wind and the sun. The fields zoomed by in a blur. The cool morning was quickly heated by a scorching sun, rising high, imprinting our dark shadows onto the darker background of the street. The shadow was our past, trying to catch up to us as we fled southward in search of our future.

We traveled through small towns and then again out into the open, gliding past rice paddies, watching the thin, bare stalks wave to us from their pools of murky water. "We are stuck here, deep in the mud, while you are flying away," they seemed to chorus. The black buffalos did not care to say goodbye, but sadness was in their eyes.

I alternated my arm positions, sometimes straddling Mrs. Duyệt's voluminous waist, other times resting them backward on the metal frame of the luggage carrier. My white Pan Am bag, worn sideways like a satchel on my shoulder, was stuffed full with my two poetry diaries, a change of clothes, two sets of underwear, and small girly keepsakes.

Hours later, I was dazed with fatigue, blinded by the intense tropical sun. My head, although protected by a cone hat, was befuddled—by the wind, by the vibration of the rattling motor, by the thumping roads that swerved and dipped underneath us, bumping and bouncing me off the leather seat onto the metal rack.

My butt was badly sore. With time, the numbing pain had spread to my extremities.

I was glad when the cyclist finally stopped to relieve his full bladder. He excused himself and, standing behind a tree, did his private business to my wondrous envy. My bladder had been pushing in agony for a whole day. But how would I find some privacy on the road?

The road took us back into an indeterminable stretch of dirt, with the leaning sun throwing patches of orange into the sky. Our past and future played a game of tag along the deserted road for the longest time, until the sun fell back into the far horizon, yielding the open space to the chillier air.

As we dizzily headed west, the sky became heavy with clouds—thick, dark, and wooly—until they blocked the horizon and blanketed us from above, pushing into our lungs their heavy dampness while the slivering dirt road slipped quickly underneath us. Between sudden lurches, slides, and brakes, the monsoon clouds burst. I restrained no longer. The warm liquid washed down me in the torrential rain, unnoticed. Thunder clapped across the darkened sky.

We pushed forward, gaining little distances, but onward, onward. I focused my will on one goal: to remain on the motorcycle. Many times, when the feverish bike skipped a track and skittered dangerously over the muddy ground, I felt myself slipping away. I braced both my shaking legs on Mrs. Duyệt's bouncy thighs, urged myself forward desperately, forgetting hunger, ignoring chill, and concentrating on only one thing: to remain on that metallic horse.

We were now one beast fighting the sheets of steely rain; our heads bent low, our backs hunched, shoulders to shoulders. In the final hour, we were engulfed in the open mouth of a large rocky mountain, its towering white walls on both sides looming like giant sentinels in white costumes. It seemed a hundred thousand years had gone by, and I had been lost in a surreal, crystallized world blanketed in a thick, liquefied substance. I strained my blurred vision to locate myself, but my senses were bewildered.

The mountain ended and we stopped by a dark roadside. Mrs. Duyệt told me to wait and walked away into the abyss. A man's eyes glistened in the cold night. Alert, I was ready to spring if the man attempted to attack. I was old enough to understand the fragility of a woman in nature, where man and beast borrowed each other's form. He inquired about my destination, the reasons for our urgent traveling. I gave him incoherent answers, making myself as stupid as I could, behaving the way of an awkward mountain goat. After an eternity, Mrs. Duyệt returned. She had found the designated house. She paid the man handsomely then led the way to a wooden dwelling on stilts.

The entrance door opened into a spacious home constructed of heavy oak. Soaring beams supported a ceiling of wooden planks. The warm abode swept me into its peaceful and orderly interior. I walked into the dancing golden halo of lantern lights, dripping as if I was freshly scooped from a deep well. At different corners of the house, the sleeping areas were readied, covered with white netting, creating an illusion of a gigantic ship with its sails unfurling; and I, the abandoned prisoner princess, was sent to its bow to be sold to foreign lands.

I bobbed gently to the host, a tiny and frail patriarch with luminous skin and white hair. He welcomed us with a benevolent smile and introduced his wife, who busied herself by pulling shyly at the bed nets. I stared in disbelief. Here was a lady just barely older than me, fresh as spring, her shiny skin gleaming under the soft light. She untied her cascade of velvety hair and began to comb through it with a large plastic comb. We nodded discreetly at each other, exchanging looks, interpreting each other's motives in our actions. She must have been curious about this lost city girl whose appearance indicated a privileged life and who was now in pursuit of some unknown happiness, while my staring eyes screamed to my peer, "Why? You ... a mere girl, wife of an octogenarian. Are you nuts?" The young lady calmly returned to her task, as I was led into the back of the house to the bathroom. I pushed open a creaky half-door to step into a small wooden enclosure. In a corner trembled the flame of a small candle, revealing in its shadowy light two fifty-gallon wooden barrels, filled to the brim with water. I closed the door and breathed in my solitude, recovering slowly from the shock of my travel, curiously inspecting the small space around me. I peeled off my soaked outfit, shivering, yet craving the therapeutic shower. There were thin gaps between the floor planks, made to drain out the wastewater. Through them reflected the black river below.

In this part of the country, homes were built above the steep riverbanks on tall columns. Many owners were fish farmers, feeding their stocks of catfish with their own waste—the best food was human excrement. The fish thrived; their fatty meat was the main item in all recipes.

I searched for a scoop and found it hung neatly by the drum, next to a small cake of white soap. Above the drum was an array of bamboo poles, designed skillfully to bring in rainwater. I washed myself slowly, and slowly my beaten spirit was restored as the layers of road grime were rinsed off. I began to savor the novel environment and tried to retain in my memory the images and sounds of this adventure, intending to retell my experience one day. In the quiet night, the sound of splashing water reverberated from below, waking the jumping fish.

I was ravenous after I had changed into a fresh set of black pants and black *bà ba*. I joined Mrs. Duyệt in the dining room. A crockpot of simple steamed rice exhaled its delicious perfume. A large bowl of soup sat waiting, wonderfully hot, its colorful contents hypnotizing my famished self. It was a simple dinner of rice and catfish cooked in a thin, watery soup of tomatoes, pineapple, ginger, and white mung-bean sprout. I finished two bowls and craved more but restrained myself as a girl should. Then I was led into a room dominated by a tall, covered bed alcove.

I was again left by myself. My bag lay on the floor, containing in its familiarity my whole universe, the home I had left far away, the soft reminder of a family somewhere waiting. I pulled out my diaries and, reading them for the last time while crying softly, tore off the pages. This is a poem I had written for my friend Huỳnh Hoa:

Here comes the sun, blanketing the universe
There! Sunflower opens, her golden light shimmering
in her slumber, such wondrous dreams
Student love, overnight emerging!

I tossed the shredded pieces of my childhood into the water below. This was the farthest in my journey that I planned to carry my treasures with me, for they belonged to my past, too dangerous for me to reveal to the authorities if I was caught.

Through the wooden planks, I spied their white shapes floating downstream, yielding slowly to the river. Then I slumped onto the thick cotton pillow, burying in it my youthful dreams, yearning for nothing more than the warm bosom of home.

The next day, I woke to a glorious morning full of sunshine. The wretched outfit that I had washed and hung out to dry in the bathroom stall had been moved outdoors. It was dancing joyously now, and it waved to me as if I was the one who needed to be brought back. I was told to change quickly so that we could rejoin the rest of the group. We were led on foot through an endless rice field. In the middle of this leafy ocean stood a small thatch hut. There, I rejoined my mother and siblings in a solemn atmosphere. Uncle Thành was fussing about something. Mrs. Duyệt questioned Mom softly about the details of her trip. Through Mom's words, I learned that Dad had been captured midway to Hà Tiên and led to the local police station to be questioned. For the sake of the whole group, Dad did not show any resistance and immediately followed the order to step down from the bus. He was last seen being escorted at gunpoint toward the village. Uncle Thành, listening in, interrupted, "Did you see him, dressed up all black like a peasant?" He waited for no reply and continued, "But underneath he wore shiny leather shoes," punching his words to give full impact.

Mr. Thuyết shook his head, clucked his tongue. "He still had his gold Omega watch on his wrist. And a gold pen in his pocket. A gold pen . . . ."

Somebody else added, "He stuck out like a sore thumb! Of course, they'd notice him." Mom's face was drained, but her eyes were intense; fierceness burned its way through. Calmly, she said, "Now I need to decide. I don't know if we should continue with you all or return home to wait for Anh Khoa's news."

Uncle Thành advised, "I think you should continue. We've come this far. He'll find a way to follow. He'll definitely join you and the kids in a couple of months. It'll be easier for him to take care of himself alone without a family."

Mrs. Duyệt's voice rose, her words well measured. "In my opinion you should go back, but let us take the children along. They'll be fine with the group. You return for your husband."

They spoke under their breath, but the air was dense with the intensity of their collective emotions. There was a long silence while Mom debated internally, her eyes closed. When she finally returned her eye contact to the many worried faces around her, her voice cracked: "I'll stay back with my children. We'll go on the next boat." It was that resolute. Short and clear. No one stepped in to try to convince her otherwise. Her determination was at once respected. The group split that night. We returned home on a bus the following day.

Mom went back to the villages neighboring Hà Tiên, searching for Dad. Patiently she visited each detention center to inquire for her husband. She found him this way: At each place that she visited, she sent in a roll of sticky rice with Dad's name on it; in the roll, she inserted a small note. If no recipient were present inside, the roll would be returned. She traveled around, a desperate wife tyrannized by love, braving insolent guards and pushing aside all doubts. Then, one day—oh joy—her roll went in without being returned. She inquired after it. She said she needed it back, because it was a mistake that she sent it there. The guards insisted that the roll was sent rightly to its recipient. To prove their point, they escorted Dad out, a haggard man with twinkling eyes. Mom had found her husband. He then knew she stayed back for him, tethered to him by her intense love which hell could not extinguish.

Months later, Mom told Aunt Sự about what had happened to Dad. When she found him, he was in a high-security prison. The guard, a Southern youngster merely sixteen or seventeen, told Mom while shoving bribed money quickly into his pants pocket, "Your husband looks docile. We did not think him risky and were soft-handling him until all of a sudden, he broke away and dashed off. He did not run fast, so we caught up with him. But the man is not what he looks. He tried to escape."

I imagined Dad running like a rabbit. I had never seen him act frantically, or intimidated by anything. It was an incredible picture that I must face, my father escaping at gunpoint across the field. I saw him stumble then try to get back on his feet, fumbling desperately for his eyeglasses. I saw him seized by despair, shaken to the core of his being, his survival instinct jerked wildly to claw at his defeated freedom.

But in Mom's stoic demeanor, all I saw was steel. It was her turn to be the family's leader.

13.

Fatherless

Fatherless children are like homes without roofs.
Fatherless children are tadpoles that have dropped their tails.

(Vietnamese Folk Adage)

The end of August dragged along in intolerable heat, oppressive and relentless. An angry sun glared in early morning; middays were scorching, white and blistery; the afternoons, finally, ceased to sizzle; the evenings exhausted, and night fell in a stupor.

The hours spun endlessly round that fiery disk, held prisoner by its own gyration, a season of irradiation. Around this invisible axis we, too, spun, and with each dizzy rotation we woke in mounting anxiety. The hours turned to days and days to weeks. Life limped on, dragged forward by the daily trivialities.

The maids asked Mom the usual questions: "Madam! What do you want for lunch?" Mom waved them off. Again, they came for instructions, "Madam! Do you want fish stew and soup tonight?" She nodded distractedly. She yielded to their suggestions. Eventually she let them decide for her. It was no longer important that the menu varied. It was now vital that she conserve her mental acumen, to keep the pharmacy going and money coming in, to protect the remaining assets, to fend off the authority's inquiries.

"Sáu, is tomorrow Friday?" she asked each time her trusted servant came to report how we were doing. With Dad locked up, Mom became even more disconnected from our lives. She lived only for each Friday; the preparations for her visit with Dad perked her up to the purpose.

She hovered over Chị Sáu, who hovered over the many bags packed to the brim for the occasion.

"Did you salt and stew the meat?" Chị Sáu nodded.

"Where is the toilet paper I set aside for him?" Chị Sáu pointed.

My mother would leave home when darkness was still thick and the neighborhood still immersed in a giant inkwell. In it, a dog's eyes were but two suspended marbles. She would make the sixteen-hour round trip bringing with her three bags full of necessities—cooked beef, dried pork, pickles, fresh and dehydrated fruit—food to supplement a prisoner's starved diet and, hopefully, prolong his health. She also brought to her husband of twenty-four years something that only he could see: her love that would give him the strength to thrive. Striving against the adversities kept her sane.

That second summer after the revolution had upended our life, our mother seemed absent even when she was nearby, her eyes looking past us, her preoccupation a glass box. Its thick, impenetrable wall kept her visible to us but off limits, incommunicable, inside which she remained frozen, petrified, pinned like a butterfly for display.

As summer yielded to fall, and our parents were still locked in an indefinite limbo, our daily care was delegated entirely to the capable hands of Chị Sáu. Chị Sáu took charge to enroll us into new schools. Patrick got into St. Thomas where Uncle Huỳnh once taught. Anne and Michelle joined a local elementary school, while I . . . .

"No! I will not go to my neighborhood school!" I rejected my caretaker's planning.

"Miss, you have no other choice," Chị Sáu insisted, exhausted from mothering her little boss. My heart was set. I had to find for myself a solution, and this time, I could not delay it indefinitely.

I biked to Uncle Mục's home at 57 Duy-Tân Street to ask him if I could use his address in the Third District to re-enroll myself into my former school, Regina Mundi, the school I had attended from first to fifth grade until Dad moved me to Collège Fraternité. Regina Mundi was now renamed Lê Thị Hồng-Gấm, after a female communist revolutionary. And how ironic: the first three words of her name were identical to the beginning of my name, Lê Thị Hồng-Mỹ, as if we were somehow related. History must have had fun at my expense.

Uncle Mục, my father's seventh brother younger than him by a few years, was a renowned professor of Vietnamese literature at the University of Pedagogy of Saigon, specializing in *Nôm*—or *Nho*, continuing in the footsteps of his scholarly father. His family lived on the third floor of a building reserved for the university professors. The two-room apartment had a whole bank of windows opening onto Duy Tân, a street made famous by legendary composer Phạm Duy in his poetic lyrics, evoking its "tall trees and lengthened shadows."

Walking in from the front door, I passed through a large dining room into my uncle's domain. I found him at his writing desk surrounded by books, his exposed neck bathing in the afternoon sun. He had his black-rimmed reading glasses on and was absorbed in his writing, giving his back to the upright Yamaha piano, its lid closed and off limits. I stood by the bookcases waiting, scanning the Vietnamese literature and *Nom* titles lining the two walls of his flat, recognizing here and there a familiar tome.

There was that book, *Bốn Mươi Năm Nói Láo,* which reminded me of an incident which had caused Mom to drive down in a fury and drag me home for a good whipping. I had come to spend a few days with my girl cousins. On that third morning the doorbell had rung, and there at the door was my brother Daniel announcing he had come, per Mom's order, to bring me home. My cousins and I were sitting around the formal dining table as usual, busily hand-copying in our notebook song lyrics we had borrowed from our friends—the only way to have our own songbooks in those days, for buying them was too expensive. We were too absorbed in our task—lettering in the song titles and having a good time illustrating our books—to pay any attention to brother Daniel and had left him waiting, looking foolish.

We startled when he called my name: "Hồng-Mỹ, do you hear what I said?"

I ignored him.

"Hồng-Mỹ, you get up this minute and follow me home."

I continued to lend him a deaf ear. After all, he was my play buddy and assigned chauffeur. He could lose his temper, like that time I had climbed up on top of his dresser and messed around while he was sleeping below in his bed. I had accidently dropped an object on his head. It was not heavy and had not hurt him, but he sprung up from that blissful place where he had floated off and was dropped witless back to earth like a plastic toy, eyes red and glazed looking up to find me atop simpering. He had had a fury the size of a tornado.

He could be furious anytime now; his calm, serene surface could transform instantly into a spewing volcano. But I persisted in my tactics to delay my time with my cousins, relying on them to stave off my brother's mood swing.

He was patient, awfully patient, with me. He did not lose his temper, but finally began stomping away while addressing the room in a curt, menacing tone, "Mom is not going to be pleased when she finds out." This got my attention, but my cousins rallied against him. Poor brother—his square teeth flashing like the African model advertising for the toothpaste brand, Hynos—was outnumbered and outwitted. The girls' teasing must have made him feel horrible, self-conscious. He opened his mouth to say something, but could not find a nasty enough word to launch at us without fouling his mouth, and closed it again. We rolled in hysterical laughter.

"Hee hee, hah hah hah," I roared while pointing at Daniel with the same Vietnamese volume on the bookshelf that I now faced, reading the title from its spine as if saying it to him: *Forty Years of Lying*. This time, I had done it. My brother clomped out of my uncle's apartment, furious. Less than an hour later, Mom showed up with a feather duster in her hand—the Vietnamese kind with a bamboo handle—to fetch her devilish daughter home for a good whip.

Ah! The happy time that I had spent within these four walls was unforgettable. The memory of it nudged toward a lighter, playful purpose. But I knew: I did not have the time to play with my cousins this day.

As my uncle looked up from his work and acknowledged my presence, I came straight to him to present my problem. He asked me about Dad. I told him the truth, that Dad was still imprisoned. I told him I needed to use his address to get into his school district, to enroll in Regina Mundi.

Uncle Mục listened to my explanation, then sternly he said, shaking his head, "It's too risky!"

He pondered his words, then emphasized again, "Too risky! I can't let you use our address. Your Dad is jailed for trying to escape the country. Our involvement will only entangle us into the dangerous mess your father has created."

I did not anticipate his refusal to help in this manner. I did not think he would flatly reject my proposal; I thought he would give me, at least, some diplomatic excuses on which I could still sway. But my uncle was firm and curt, and I could not pursue my topic further without sounding like I was begging.

"It's alright," I said to him as politely as I could and gracefully ended our conversation. "I understand."

The country was in turmoil and, in this topsy-turvy situation, all lives were threatened. No one was less endangered than the others. It was acceptable to refuse to help. My uncle did not owe me any obligations. And yes, we all needed to prove our loyalty to the Party, for it was either *it* or doom.

Walking me out, my uncle pulled me close and murmured into my ear, "Remember, Hồng-Mỹ! Do not let anybody know about your relationship with your cousins. Don't even say hello to them in the streets if you see them. You promise?"

Like a leper. I did not see myself an outcast until I talked to my uncle. I felt so helpless, lonely, and deeply disappointed. Until that day, we never had to rely on help from any of the other Lês. Dad was always the most successful member of the large family, the one who provided and aided, never the other way around. I was embittered for the first time toward my uncle. We were supposed to be of the same root; his branch should shield my tiny twigs from the burning sun.

The next day, after much musing, I took my chance and biked with Chị Sáu to my old school. I found one of my teachers working in the registration office and presented my school records. Although three years had lapsed since she had last seen me, and although I had grown much since we last said hello, Ms. Của recognized my face and accepted my documents without an inquiry; my home address did not bring any questions to her mouth. She just took everything from my trembling hands, smiled sweetly to my anxious face, and said, "Welcome back!"

14.

School Year 1976–1977

With Dad in jail, Mom felt vulnerable as our family would be specially targeted. Dad, her optimistic partner, her only source of comfort, was now her source of worry. She was alone in her fight against the constant onslaught of government inquiry and countless other policy changes and requirements.

Mr. Hoàng Văn Thụ came into our life during this difficult time. He was a distant cousin of Mom's and, due to circumstances, had stayed back in the North until now. At his proposal, she let him stay at the deserted pharmacy which had ceased its operation sometime after the monetary change. He would be useful in keeping the building safe at night. Within a few short months, we heard rumors that the philanderer had brought "ladies of the night" into the facility for improper activities.

We children disliked Mr. Thụ from the very beginning. It was hard to explain what had caused this, except to say that we saw in his friendly manners an unfriendly purpose. Mr. Thụ did not come on the scene carrying a dark suitcase, nor was his appearance announced by the nerve-shattering base notes—*Pom-pom, pa-ram, pom-pom. Pompom, paa-raam, pom-pom*—of "Mission: Impossible."

He was well proportioned, tall for a Vietnamese, wearing simple but neatly pressed clothes—a proper civilian. He flashed his attractive smile easily. When he did, furrows appeared at the corners of his eyes and two dimples deepened, enhancing his sex appeal. The jaundice in the whites of his eyes and the grayish color of his face, however, betrayed him and gave away his corrupted health, possibly hepatitis. He had two missing fingers on his right hand, self-amputated to avoid the military draft. We knew from the sharp instinct of children that he was conniving—out of necessity mostly, then out of habit; or maybe he was a born opportunist.

Mom hoped that as a citizen of the North, Mr. Thụ would be able to keep her pharmacy out of the inquisitive hands of the starved government, and he profited on her naivety. There was nothing a plain-clothed citizen with two missing fingers like him could do to help my mother safeguard her hard-earned store; the store she had dreamed of and built child after child, labored for, climbing the high stool to take down the medicine for her clients up to the day of each childbirth.

We lost the pharmacy a few months after Mr. Thụ moved in. He had but a few possessions to carry out. Bag in hand, he presented another proposal to Mom. He wanted to purchase Grandma's house to move his family south. Of course, he would pay. Give him a reasonable price, and he would take care of this extra property, before it too was confiscated.

This was to my mother a sensitive topic to discuss with Grandma. Grandma's house was, after all, more than a home to her. It was a monument of love from her son. It was her independence. It was her life. Mom would take away from her mother-in-law all of those things by selling her roof—and to whom? A distant cousin on her side of the family.

"My mother-in-law is going to accuse me of bad things if I talk to her about this," I overheard her whining with Mr. Thụ. "But you're right; I will have to do it."

He nodded approvingly, dimples deepening on his yellow-toned cheek. "You will have to. It's difficult . . . but it's better for both of you in the long run."

Mom murmured, her voice full of longing, "Ank Khoa would know how to approach his mother. She would not doubt him."

Her villainous cousin did not encourage her longing. His next sentence brought her back to reality: "He's not here. And we can't wait too long."

Mom dragged herself out toward Grandma's home. Her leaning shadow followed her closely, but it was of no use to her. She understood fully, through Mr. Thụ's hint, her new role. She was no longer a wife with a husband by her side in the next storm. And she was not the only one, so that she could cry on sympathetic shoulders. She was one among many thousands of wives whose husbands had been taken by the system.

But Mom's task was done within days. Grandma, surprisingly, did not put up a nasty fight or even protest. Her resignation was harder to see. She was quiet the whole time, her hands smoothing out the invisible wrinkles of her pant legs, her silence punctuated by the fifteen-minute and then the half-hour chime. Mom did not use hinted words but, true to her nature, told Grandma she was too old to be living alone. Grandma acquiesced readily, but her hands showed their reluctance. They stopped ironing out the wrinkles, as if they were pondering the meaning of Mom's words, their action suspended by the condemnation to a life of dependency.

When the clock sang "Ave, Ave, Ave Maria" to announce the hour, the conversation between the two women concluded, with Mom adding, as a consolation to Grandma, "You can bring everything with you, Mother." But she remembered what had been discussed earlier with her cousin, and softly added, "Except the divan. And all the furniture. They want the house furnished."

Grandma flashed her words, showing her mounting temper, "Enough said. I'll do as you advise. My bed goes with me. And my clock."

Slowly, Grandma's meager belongings were moved across the yard, where they stayed until they were moved into our downstairs bedroom, the baby room. The cuckoo clock came first, bringing with it the hourly prayer reminder. The larger clock with its beautiful "Ave

Maria" tune was left behind. Grandma could hear it calling out to her each quarter hour, and she knelt at the hourly moaning, "Ave, Ave, Ave Maria." Her bed came next, occupying a large space in the room that, until then, had never had an adult occupant. She would have to be content with our older blue living room set. The rest of her furniture—her living room set that was still wrapped in the original plastic, kept from wear and tear; the divan on which Grandpa had lain during his sickness and until his last breath, where Grandma napped daily, and where all of us gathered to play cards each Lunar New Year—all of it, like Mom had warned, was left in the house as dictated by the terms of sale.

After over twenty years of constant begrudging, Grandma's ceiling fan was finally ours to keep. Daily, on her way out to church, she saw it spinning lazily, a token from a past. She still pointed to it with her folding-paper fan and reminded us, "Your father said it will be returned to me once I settle in." Ironically, had my father kept his promise to return that fan to his mother, it would be totally lost to a stranger's possessions.

I was ashamed to admit this, but while Grandma's belongings were temporarily set in the courtyard, I had noticed her favorite Chanel No. 5 lying unguarded and had pocketed it for myself. Grandma searched for her flacon multiple times; she missed it dearly. I was mortified by my act—horrified by it. But I had no courage to admit it to her, or to anyone else. I had no heart to wear that perfume. It was hidden in a small drawer of my sister Mai's beauty desk on the third floor, away from my sight, my secret unconfessed, even to the priests. It represented the mortal sin of my youth. And I could hear, each time Grandma mentioned it to us, missing it, baffled by its disappearance, the swinging pendulum of the eternal clock in hell, and these words from Grandma's mouth when had she told us about its existence: "It is a place of eternal condemnation. A place where the pendulum of a clock would chime 'Forever and ever,' eternally."

I was, for a long time, a tormented Christian.

To have Grandma living right in the heart of the family was a big change for all of us. In the past, every time the church bells rang, summoning to God his devoted servants, we would scurry out of Grandma's path. If stuck downstairs, we would hide behind the long sofa in the living room until she walked past the large French door. Although guilt weighed heavily on our innocent souls—to see her emaciated frame, a lone, absorbing figure with its slow walk swallowed up by the Green Gate, holding in one hand a white, folding-paper fan and in the other, her worn Bible—it was easier to dismiss it than being trapped inside the church with her in the first pew while precious play hours slipped by.

Each day, our feelings were thus balanced delicately on this scale furnished by our conscience, which the church bell made impossible to ignore. We were either guilty or sacrificed.

I don't quite remember how we resolved the problem of daily church attendance once Grandma moved in with us. I guess we stayed out of her sight when the seven o'clock Mass time approached in the evening. We had plenty of warnings; the quarter before the hour was chimed loudly at first by her musical clock, then by the heavy clanging of the church bell from its high tower, pulled by some urchins glad to swing the long, thick rope. At the hour, the cuckoo jumped out from its tiny hole and coerced us again with its joyous counts: "Cuckoo, cuckoo, cuckoo, cuckoo . . . ." No one could escape the reminder of the seven o'clock Mass, for even the changing color of the sky at twilight would invoke this important time. There were red patches of blood in the clouds, warning of the hellfire in the afterlife for those kids whose hearts did not heed the church's summons.

But soon, Grandma's cuckoo clock became more an attraction to us for, like her, we were conditioned to enjoy the cuckoo's song and its movements at each hour. Our urge to check out the cuckoo every time we passed Grandma's room soon turned into a source of irritation for her. Interrupted from her prayers by the sound of her opening door, she would look up only to see her door closing. Perhaps she was lonely and expected a visitor. Perhaps she had nurtured a plan to instill a religious sense in us, to educate us in the way of the church, and was disappointed to see that her proximity to us did not help her achieve her wish in any way. Either way, she was not amused to be disturbed by a stream of kids who did not care to address her.

One day, she confronted me with my nose half-caught in the door, her doorknob suddenly cold in my palm. She ordered me in, and with both hands smoothing her pajama pants—the way a cat twitched her tail at a mouse—she eyed me severely. Then she asked, "Do you think I am a monkey? Or do you think this room is a zoo exhibit?"

I babbled an explanation. "Grandma, I'm just checking."

"Checking what?" she demanded.

"Time. Just time, Grandma!" I blurted, realizing my implausible answer, since a large electric clock hung conveniently in our dining room not far from Grandma's room.

Grandma nodded, unconvinced, but nodded anyway, then gave her advice: "Next time, if you open my door, step in properly. Say hi to me, then you can look up the time and leave. It is very impolite of you to sneak away like that." I bowed and left. What a difficult lady, I thought. As soon as I took leave of Grandma, I ran to inform my siblings about the unexpected confrontation, to prevent them from any future mishap.

Each day, Mom came into Grandma's room to check her stock of medication. Grandma had a weak bladder and depended on a constant supply of Western medicine to improve its function. It was one of Mom's concerns, since the supply we had saved from the pharmacy had dwindled greatly. To delay the inevitable, Grandma started to drink the liquid from boiled corn silk as a supplement to her medicine.

Despite her age, Grandma endured the economic hardship extraordinarily well. She, a meticulous and punctilious woman of eighty, who demanded her meals cooked precisely the way she had been eating them since childhood, did not once complain about the abrupt accommodation imposed on her. Like all of us, she limped along, adjusting to the ever-growing shortage of goods. Had the civilized world ever been exposed to such crude living conditions? I often thought. Items once considered utilitarian had become precious commodities: from lifesaving medicine like antibiotics and quinine, to soap, toothpaste, needles and thread, even rice. Rice, the essential grain that had made South Vietnam beam with pride as the granary of the world's agriculture, was now lacking.

We faced it all day by day with good humor, ingenuity, and prayers. Slowly, toothpaste was replaced by salt. We washed our clothes in plain water and saved the soap—even detergent—for shampooing our hair and cleaning our bodies. When even detergent became rare, we replaced it with the boiled liquid from honey locust seeds, whose slight aroma and slimy texture were at once favored as a fine shampoo. It was hope and Saint Martin that sustained us through these years. Through Saint Martin, we supplicated to heaven. And miraculously, our hope was kindled, embossed in the thin letters of our brothers and sisters from overseas.

I used to bring each new letter to school and share it with my new friend, Thanh-Tâm. In return, she read to me her sisters' correspondence. The letters were a constant source of solace, a common denominator in both our lives, creating between us an unspoken trust.

The unsettling condition of our city, coupled with the unavailability of a telephone connection, cut me off from my old Fraternité friends. As the time passed, a new alliance formed between me and the new girls I met. The fact that we all were transferred from different schools shut down by the new government bonded us together. Together we became a rowdy group in the back rows of our ninth-grade classroom.

I barely studied but managed to pass my math class. Probably my effort was boosted by my challenged ego. I had returned to Regina Mundi with a feeling that I had something to prove for leaving it, supposedly for a better school. I had the impression that the circle of girls who had shared my elementary classes had been watching me carefully for any signs of mediocrity. I managed to maintain my grades by cheating skillfully in history, which I abhorred, since all we learned about were the victorious battles of Việt-Cộng against the French and the horrendous deeds of the "Imperialist Americans."

The nuns previously heading the all-girl Catholic school were now only the State's servants, allowed to continue their profession of teaching as laywomen. They were prohibited from invoking their religion in whatever they did or portrayed. They were not to don their robes and headgears in class, had to strip themselves of their infamous crosses and rosaries, and had to control their language so as not to mention any religious sentiment or names. The students were to address these nuns as Ms. So-and-So, not Sister X or Mother Y as in the past. Gone was that sacred boundary reserved for god-servants, replaced by a universal utilitarian class where every member was treated equally as "Comrade," without any human feelings.

Mother Joseph, our French instructor, was then addressed by her maiden name. Mother Alexia, our math teacher, was now Ms. Hồng-Quỳ, nicknamed "Four Coordinates." We referred to the science teacher, who hearsay told us was a fervent revolutionary straight from the Hồ Chí Minh Trail, as "The White Devil." She could easily kill us with her kind of background and being who she was: cold, distant, and strict with her grades.

In our hearts, our little gang and I pronounced ourselves enemies of the "Little Red Pioneers," the good children of Uncle Hồ, recognizable by their red scarves. We spent the day devising plans to outsmart the Red Scarves students, to cut classes, avoid the gymnastic sessions, secretly disrespect the flag salute ceremony. Our feelings were even hardened toward the poor nuns, whom we accused of being traitors for allowing the system to transform them into dutiful teachers of the state without rebellion. We pinned insulting labels to these teachers' backs, disturbed their quiet nunnery, placed bets on who could verify whether the nuns did wear something underneath their robes. We were at that age when normal children grow up challenging authority; and with the excuse of our communal anger against what had happened to us with the loss of our beloved South, we were but rotten spirits awaiting occasions for revenge.

I was roiled with plans to spoil the classroom's atmosphere!

During class, my eyes constantly wandered to the blue expanse outside the windows, traveling from rooftop to rooftop to the land of naught, where nothing would ever materialize, would ever exist. The only thing left in the land of naught was destruction. My fertile mind was stirred with original ideas to corrupt the orderly class in session, to cause mayhem, to wreak havoc in the capacity of a small, powerless girl, shy and trembling with her rebellious plans. Yet, I had acquired a daredevil attitude from witnessing the multiple injustices that had taken over my life. I thought about Dad behind bars, about Mom half-lost in the maze of the new politics, about our reversal of fortune. I thought of my classmates, these well-raised girls now dutifully counting the victorious battles against imperialistic foreigners, learning to hate, pledging their innocence to the Red Party. I thought of the red scarves tied neatly around so many slender necks like blood-soaked nooses. I was desperate, and I was terrified at what was to come.

I had my gang to back me up, emboldening me. Our acts were but childish defiance, not serious enough to be personally persecuted by the politically charged student body, but disturbing enough to disrupt our class order, thus satisfying our hunger for revenge. My friend Thanh-Tâm would whistle softly to challenge me. In response, I would meow—softly at first—but seeing it made no impact, would raise my volume a notch higher, then keep raising the throaty sound until the girls at the front row looked round. Ms. Hoa interrupted her lesson and investigated, "Who did that?" To cover me up, my back-row friends would point out an invisible cat. Unconvinced, but unable to pinpoint the source of the animal sound, she wrote into our class notebook, "Someone meowed in class."

My innocent appearance and my habitual shyness many times saved me from the teachers' inquiries. They never suspected and sought in this fair-skinned Hồng-Mỹ any trace of belligerence; she looked almost like an angel with her soft, effacing manners, almost a perfect studious girl with an excellent command of language arts, but mediocre in math. Thus, I escaped most punishments for my first experimentations in the art of deception.

To avoid Gym, I told the head student, a Red Scarf, that I had a serious accident on the way to school and my leg was too sprained to exercise. I had always been an exceptional tale weaver, so my words were absolutely convincing, and now, with the collaboration of my gang, I put up a first-rate act of limping and wincing. I was such a good actress that the girl offered to carry me home, which of course forced me to think up another sets of lies to decline her good will.

I had no remorse for causing trouble in school. I thought a wrecked life deserved at least its right to contaminate the orderly lives of others; I should be given medals of honor for saving many kids' brains from being white-washed and red-stained. I was that angered against the new system. Anger and powerlessness found in me their outlet for revenge through harmless acts.

Under the new regime, the high school students had to be responsible for their school's cleanliness. In the new education system, we were trained to eradicate the barriers between the mind and manual labor. In fact, the future generations of our nation were to be well prepared to handle any tools of our nation's rising class, so a mop in hand in the bathroom was no less effective than a pen on the desk of the factory. There would be no separation between those who worked with their brains and those who labored in the fields. The people of Saigon concurred: "We are all equal slaves of the State."

After class, we were allowed an hour lunch before reporting back to school for janitorial duties. This included sweeping and mopping the classroom, emptying the trash bins, and cleaning the bathrooms. Our work was checked by a Red Scarf and a teacher on duty.

Frankly, these working afternoons were fun-filled for us. We chit-chatted while laboring, teasing each other as if there were no tomorrow. Kim-Bình had a bad habit of squatting immodestly when she mopped, showing her undergarment. We would wait for this opportune moment to bring Mr. Duong up for inspection. From the other end of the hall, he would walk in, eyes alert, and confront this girl in a most provocative posture, looking up sweetly from her duty. We could see the young male teacher's inability to react, to back down, or to advance, to scold severely, or to ignore the scene, feigning sudden blindness. One of us would gesture to Kim-Bình to lower her thighs and straighten her skirt. She, face red as a tomato, awkwardly dropped on her knees. She looked like a sinner who had fallen forward, begging for forgiveness, when God finally appeared wearing his almighty halo to deliver us from this imposing chore, this ridiculous job, this unbelievable humiliation.

Thus, I grew, living a worthless life, while Mom devoted her boundless energy to saving Dad.

One Friday, she told Patrick that he would be going with her to visit Dad in Rạch Giá, about 57 miles north from Hà Tiên. She said Dad had been asking to see the children, but she could only afford to bring one of us, a boy better than a girl, to help her with the loads of supplies. Secretly, I think Mom felt more protected with the presence of her favorite son, although Patrick was merely 12. There was a sort of natural rapport between the two of them, Patrick being diplomatic like Dad, optimistic like Dad and, like him, knowing how to be funny.

I was of a different breed—too serious, too idealistic, hardheaded, and combative. I remember those times when Mom got angry, which happened frequently for one reason or another. Once her temper flared, its flame would undoubtedly spread upwards, galloping by leaps and bounds to her voice, then exiting sideways to her right hand, fast as lightning, and *slap*—the blow would send stars to one's eyes. The minute my brother sensed the approach of the motherly storm, he would spring off unabashed, faster than the Gingerbread Man.

Mom would chase after her victim, interjecting, "Stop! Don't you dare run away. I said stop!"

To which Patrick would retort, grimacing like a tortured monkey, "You think I am crazy to stop? Who wants a slap from those hands?"

This would send Mom into unstoppable laughter, her flame skillfully extinguished. I, facing her unjustified anger, would brace myself like steel and, eyes fiery, challenge her to hit me. Which she would. *Slap, slap.* The stinging blows could not make me any wiser, I, a warrior in the name of justice.

When Patrick returned from his once-of-a-lifetime trip to visit Dad in Rạch Giá, I anxiously inquired about the details of his brief fatherly encounter. This was what he reported:

We had to take a ferry across the big river, Mỹ-Thuận. That night we stayed at Aunt Hỷ-Phụng's house in Rạch Giá city market. The next day we woke up early to line up at the prison's visitor center, right next to the main jail. There stood a huge black double gate. Behind it, there were long lines of prisoners waiting their turn to see their family. We waited for about an hour. Then we saw Dad queuing at the end of another line. His hands and feet were handcuffed so he could not move fast. Mom started to sob, and I joined right along. Dad came out with his eyes all red, but he did not cry aloud. He smiled at mom and kept nodding. He placed his hand on my shoulder and told me 'Take good care of your mom.' Then he kept pinching my nose. It was so annoying. The fifteen minutes went by fast, and Dad was ushered back behind the black gate by the guards. Mom and I left the prison still sobbing.

15.

Mother Hen

My mother was a distracted mother hen, one who supervised only from the corner of her eye while tending to business, clucking a warning now and then to remind her chicks of her existence.

We grew up like weeds. Wildly scattered and windswept, riding on bird feathers, on the tails and paws of animals trampling by, we were like seeds deposited chancily on moist soil to grow into trees, hardy and stormproof. Aunt Khôi used to tell us: "One day, I visited to find Khải, about four years old at the time, wandering in the yard alone with a dirt-smeared face. I came upstairs to look for your ma, but she was nowhere to be found. Instead, Daniel, barely two, was dozing on a bed by himself, burning with fever. The first thing on my tongue when we bumped into each other was to tell your ma about your brothers, thinking she was unaware of the fact, but she just laughed and waved me off. Do you know what she said? She said, 'Oh! Children are resilient. They'll be all right!'"

That was our mother, a practical woman unfussed by details. She tailored our clothes several sizes larger with the practical expectation that we would eventually grow into them. Meanwhile, we stumbled about with too-long sleeves and oversized pants that we rolled at the waist and legs, dragging our clothes along with us wherever we went. By the time our clothes fit us, they were too tattered to look good.

With that same cheerful logic, she cut the girls' hair short, a style she called *garçon manqué*. The haute coiffure given us was simply a boy cut. I used to cry each time she sat me down for a trim. Her fingers were rough, arbitrary, her long nails unmerciful. The scissors made a *swish swish* sound in my ears, and snip and snap, locks of hair rained down and blackened the floor. As if that wasn't enough, she whipped out her preferred razor-comb to pull harshly through the remaining short hair and thin it further. My hair blanketed the tiled floor, as my tears tasted salty in my mouth.

By the time she handed me a mirror, there remained only a whiff of soft, skull-hugging mane, my huge black eyes brimmed with tears in the face of a boy.

Our feelings meant nothing to her. We would get over the tears. Her prime concern was our physical well-being. She would be watchful for the first signs of illness. Her hand constantly touched our foreheads. She peered into our mouths, checked the gums, wiggled our teeth.

"Let me see," she would say, and the wiggling tooth would come out in one quick yank. Or she would chase you around the house for that tooth.

When her palm was too cold for our heads, we knew—it was time for the white powder, crushed from round pills. Disgustingly bitter.

If that wasn't enough, she would order the afflicted to lie face down, bottom up. A hard, slimy thing was pushed into our rectums. Resistance was useless. One, two, three. Done. The stick was in. We were released with a sensation of burning and warmth, feeling like butter was leaking through our rears.

That might be why I had decided to become a different type of mother hen—a kissable, huggable one, a mother who would reach out to her children's fantasies and fears and believe they were real, as real as feverish foreheads. I practiced my maternal skills on my three younger siblings. I wrote down their daily schedules and assigned everybody a timeline for completing their tasks. Each morning and night I reminded the three kids to brush their teeth. I encouraged Patrick to keep himself clean and presentable. I mended his torn pants. I arranged his schoolbooks neatly each night and made sure he went to school equipped with a pencil pouch, tucked nicely in a bag. All the special cares that I longed for from my mother I provided to my siblings, no matter their needs.

Patrick did not mind my pestering him. We got along wonderfully. Anne, she was stubborn. A bamboo stump. However you hack at their roots, bamboos cling to the earth, insisting on having their way. She was my big headache. Uncheerful. Uncooperative. Passive aggressive. With her, I had to resort to all kinds of tricks, alternately cajoling and threatening. Sticks, carrots— it didn't matter to her. She just sat there, arms crossed, ignoring me and my authority. To her, I was just another obstacle to circumvent.

Michelle was my favorite dear little sister. She wasn't pretty as a child, but docile—a doll easily persuaded. The ninth child, born after my mother had a full house of bouncing children and a pharmacy to operate, she received very little attention from my mom. A maid provided her care, and I acted as her surrogate mother. I was the one wiping her after she was done using the bathroom—sometimes willingly, other times prompted by her futile calling after the maids, "Chị Dệ, I'm done."

Each morning, I selected her clothes, and she put them on happily. Done dressing, she would come to me for inspection. She accepted my supervision good-naturedly and always tried to please me. I would never have guessed that my good intention—to raise her into the impeccable doll of my imagination—had almost cost her the few social contacts at her new school.

For a while longer, I continued to live walled inside my beautiful garden of the old lifestyle: to come home each day to my own room, and, while waiting for my meals to be cooked and served by the servants, playing with my siblings in our yard. I went to the school I had attended years ago, my scholarly circumstance not much altered.

Most of my old friends were still there. I still dressed in the uniform of white shirt and blue pleated skirt.

But Anne and Michelle had been uprooted and transplanted into Cơ-Đốc Elementary with the local children of blue-collar families—two lilies in a patch of crocuses. From the start, my two sisters were objects of curiosity at their new school and kept at a safe distance. I was unaware of their desire to fit in until one morning when, as usual, I laid out Michelle's dress for her. When she failed to return for the final checkup, I went looking for her. To my amazement, she was still in pajamas. Thinking she had forgotten to change, I scolded her. She let me huff, then when I was done with my lecture, she said in a tiny voice, "I can't wear a dress to that school. Everyone looks at me funny!"

I was crestfallen. I understood her dilemma, her feeling of isolation. The world that she was growing up in was no longer the same world we had been brought up to inherit. What she said was true. To survive, we had to change our way of thinking and behaving.

For once, I refrained from insisting on having my despotic way. I was seized with sympathy for her and wanted to be her guidance in life. I wanted her to be able to speak heart to heart with me, if not with Mom, so that she would not be afraid to share the unmentionables: the breasts, the menstruation, the attraction to boys, the various and indescribable emotions. I did not want Michelle to go through my lonely path toward womanhood.

Unknowingly, I was beginning to heal from a deprived maternal attachment by my new dual role: I saw myself in my little sister, and at the same time became to her the ideal mother I had longed to have.

16.

Amidst Turmoil, Father and Mother

We lived through drastic changes only superficially. We learned to build for ourselves an impenetrable wall behind which our hope stayed strong. Behind that wall we could still hold on to the values and notions we had lost: our right to exist as unique individuals, love for oneself and others, a broad-minded education, God, angels, ceremonies, fashion sense, and basic hygiene.

It was a constant struggle to tenaciously hide the ebb and flow of our inner lives and keep our heads higher than the tides of mud. Safeguarding our souls required vigilance, a strength of character, a will unsurpassed. It was the mental weakening, the inability to fill in the gaps between who one was and who one seemed to be that had ruined many. The dual identities, one real and the other fake, had caused many to give in and commit suicide—die to preserve, or conform and live a treacherous life, hating oneself.

By tightening our rations, the government succeeded only in making us physically dependent. The sanctity of our souls was still ours, hiding behind an invisible fortress. Though we cheated and lied to survive, we had never given in—only playing a game of smoke and mirrors; never becoming a part of the new society, like joining the much-hyped Red Guard Movement or the Little Pioneers, enthusiastically heralding party slogans while in a crowd, or showing off a zeal for reform. But how long could we persevere?

Daily I rode my red bicycle through the back alley from our home to school, passing unlit homes, encountering the neighborhood's children in scant clothing, barefoot, dirty, and destitute. I noticed but never thought much about the difference between us and our neighbors. It was, for them as well as for me and the people in our circle, accepted, our fates immutable, preordained, as expressed in this Vietnamese proverb: "Royal children will go on being kings; the offspring of the pagoda's keeper will continue to sweep the banyan leaves." But now, now . . . it was only a matter of time. It was the settling of a new world order, where we would taste the bitter bile of poverty and ignorance, while our neighbors' lives, though little they knew, would be anything but improved from their current conditions. The economic difference would level out at the bottom of the measuring stick. The only winners would be the top cadre members. But I didn't know that myself, back then, a mere girl pedaling alone in a doomed city.

Our life is on the brink of destruction. This dark thought accompanied me each morning as I pedaled into streets choked full of cyclists, crossing intersections controlled solely by motorists' wits and quick reflexes. I could not escape this gloomy feeling as I traversed through the familiar Công-Lý, following my usual route to school and leaving behind the sprawling avenue leading to Tân Sơn Nhất International Airport. It had been more than a year since the last intercontinental plane departed with its load of passengers: war refugees and military personnel leaving in terror and chaos. The airport since functioned as a port, a place to bring goods in. These were not commercial goods but gifts sent back from Vietnamese overseas to starving relatives. These cargos were the only link we had with the international community and the only means to keep us economically afloat, and without them I would not be typing these lines, alive and reminiscing.

But we hung on with dignity. I continued life as a high school student. Mom continued life as our family's caretaker, weekly lugging her love to Dad. Dad continued life with his feet shackled, his febrile mind working a plan for the future. Grandma continued life through her prayers, delaying death with her last supply of medicines.

Chị Dệ finally left us to join her family in a new settlement. The government had launched a campaign called Kinh Tế Mới—New Economic Zones—to promote settlements in the uncultivable zones still rigged with mines. The new settlers would be guaranteed full partnership to community-owned lands. There was promise of financial assistance. These offers of lands and monetary assistance tasted like sweet sugar to the hungry mass. Country folks, destitute and barely scraping a living in their villages, decided to hop on this opportunity. It did not take long to unmask the ugly truth. The local government pocketed the money, and the agricultural equipment promised by the central branch never arrived, leaving the people with nothing but the right to illnesses, partnership in famine, and guaranteed exodus to the world above.

But it was too late! There was no way for the people to retreat to their lives before.

Chị Sáu and Chị Bẩy chose to stay back with us. Chị Bẩy cooked and cleaned, performing the routine housekeeping tasks. Chị Sáu, with her keen intelligence and devoted heart, assisted Mom in keeping the family afloat. She helped Mom fill out paperwork, attend meetings, or spend time lining up for numerous things: rice, sugar, salt, charcoal . . . , the list went on.

We were mired in hopelessness. I had had enough! School, what would it do for me? We were starving for rice, for heaven's sake! Fed up, I decided all of a sudden, "Enough of this nonsensical schooling." I reasoned I had better things to do staying at home, learning realistic skills like cooking and cleaning—in short, keeping a meticulous home. So, I stopped attending school. Every day, I busied myself in the kitchen, rearranging the cupboards, clearing the mess that had been buried there over the years, which the servants could not see as disorganized or dirty. I learned to bake cakes, fanciful sweet dishes that I proudly brought to the dining table.

Mom did not notice my new activities for a while, but Chị Sáu finally alerted her. I thought Mom would be proud of me for taking such a drastic act as revolting against the system. But no, she was displeased by my decision. For some reason, though, Mom did not use her authority to force me back to school. She persuaded me softly, telling me that, at my age, school is where I should be, however bad it was. Then she enlisted the help of Aunt Sự, asking her to come home to discuss with me my sudden decision, my motives for staying out of school. I had skipped almost two weeks and had begun to get bored in the kitchen. My friend Thanh-Thủy stopped by each day after school, keeping me abreast of classroom news. The embroidery assignment was due, but she had embroidered an extra handkerchief and turned it in on my behalf. I decided I had caused too much hardship for too many people and went back to school.

We spent Christmas without Dad. Mom did not let his absence spoil our spirit. She brought home eggs and flour to bake us a cake, a proper one with icing whipped from real butter. Even when we were knee-deep in an economic crisis, to the rest of the populace we were still the lucky ones, our privilege having sustained for a while longer. We were not terribly affected by Dad's absence per se. However, we lived in suspense, waiting for his return, fearing the worst. He could be sent to the North. Or he might perish—succumbing to malnutrition, to disease. A million unknown things could happen to a man behind bars in a lawless world, having no justice on his side.

The months flew by uneventfully. My friendship with the new gang at school blossomed. Emboldened as a group, we engaged in the worst of behaviors, from smuggling snacks into the classroom, copying each other's homework and cheating in class, to stealing candies from the little canteen shops run by the nun's helpers. We took pleasure in teasing the properly behaved girls. Often, we drove in groups to Gia-Long High, where we waited like a bunch of smitten teenage boys. Once the school bell rang, out poured the stream of white-tunicked students, graciously mounting their wheelers. This was the signal for our gang to spring into action. Two on a bike, cycling hard, we accosted the girls, whistling impertinently, shouting teases. Then as the girls looked on disdainfully, ignoring our verbal abuses, we started shooting them with paper bullets, aiming at their shapely behinds. Then, roaring victoriously, our laughter soaring high above the scene of escaping white doves, we vanished into the neighboring streets, intoxicated with glee.

Returning home one day from such an escapade, I found Chị Sáu at the Green Gate, her face beaming with a great joy.

"Your father's back," she announced.

I could not believe my ears. "Where is he?"

I threw my bike to her and galloped upstairs to search for him. I found him sitting in the master bathroom, stark naked, enjoying a bath. I was shy to find my father so strange, thin and tanned. He looked up and saw me. As in the past, he asked, "Want to join me? Jump in!" I shook my head, declining. I could never take a bath with him again, now that I was changed into a grown woman, unbeknownst to him. He seemed surprised, "No? Come on. It's cool in here." I again said no. Then I backed out, feeling utterly peaceful.

My father was home, safe and sound.

17.

An Offer of Asylum

I flip the pages of my mental album, yellowed now with age and shoddily preserved—the results of an amateur's job. There is father, back in the warm bosom of our family, bringing with his return a certain normalcy to our life. I saw him each morning through the open door of the master bathroom, sitting on the toilet, left hand cupping his genital and right hand holding a book, thoroughly enjoying the simplest pleasure of existence.

The windows of the bathroom were left open to invite in the bluest sky, serene as a silent sea, its waves of foamy clouds stretching to the horizon. On mornings like these, life was again full of promise. I recognized the old freedom in the sky—the birds were soaking it in through their wings. I could almost glimpse the metallic silhouette of a Boeing 747 among the minuscule black-winged creatures. I thought I saw its jet breath trailing in the billowy puffs, coming in our direction. But my vision yielded to a reality in which the wings of freedom were long clipped. Only migrating birds were heading off, carried by the northern wind.

Pausing in front of my mother's vanity table, I glanced at my reflection and spent some time in arranging her various cosmetic products. I enjoyed touching and sorting the beautiful lipsticks and nail polish vials, running the little brushes over my palm and sampling the various perfumes. However, these products had remained with a vainer world, a world of color and fanciful dreams. Inside the cute containers, the lacquer was beginning to cake. And the girl of fourteen staring back at me from the mirror—who will she be? Will she also lose her freshness and slowly degrade, like those dried-out chemicals, into a proletariat, the perfume of her life evaporated, her mind dulled and common, her body thick with working muscles like a field buffalo? I had seen a sample of my future parading in the streets, a soldier, *bộ đội*, wearing her telltale black braids and green army uniform. Northern soldiers like her had entered our city's villas to puzzle at people's bidets and bras, to use the former as a sophisticated sink good enough for washing vegetables, and the latter as modern, dual-cup coffee filters. She had been raised in a utilitarian culture and could not think of other purposes for these objects of luxury. How I had laughed when my friends told me these life's vignettes.

I interrupted my daydream to inform Dad that his breakfast was waiting.

To rebuild his strength—to a Vietnamese, it means to fatten oneself up—Dad ate two soft-boiled eggs served with buttered bread at every breakfast. He drank condensed milk, which was the only kind available in Vietnam, a luxury supplied solely by the black market. His expensive breakfast was justified by the need for a rapid recuperation from his near-starvation jail diet until his pot belly would grow back.

Slowly, Dad resumed his former activities. He did not forget the reasons for his capture. But he was determined to try for us to escape again. The news that traveled to him from the old connection was both exhilarating and discouraging: the group that we were with the night Dad was arrested had reached Thailand. After that, a third boat was organized. Unfortunately, that one had capsized, and the captain as well as all his passengers had perished. That was the end of my father's first fruitful connection.

Meanwhile, through our siblings' letters, we learned that Aunt Diệp, together with the family of Aunt Kim, had relocated to Camp

Pendleton in California. Brother Khải, who at the time attended Harvey Mudd College as an electrical engineering undergrad, had helped to sponsor them. Grandma doubled her quota of prayers to give thanks to God. But Dad sank into a deep melancholy, musing long in front of his chess pieces about the ironic fates of various members of the family. Aunt Diệp, the baby sister who had depended on his support most of her life, was now a free member of Western society, while he, the know-all brother, the guru of the Lê family, was hopping mad inside a closed-border Vietnam, wasting away.

His lethargy did not last for long. An unexpected visit from Aunt Trọng shook Dad out of his retreat from life. Aunt Trọng was the wife of Dad's second-youngest brother of ten siblings. Like everyone else in the Lê clan, she turned to Dad in times of need. This time, he was to counsel the haggard sister-in-law on what to do to safeguard her husband, for staying at his home was no longer safe for him. In the past, Uncle Ngân had belonged briefly to the South army's corps of medical personnel, working as a pharmacist. By the state's order, he should have reported himself to a re-education camp like any ex-officer. But he had procrastinated, and while he was buying time, had learned about the sad fates of imprisoned relatives and friends, which caused him to think of going underground. Where could he hide, for the local police would surely come looking for him at his residence?

"There is no time for lengthy debate," Dad had told Aunt Trọng. "For his immediate safety, move him here, until we can help him get out of the country. Do it soon."

Though still a child, I could measure the dangerous implication of this offer for asylum by the terror I saw in Mom's eyes when she learned of the fact—after it was decided. For a brief moment, she opened her mouth as if to suggest the possibility of retracting the offer. But the imploring look from Dad silenced her. Evading this responsibility was not a choice. She knew her husband and had been long enough with him to know the futility of her words against his decision. Had she not, from the very beginning, accepted the Lês as part of her life, to have and to hold, till death do they all part? Her loyalty was often tested throughout the course of their marriage, for her husband's generous assistance to the many needy members of the clan had encroached on our family budget, and had worried her. But this time, it was more than she could endure. This time, Dad was risking the safety of his wife and children. How could he?

Their opinions clashed again over dinner. Mom kept up her argument. "Tell them we were targeted ourselves. The servants, the children . . . Things would leak out. It would be imprudent to bring Ngân here. If he gets arrested from our home, his wife will never forgive us." But by the next day, Mom was again her husband's support pillar. Looking at my parents wrestling with their burden, I thought of the story I had heard long ago, of a man caught in a terrible storm on a boat with his son and wife. As the boat began to sink, he realized he had to sacrifice one of the passengers in order to save the rest. We used to poke fun at the ending, my brother calling out, "Sacrifice the wife, of course; she is a female." While all the girls chorused, "The son. He deserves to die." My own father was now that man in a tragic time, caught between two conflicting calls of duty.

Did he weigh the pros and cons of this decision? Probably. Was he tempted to not extend his protection to his brother? Perhaps. Did he think of shying away from this responsibility? Definitely not!

The call of duty was deep in his heart through years of growing up side by side with his ten siblings and struggling with them through the depression years. And what was dear to him should be important to his wife and children.

As branches of the same tree, we would survive or succumb together.

18.

The Curtain Came Down

I lost my bedroom to Uncle Ngân. That room used to be sister Marie's. After she left in 1969, sister Madeleine lived in it until she departed Vietnam in February 1975. With all the bedrooms in the house vacant and available for use, I had been moving from one to the next, experiencing the uniqueness of each—each looking out to a different angle of the yard, each with its own special amenities. Successively, as I claimed each room to call my own, I discovered that I loved each with an innate love that a captain has for his ship, that a farmer has for his fields—a love that I had spread to each wall with my childhood signatures; the corner cupboard that had been used as the graveyard of unused books but was to me the treasure cave of Ali Baba; the soaring staircase at the bottom of which I had stood, ringing my improvised dinner bell to avoid bellowing, "Mai, Marie, Khải, Daniel, Madeleine, Patrick, Anne, Michelle, down for *dinnnnnerrrrrr*."

We now called Uncle Ngân "Tenth Uncle" to protect his identity. I was proud when Tenth Uncle moved into my universe in which, with a teenager's zeal to express herself, I had glued, scribed, pinned the verses of many poets, French and Vietnamese, including my own muse, on the four walls of my room. I was proud to invite Tenth Uncle into that special room with its good-size L-shaped balcony, screened to block out insects—a cage with us inside, hanging amidst the leafy branches of a guava tree, while outside were the happy sparrows, coming back and forth from their nests, alighting briefly then skittering away; their *Eep, eep, eep, wit wit too wit* intensified one moment then fading into the thin air.

The house opposite did not belong to Grandma anymore. I had taken the precaution to block the view of my room from the spying eyes of Mr. Thụ's grown son. And now I was glad that the makeshift curtain I had sewn from some flowery bedsheets would help shield the presence of our new refugee. Behind the shuttered balcony, my uncle hunkered down in the stuffy, darkened room, chain-smoking cigarettes, listening to music using an earphone. Sometimes he hunched under a small lamp to read while waiting for his wife's daily visit. When the maid knocked on his door to take down his breakfast tray, he always asked, "Did you see my wife in the alley yet?"

Except for the time in the morning when he expected the arrival of his love, my uncle looked lonesome and fearful. At each bang at the gates, we would see him stiffen, eyes darting about for a place to hide. He often jumped into the large, built-in closet in his room in anticipation of the worst. His nervousness was palpable, and his alarming dashing about frayed even our juvenile tough nerves. His delirious fretfulness irritated my Dad a little. Dad was a man of composure and even temperament. He could not tolerate his brother's unreasonable lack of confidence in the safety of his refuge. "Say they come to find you here—so what? Doesn't a man have the right to visit his brother's family for a fortnight? You only attract suspicion when you act like you do, like a chicken with his head on the chopping block."

Despite Dad's reassurance, Tenth Uncle could not shake off his dread. Instead, he hid from Dad to avoid the lectures. Also, the difference in age may have separated them, as age does in a Vietnamese family, giving the older brother a certain dignity, a certain authority, a rank that the younger brother cannot trespass to build a bridge of close friendship. Thus was my uncle, a mouse in a hole, darting in and out for a quick meal, to scurry back witless from the mere shadow of a cat.

The presence of his wife brought him temporary cheerfulness and hope. He often called one of us into his room to give us a piece of fruit from her basket. His face was flooded with happiness in the shadowy cell. But as soon as my aunt departed, he dragged about gloomily. Now and then, the need to be up and around overtook my uncle. A new bravery flowed through his veins, bringing his quick step downstairs. As I saw him lurking above, I would dash to the French door to close the yellow curtain and the windowpanes. He walked about softly, stretching his arms, flexing his legs, inhaling the fresh air, enjoying the open floor plan, a rare moment of freedom, releasing himself from the grip of fear. Then, as quickly as he had descended, he would fly back to his hiding cave.

My uncle's self-imposed exile ended within a year. He departed with his wife, saved by the necessary documentation that she had procured with a handsome amount of bribery. Often, I waded back in time to peer into the sieve of destiny. Many of my other relatives had fallen through it into the swirling molten stream beneath. My uncle was rescued, in the nick of time, from the fateful abyss that had swallowed Uncle Khôi, Uncle Linh, and my cousin Quý. More than ten years would trickle by until any of them could walk back home again—toothless, lungs infested with diseases, barely living.

Yet, even in our direst situations, we recognized good opportunity when it came smiling to us. For years, Dad had wanted his children to learn to play a musical instrument. He had purchased a Yamaha piano and brought home one teacher after another. But none of them stayed long. Their causes for dismissal ranged from personality clashes and archaic methods to bodily odor and mercenary attitudes. It had been years since the last teacher had come and gone through our living room. The chance for music learning had never knocked on the doors of my older siblings. Despite this, Dad kept the Yamaha with the thought that, "As long as it sits in the house, it will serve someone." For many years, the walnut-colored upright had served mostly Uncle Mục, who could play any musical instrument.

Through sheer serendipity, music came into our lives at a time when my desire to learn an instrument was peaking, mainly because my friend had impressed me one day with her skill at the piano. I wanted to be able to play at least as well. Within days of my demand, Dad found me a piano teacher whose studio was nearby our home. Because what I did usually influenced the younger ones in the family, all four of us signed up for the weekly lessons, becoming one another's fierce competitor. Our new teacher, Ái-Minh, was a gifted twenty-year-old piano student at the Conservatory of Music of Hồ Chí Minh City. She came from a family of musicians and was eager to get more students. Although young, she was earning for her entire family, being among the few lucky people employed during that dark period.

Ái-Minh's method was traditionally used by all piano teachers in Vietnam. She started us with *Methode Rose*, a preparatory book. However, unlike the previous teachers who had failed to keep up our interest, Ái-Minh's personality, her charm, her confidence, and her music sense combined to enthrall and motivate us. We enjoyed each lesson with her, practiced eagerly and steadily made progress, persevering through the difficult levels of *Les Classiques Favoris* series.

Ái-Minh was a talented but hot-tempered teacher. Her furor when we stumbled badly on the keyboard was made of the same fire that fed her zeal for music teaching. With the same stick that she used to beat the rhythm, she slapped our awkward fingers. When she could no longer contain her temper, she had us lie flat on the piano bench, buttock up, then *kachack*, she smacked down the bamboo stick. I, being older, had never received this punishment, but poor little Michelle had to face it regularly.

One day, unable to endure my pathetic performance, she sent me home with the order never to return. I took her words seriously and, for the next few weeks, pedaled miserably to her house for my weekly lesson with music books in hand, only to dawdle outside her studio, until she inquired after me. When Michelle told her that I had been coming but waiting outside, because she had banned me from the lesson, Ái-Minh threw her head back and laughed, as if Michelle had just told her a joke.

The fast-moving pace of our piano learning regulated my life, giving it the focus and challenge that school no longer offered. Sweet water for my parched throat—it gave me hope for a better day and anchored me to the safety of an older time. I was of that age when I needed to be touched by a radiant love. I was satiated—in love with music and my beautiful dark-eyed teacher.

A high school placement test marked the end of my ninth grade. It was an important city-wide examination to separate the students into three main fields based on their academic strength: Math, Science, and Languages. There was great anxiety among the girls; all vied to be placed into Math and Science. I had no regard for my future in Vietnam. I took the exam with a lackadaisical attitude.

We returned to school in September 1977 in trepidation, only to have our fear confirmed. Our gang was no more. I was placed in 10B, the sole Language and Humanity Studies class, destined for a teaching career. My friends were dispersed into the various Mathematics and Sciences classes. Our school, until then an all-girl establishment, started enrolling boys. It was quite a sight to see the girls in our school mixed in with boys from all corners of the districts. Little did I know that the changing landscape of my scholastic life was only the precursor for more impactful events. The curtain was coming down.

Behind this blood-red curtain, the iron fist of the government again tightened. The new campaign, named "Campaign of Love," proved to the populace that the heads of state did have a sense of humor, though a sick one. This two-pronged campaign, with the goals of cultural and economic cleansing, targeted business and affluent household owners as exploitive "comprador capitalists."

One morning, five or six teenagers, members of the Vanguard Youth Group, knocked on our gate and demanded entry. Accompanied by a uniformed policeman and brandishing their clipboards, pens, and paperwork, they cited an order for a mandatory home audit. We were immediately surrounded and placed under house arrest inside our dining room, while they marched upstairs. Their footsteps echoed loudly in the rigid and heavy silence that choked our breasts, and brought tears to our eyes as they defiled our private sanctity. I stuck close to their heels in my mind's eye, saw them pushing through each bedroom merrily like bandits on a bounty hunt, tearing at our closets and drawers, gawking, touching, snatching—foaming from greed. We heard the sound of their voices intermittently, the thudding of books being thrown on the floor, the rattling of pills inside the bottles as they gathered them. As they moved downstairs, their cheap jokes reached our attentive ears, like young mothers' ears listening for the distressed cries of their infants. Their mission was to inventory our household goods, meticulously counting and recording the number of household goods like bedsheets and soap bars.

They were looking for ways to pin us for indulging in "imperialists' soft and degrading media" and "stockpiling"—the latter a crime punishable by eviction to the new economic zones—a place of death. But what interested them most were our valuables: the electric guitars, stereo and TV sets, and typewriters. These they plundered and sacked. We endured. Patiently, our parents submitted their will. It would not pay to rebel. What was material loss to us? We were hanging on to dear life.

Cowered there by my family's side, I was secretly thankful for Uncle Huỳnh's vigilance and the bonfire that had robbed us of our past. Although we had burned as many foreign books as we could, there were numerous more, gathered by the Vanguard's zealous hands from various bookshelves in the house. They brought them down by the sack-full and scanned through each volume looking for any with a pro-Western theme. Then they proceeded to count the medicine bottles they had gathered. The counting soon bored most of them and the leaders left with the pilfered objects of value, leaving the books and the uncounted bottles of pills behind for one youth to guard.

The yellow-costumed policeman tossed these words at us, "We will let you know the verdict in a few days. Looks like you capitalists are leading a life of debauchery, wallowing in American luxury." We were allowed to go to the bathroom at request, one at a time. Upstairs alone, we gathered as many vials and containers of medicine as we could to flush their contents down the toilet, destroying any possible evidence of stockpiling.

After a few days we were allowed to return to school. We stuffed our knapsacks full with the medicine bottles and took them to the school garbage. This went on for about five days, before the last of the youths finally left with goods that did not belong to them. They despoiled our home and left behind poison in my heart. I was born to love. I was still a budding rose, soft with velvety petals and yearning to perfume the world. The sting from these scorpions hardened my heart and filled it with hatred. I despised myself for being too cowardly to stand up to these invaders of my home.

The legal proceeding that would decide our fates never materialized, fading into thin air together with our possessions. Afterward, I could not locate many of my belongings. My new wooden high heels that I had saved for special occasions were nowhere to be found.

We had been robbed by thieves in broad daylight.

19.

The Returned Prisoners

Aunt Bích returned home from Bạc Liêu Jail around the end of 1977, almost two years after she had been captured trying to cross the border. My sun-scorched aunt was as young and pretty as ever in her *bà ba* costume. Her black eyes were two gemstones, lively and cheerful. She still smiled easily like a child; her dimples enhanced the fragile features of her beautiful face. The hard life in the prison had made her hands thick with calluses, but she remained a fluttering bird in need of protection.

She arrived home with only a few plastic bags, which she hugged tight to her wherever she went. When I asked her what she had in the bags, her smile flashed sweetly as she confided in me its content, "Look! These are valuable things I kept." From the bags, she pulled out bits of trash: little twines, plastic bags, a broken spoon, a half-finished handicraft. I stared at her treasures in disbelief, not knowing what to say, but, being a polite girl, I showed enthusiasm. "You made that? It's lovely!"

She carried on happily, "Yes! I've become good at tying knots. Don't you think it's something?"

My mom steered her away from me gently. "Let your aunt rest. It's been a long day." When Mom told her that a room in our house was readied for her, I was surprised to hear my aunt's refusal: "A room? Oh! It's so generous of you. But it is not necessary to fuss for me. Really, I can wherever."

This adaptable person was the same person who, in her first few months after returning to Vietnam from Paris, drank only soda to avoid getting sick from our water. This country woman who knelt down to caress our floor with wonderment on her face used to walk through here daintily on high heels, scenting the air with her expensive perfume. She who lived surrounded by boxes of chocolate and silky clothing now lovingly fingered the coarse cotton towel Mom handed her, eyes twinkling with pleasure.

Mom firmly insisted, and my aunt followed her into my room. She took her bags and placed them carefully on my bed. Then she took an outfit from Mom and went into the adjoining bathroom. I waited for her with an adoration that had not diminished, but now was tinged with a new pity. When she returned, fresh but ridiculous in Mom's clothes, she beamed, "Oh! Your house is so lovely. So impeccable."

It took Aunt Bích about a week to become somewhat normal. When she said I could have her prison treasures for playthings, I knew she was coming out of her shellshock. By then, my pretty aunt had developed a new phobia. She was sure the prison people would come for her again. Like Tenth Uncle, she was consumed by fear. She begged Mom to find her an apartment inside the French-expat building where she would be protected by the embassy. The day she reclaimed her French citizenship was a day of joy and relief for all of us. My aunt moved into the foreign-occupant building downtown and left the country within six months.

I did not dare approach my parents to ask them about my aunt's reaction upon learning the terrible news of her baby's death. Not then, and never afterward. I had waited for the subject to come up naturally in our family conversation, but my parents were forever tight-lipped about it. I did not meet my aunt again after she had moved away until years later. She had left seemingly without the knowledge of her loss, leaving the hellhole as a butterfly, shedding the last shreds of her tormented cocoon, blissfully flying away.

After her departure, Uncle Chấn and Uncle Kiểng also returned from prison. Altogether, they had been locked up almost three long years. As soon as Uncle Kiểng set foot in our house, he flung questions at us about his child. The pain of unquenchable love and impatience ravaged his face already battered by the years of confinement.

"Quốc-Phái—tell me, how is she? Who is she with? Is she with Bích? Tell me quick." His breathing was shallow, his face burning with desire for his daughter's news. What he must have seen in my parents' agony shook him.

"What's going on? Is something wrong? Is she not yet in France? Say something."

I stood at the lower stairs landing, sobbing. He would soon know. My parents brought him inside Dad's bedroom and broke the hideous news to the beseeching father. I heard his wail, a wounded animal's howl. He hurled his body out of the bedroom, staggering downstairs, sobbing like a child, his face smeared with tears, mucus pouring out his nose. He ran out to the street, screaming: "Quốc-Phái! Oh! My love. Oh, my darling!"

He never returned home or renewed contact with our family. My aunt and her husband never met again. How could they reconcile with such deep holes in their hearts? Their love story was buried with their only child in unmentioned compartments of our memories.

20.

The Boat People

Over the bottomless seas, beyond the familiar sky, a new horizon beckoned daily. 1978. Three years dragged by without an ounce of worth added to our lives. We realized that we had only been putting our necks to the grinding of time—like farm stock, for mere hay, for grain, for water. We were getting older, wasting our minds in classrooms that functioned more as brainwashing factories. Dad had become even more impatient as favorable news was sent home from abroad. "We started working and making money," said one letter. "The kids did not take long to learn English," boasted another. "And how have you been?" inquired my aunt.

If it had been permissible for me to reply frankly, this would have been my letter:

Dear Aunt,

The summation of our days is spent at the lines of the co-ops. At home, the majority of our time is spent in helping to sort out the pebbles from the best rice we could get on the black market. Lighting a charcoal fire is also a time-consuming task. And although we have learned to build an effective coal pile that catches fast, I cannot relay to you in enough detail how inconvenient it is, its black serpent of smoke curling and rising up to bite one's eyes with its venomous fangs.

Our school has been informative about how we had courageously beaten the mighty nation of USA with bare hands.

Pardon me for the running ink. I did not seem to mix it well, and my quill pen is pretty shabby.

Yours respectfully,

Hồng-Mỹ

In reality, my father's letter to my older siblings read:

Dear children,

I write you this letter to inform you that Fifth Uncle and his family have gone to the countryside to work in the rice fields. Hopefully, the soil condition and the weather are favorable to them, and soon they will have a bountiful harvest.

Love, Mom and Dad

As I entered eleventh grade, as the seas became safe again to cross, we again packed up. Anne and Michelle had left for Gò-Quao, a sea-bordering district deep in the heart of the Southland. Grandma followed soon after. For her, it was a matter of life and death, her medicine supply now long exhausted. Long, my 15-year-old cousin, Uncle Linh's second son, arrived at Gò-Quao shortly after. He, too, wanted to be a part of this adventure. Our parents, Patrick, and I were the last to leave home for Rạch Giá, a commercial sea town neighboring Gò-Quao.

We boarded a top-heavy bus from the crammed Bình-Đông Depot. These commercial buses were utilized to their limit. Their roofs were first loaded with bulky merchandise. On top of the heavy items, bamboo crates, crowding with clucking chickens, were loosely attached. Then plastic goods and smaller luggage were loaded onto the already towering piles. The people were stuffed into the passenger compartments, three per bench. The children sat on the adults' laps. The last passengers were almost shoved in, dangling halfway in and halfway out, looking like huge meat flaps spread for drying. I inhaled the ever-present stench of sweat, the smoky flavor of fuel, and fought against the flies and puffs of airborne poultry feathers. Food peddlers knocked on the windows, singing out the contents of their baskets. They fell behind as the bus lumbered out, moving like a gigantic buffalo toward the rice fields.

I was preoccupied with the twenty-four-carat gold ring Mom had fitted onto my right finger. It felt foreign and heavy. A layer of crude paint had been hastily pasted over the golden luster to make it less conspicuous. Afer a while, I diverted my attention to the surroundings, trying to record in my memory the scenery of the Southland that we were about to leave behind forever. I fought a dull sleepiness as the green fields rolled by, revealing the beginning of a new workday in the countryside. Nothing seemed to have changed. My people were bent on their tasks, crouching under paddy hats, their faces invisible. Lulled by the heat of the afternoon sun and the endless road, I drifted in and out of an unsuppressed slumber.

At a roadside public bathroom, we stepped down wearily from the crowded vehicle, joining other ladies. So horrendous was the stink that I had to cover my nostrils as we lined up. Behind a high plastered wall, people started to pull down their pants, squatting where they could. Our intrusion frightened the flies sampling the feces; they swarmed up in a whirl of air, buzzing loudly. I tried not to look, not to hear, not to smell, did my private business quickly and hastened away. As we returned to our seat, little boys selling roasted ears of corn offered them to us, chanting, "Fifty cents one, one *đồng* for three."

Mom called for banana rice cakes. Patrick asked for a cup of pressed sugarcane with ice. We ate hungrily, enjoying the rare opportunity to eat roadside food. Then we again boarded, leaving the little town behind, moving southwards. After about six long hours, our bus queued to enter the largest ferry, Mỹ-Thuận, connecting to Rạch Giá. Before the crossing, we were advised to get down from the bus to eat in one of the many restaurants lining both sides of the street. The one-hour wait was well spent. We relished the hot food, trying a variety of Southern rice cakes, wrapped in banana leaves in a pyramid shape. On the ferry, I joined the other passengers to climb a small stair to a higher deck. The Fore River carried us gently across. I shielded myself from a chilly breeze rising up from the grayish water. People's voices rose above the *thud thud thud* of the laboring motor, and the chickens roosted over the buses, flapping their wings in alarm now and then. Soon, we remounted our bus and entered the heart of the Southland's Mekong Delta, where people's lives intermeshed intimately with countless rivers, and reached Rạch Giá at sunset.

The bustling town had already been lighted for the evening, throwing half-shadows into the deserted bus station. I lost track of how we had found ourselves bobbing along the dark river in a hired wooden canoe for the remaining leg of the trip. A small motor chugged softly, coughing its diesel breath into the cold night. The incessant croaks of bullfrogs chorused in an inharmonious melody with a family of crickets.

Our paddlers spoke to Mom in a soft and Southern-accented voice: "Where are you going?"

Mom hesitated then answered, "Um! Visiting relatives."

Catching her urban dialect, the peasant proceeded, "Are you from Saigon, ma'am?"

Mom ignored the man's idle talk with questions of her own. "Has the flood water receded?"

"It's been really bad this year," answered the man.

We spied the flickering of lanterns, glowing like animal eyes through the dense shrubbery on both sides of the riverbank.

"How do you cope?" inquired Mom.

Another canoe, transporting passengers, floated by, carrying a conversation upstream. The indistinct sound reached us, bringing with it a soft humane assurance, a certain casualness, easing our apprehension. It was a moonless night, heavy with clouds. Everywhere, the people might have gathered with their families around hot dinners—steamed rice with bits of salty meat and freshly boiled water spinach—which more or less subdued their appetite.

Life carried on simply, so simply. Why had it been so complex for us? Why this distraught feeling, this unsatisfied hunger for something more, something else, beyond the hot nourishment, beyond the warmth of home?

I was jerked back to reality by the boatman's twang.

"Badly. We survived. My wife goes down to the market to sell whatever she caught from her bed. Water rose past our kitchen door. We've been living in the water mostly."

He steered the small vessel onto a muddy bank, switched off the ignition, and jumped nimbly down onto the shallow bank, guiding the boat along until it collided lightly into a rickety wooden ramp.

"Here we are!" he announced simply.

Patrick stepped out first. He cautiously maneuvered his steps so not to offset the delicate balance of the canoe. As Patrick jumped off onto the muddy bank, the boatman, standing at one end of the tiny craft and digging in the shallow river bottom with his long pole, expertly counteracted the sudden jerking. Dad followed next, awkwardly dragging his legs. He gave Mom a hand to hoist her out, jiggling the boat violently in the process. I waited, both my hands gripping the wet bow. I observed the others carefully to learn my move and then proceeded cautiously. Once landed, I was exhilarated. It had been a rewarding experience.

The boatman received his pay and patiently explained to my parents the way to go, gesticulating wildly. "It should not be hard to find the place around here," he said, "Just ask your way in. People are friendly and know each other well."

We descended into a quiet village bordering the swift river. We followed each other gingerly in the dark, peering hard, hoping for a scout from the host. Sure enough, about a dozen steps up, we saw an approaching lantern, heard a couple of slight footsteps and then a voice, "Here, here. This way."

Dad hastened up for a handshake. Following a worn path through a large weeded field, we stumbled upon a low bamboo-frame dwelling. A delicious aroma of freshly steamed rice and fish stew greeted our noses. A group of people had already arrived: a middle-aged couple, a man of about twenty-five, and two pretty ladies. We were welcomed heartily over a Southern dinner, spread on top of a large wooden bed. I have never eaten so well. After dinner, we divided sleeping places. Patrick and I slept with Mom on a bed by the large entrance door. A green army net blanketed us, giving us a certain amount of privacy. Dad hunkered down with other men in the kitchen, speaking in soft voices. The music of nature lulled us softly into a carefree dream, our senses deadened to the world.

We spent the next few days as if we were on a long summer vacation. With our clothes on, we splashed and swam in the cool river amidst the locals. For the first time, I realized the difference between swimming in a pool and swimming in a flowing stream. The water carried everything downstream; to go against its current I had to be a strong swimmer. Alas! My swimming skill was almost nonexistent. I barely floated, so downstream I was swept, away from the reference point I had mentally marked to return. I realized this soon enough to struggle back to shore, before I was completely taken to another part of town.

Traveling downriver opened my eyes to the reality of river life. One should stay upstream to bathe and wash and go downstream to use the public "catfish latrine." A lesson learned. In this part of the Mekong Delta, most household latrines were simply raised above water, constructed with bamboo and other cheap woods and walled in with dried coconut palms. As the waste dropped, it was almost completely consumed in midair by the school of catfish farmed by the locals. This symbiotic dependence created a perfect and economical solution to the age-old toilet issue. The fish, once reaching maturity, would be transferred to some caged-in part of the water and starved, thus their systems were completely rinsed out before they became fit for human consumption. This way, the fish ate what the humans ate, and the cycle continued. If the human food was nourishing, then the catfish would be fat and tender. If the catfish were tender and juicy, the humans would eat well and produce good fish food. This had been the traditional way of life along all rivers of South Vietnam.

To city dwellers like us, it was different. I stopped enjoying my meals for two reasons. First, when I sat at mealtimes, staring at the delicious-looking dishes—catfish soup, catfish stew, stir-fried catfish—all I saw was the frenetic midair feeding. Second, eating meant filling up your digestive system, which in time, would need to be relieved. Here was another of my problems. When nature called, I followed the example of the locals to the above-watered public toilet. There I squatted, humiliated in my primitive position and morbidly embarrassed, taking great effort to hold down the noise.

Although I tried hard to hasten the process, my bowels did not cooperate, partly due to a breeze that teased my buttocks, causing an uncomfortable sensation. My legs, tingling from the lack of circulation, slowly drained of any sensation. Finally, when I felt that my legs would no longer support me, my bowels started. But lo and behold! Spying their food, the school of greedy catfish leaped into the air as tiny dolphins, snatching as they flew. Under me the water boiled like a hot spring. Not yet recovered from being splashed wet with water, I next became the fishes' target in their fight for food—they aimed their whiskered mouths straight at my nakedness! I quickly raised myself up to escape their jaws, then immediately ducked as now my white flesh was mooning above the low coconut wall. Spotting my lowering body, the hyper catfish again catapulted like untrained dogs at a child's face.

Experiencing this once was too much. I could not bear to go through this experience another time. But how could I escape the call of nature? Miserably, I shared my problem with Dad. Like always, he was quick with a solution. We agreed to share bathroom time one afternoon so I could learn his "superior technique" for a peaceful toilet moment.

"Like sitting at home," he said confidently.

At the appointed time, Dad entered the toilet stall, equipped with a long bamboo stick. I claimed the adjoining stall to benefit from his teaching. The trick was to divert the attention of the fish away from us. So far, so good. The scheme seemed to translate well from theory to reality. The malign cat-faced swimmers were easily fooled; they stupidly rushed to the artificially bubbling water as Dad stirred the water with his stick. Dad balanced himself, one hand securing the stick, the other pulling down his trousers, ready for the actual deed of unburdening his digestive system.

As he lowered himself, he repeated his test, stirring vigorously. This time the fishes' attention seemed to be divided, half them diving into the diverting surge, half focusing elsewhere. But the instant Dad was completely squatted down, they shot up in one tumultuous, wiggling mass, aiming at the unintentional bait, which was nothing but Dad's reproductive organ. I witnessed his leap, white butt up in the air, face constricted in horror, as he dropped his stick into the river below. I could not help but roar with laughter.

We returned from this comical experience feeling insightful. Dad realized that his background in agriculture engineering had not taught him much about the intelligence of swimming vertebrates, while I acquired a new bravery to face my food source each time I had to act their feeder—I gathered this new courage from my realization that when I could not run away from my fear, the only option left was to face it.

I was what the Vietnamese called "a hero created out of difficult circumstances."

* * *

Sometime in the middle of our third night in Rạch Giá, Mom woke us up and murmured, "We are leaving!" My eyelids weighed heavily, and the bed was nicely warm, but I understood and grasped my small bag. The moment had come—only a step forward, one moment, for one's destiny to be transformed entirely. Patrick's diffused voice was almost a tickle to my ear.

"Where's Dad?"

I ignored him. Mom should know about the arrangements. It was not the right time to ask questions.

The night was crisp and dark as a cave. Mom followed the guide, a small man furtive as a tomcat. Patrick and I pushed into each other as we filed after our leader like Indians, through the damp weed field, separating the curtain of tall grass around us as we stumbled forward, using the person in front of us as a guide dog. Nobody uttered a word, until our guide, in his throaty voice, instructed us to step into a paddleboat. Suddenly, I realized that we had reached a marsh, well covered beneath a low forest of reeds and cattails. A boatman held out his strong hand silently to help the three of us into his shifting canoe. Once handing us over, our guide retraced his footsteps and vanished into the darkness. We held our breath as the paddler pushed his long oars skillfully into the swampy land, left, then right, prying a path among the dense grasses, shoving knowingly this way and that in the shallow water. My eyes adjusted to the darkness, and my ears started to detect the faint movements of some flying insects. Their presence was at once confirmed by painful bites. Upon their first sip of warm blood, the army of mosquitoes returned for a second round, then a third, stinging us on all exposed body surfaces, on our faces, along our arms, behind our necks. We sat there hugging ourselves as a mother hugs her child, collapsing into a ball to shield ourselves from further assaults. The silent attack and the quiet submission went on, keeping us too busy to notice a gradual transformation of the surrounding landscape.

We soon found ourselves in an open space, on a full and opaque river. Our canoe met up with a larger fishing boat and again we were transferred over, one by one, climbing clumsily up a taller stern. In this watercraft, we met up with the Phạms, the middle-age couple we had cohabitated with the last three days, their son Tuấn, his fiancée Phương, and his sister Châu. On the boat were two boatmen, young, muscular, and dark. They informed Mom that their job was to taxi us out to the mothership, waiting somewhere in the open sea. There, we would be reunited with Dad's group, and another coming directly from Gò-Quao, carrying Grandma, Long, and my two youngest sisters.

The engine was started—*pup, pup, pup*—sounding the drum line of a victorious Freedom March. We settled down contentedly. The boat picked up speed as it moved under a rising wind, zipping through the water. We were transported thus out of Rạch Giá's river mouth into the open sea, traveling at good speed for about an hour.

Then, suddenly, the boat slowed to a cruising speed. The rendezvous place, we were told. We waited silently, until the fishermen's patience began to wear thin. One man cursed under his breath. As the minutes ticked by, the two men started their discussions softly, exchanging information and unanswerable questions. Suddenly, there was a lighted signal, faint and far away. The men seemed to be startled, confused. Hastily, they whipped up the engine and drove at great speed. As we flew through the dark, they explained to us what they had learned through the coded signal. The border patrols had captured the mothership and had immediately blanketed the area with force, looking for more taxi boats. Therefore, the men had decided that they would not risk returning to land but push out to the international waters. The boat would hold up in this weather. We would be in Thailand before we ran out of fuel.

"There is enough water for everybody," they said, "if we all drink conservatively. And there is a good reserve of food. We can supplement it with fish."

I started to say my prayers, feeling Mom's cold hand squeezing mine so tight it hurt. I knew what she was thinking. Dad, Anne, Michelle... Where were they? Did the police catch them? Or were they on one of the taxi boats like ours, braving the brine toward freedom? The Phạms looked up hopefully. Seeing the anxiety on Mom's face, Lady Phạm reassured her.

"Don't worry. These people are capable fishermen."

It was pitch-dark. One of the men confidently showed us that their boat was well equipped, as all fishing boats should be. Below deck were nets and fishhooks, repairing tools, a portable stove, some utensils—tools of a fisherman's livelihood. We sat on deck, breathing the salty air and adjusting as time went by to the immensity of the space around us. The horizon was nonexistent. I experienced the odd sensation of being trapped under a gigantic frying pan, seeing nothing but the dark enclosure, unable to differentiate where the sky ended and the ocean began. We were each a tiny dot in all this—a nonentity with a faint, beating heart. I felt vaguely anxious, but like all tiring children with too much exertion and the assistance of the four elements, I shifted away, pulled into a drowsiness with each climb and dip of the boat. Half-unconsciously, I lay down on the cold planks of the deck, with one leg hooked onto the square opening which was the access to the hold below, for fear I would slide off into the dark water. Then I merged into nothingness, a speck of dust zooming across the Milky Way, unconcerned and unguided.

It was still night when I woke, sensing my full bladder. The boat had stopped in the middle of the ocean. One fisherman had jumped into the sea to survey the motor blades, mentioning something about the possibility of them getting caught in the seaweed. He reemerged, shaking his head to his companion, "Nope! No damage there!" They both went below deck, this time to restart the engine. I heard the chain shearing the motor gears. The engine only coughed weakly, unable to catch on.

"Motherfucker," cursed the thinner man. He climbed up on deck and then threw himself down heavily to a sitting position. "Well! The thing is dead, overheated!"

"What do we do?" Brother Tuấn asked, man to man.

"Nuthin'! Just wait till another boat comes by to assist us. Thank heaven, it won't storm tonight."

I followed his eyes upward. Suppose it would? I held that question caged inside my pounding heart and let it claw at my life source. But I instinctively knew, even if I had opened my mouth to free my fear and dump it there on the cold, damp deck in front of the other people, there was nothing they could do to dismiss the terrifying possibility. Suppose that it stormed—would we stand a chance?

Fear was now emboldened. It was better equipped than I, more cunning and faster. It had years of experience that I did not, being merely sixteen and well protected in a cocoon of health and wealth. It broke out of the poorly constructed concealment that I had raised to protect myself and my remaining family.

And Fear had the child in me by the throat, its hateful eyes staring down my soul until I trembled, losing my mind to it, inwardly supplicating it to let me go; let me go, and I would not tell where I had seen it, among us, sharing the crowded deck of the immobile boat. I dodged and ran with all my might to the angels, to Mother Mary and Saint Martin, and I collapsed in front of them, giving myself up to their protection.

We waited for the night to pass.

"Well! I'm hungry! Let's catch some fish!" announced the thin fisherman.

By now, I had learned that his name was Tâm (Heart). He tugged at the tangled net, skillfully unfurled it, and with one swift movement cast it to the sea below. Then, back in the hold, he lit the stove and set a pot of seawater to boil. He surveyed the stove and hollered for his companion to haul up the net. We all *oohed* and *aahed* at the jumping fish, about five or six small ones, gasping their last breath.

For a moment, the cooking task occupied everyone's minds. The leaping flames of the small stove created a new source of hope. And Fear and its untamed questions were held at bay. We ate simply that night, just plain boiled fish in salty water, drank a little, and then resumed our wait. All the males took turns urinating into the sea with their backs turned to us. I held on to Patrick's leg when he stood up.

"Be careful," I whispered to him.

Suggested by the good-natured Tâm, one by one the women descended below deck to empty their bladder into a trashcan. I resisted, but finally I, too, yielded to the demand of my body.

As the first morning light peeked through, we spied the mast of a large fishing ship. We hollered with our hands cupped. It came briefly into sight and then disappeared. Another ship came into sight; it, too, sailed quietly away. The afternoon sun provided us with warmth, then as the day prolonged, the heat became more intense. I pulled down my long sleeves and hunkered under my cone hat. By early evening, we were all worried. It seemed that we were unable to attract any attention from the marine world, and another night was about to come. The two fishermen attached a white shirt to the end of a fishing pole and waved it wildly at the passing boats. Our white flag, like a headless ghost, flapped its arms in a mad dance. Another large ship came into view. It seemed to be heading toward us.

Yes! It was coming.

We were instructed to go below deck, making ourselves inconspicuous. Finally, we heard a voice, asking the fishermen through a loudspeaker what they wanted. Tâm's voice projected loudly: "Our engine has failed. Will you help to pull us to shore?"

"We will inspect your boat first. Then decide. Anybody else in there?"

A silence.

"Anybody else on board? Come up by this order."

The adults looked at one another with a tangible desperation. Then, one by one, we showed up on board, all nine of us, including the boatmen. The ship came into full view. Its name was painted clearly on its hull, Mekong Fishing Boat—Socialist Republic of Vietnam. It was a modern-equipped ship, its engine roaring boastfully with strength and arrogance. As it approached, the authority directed us clearly: "Children and women first, then men. Fishermen remain on deck with hands up."

The course of the huge ship sent large waves onto our little boat, shaking it violently. Finally, the ship tied our boat to its side. A plank was sent down, and we mounted it on all fours, scurrying up like rats. Once we boarded, we were stripped of our belongings and sent to the front of the boat among the passengers, to be guarded by a seaman. Tâm and Hoa, the two fishermen, were immediately handcuffed and sent toward the back of the boat. Thus, we were captured.

As the ship blasted its propellers and sailed full course toward Phú-Quốc Island, we witnessed with horror the drowning of our little boat—it was tied by a thick rope to the back of the steamship. Then, like a cheap toy, it was quickly overpowered by the force of the waves.

Had we remained below deck, we, too, would have drowned, mere food for the sharks.

21.

Phú-Quốc Island

It was really over—our hope, our dreams, our future. The ship, like a victorious devil jubilant with its new prize, bore us toward Phú-Quốc Island. Its passengers, commuting merchants and islanders returning home, gathered around us and eyed our wretched shapes until deck officers dispersed the crowd.

We were thankful to have survived. I could see a million thoughts coursing across Mom's face. She looked lost but not panicky—a mother cow facing a pack of wolves. This was not the first time my mother had to fight back an enemy to defend her family. Looking at her pale face and clenched jaw brought back the memory of her raising a broom to a drunkard who had invaded our pharmacy one late evening and shouting, "Get out, else I'll hit." To scare the bewildered man further, she bellowed into the back of the pharmacy as if addressing to my father (who was never present at the pharmacy, which was Mom's territory), "Bring me a gun, Father. This criminal wants death." The witless drunkard fled her ferocity on the double.

As we were left by ourselves at the front of the ship, she leaned closer to me and took off her conical hat. Shielded by my body, Mom quickly unknotted one side of her cloth chinstrap and slipped our gold rings inside the strap's hollow; with her trembling hands she tied back the knot, making sure to keep the rings hidden within it. How did she manage to keep her presence of mind, when just one glance at her furtive operation had pumped me with such a frenzy that my heart leaped wildly about, thumping loudly in my ears?

The ride grew rougher as the sea rolled inland. Like a lump of dough being kneaded into bread, I was tossed and heaved. I only had the strength to crawl toward the ship rail to vomit until I had nothing left to retch but the bitter bile, yet my stomach twisted itself still more violently. My face was caked in cold sweat and dried tears. My lips grew parched. I thought I had finally reached the bridge to the other world, as I was beyond exhaustion. Mom massaged my contracted hands and feet stoically, patiently, controlling her emotions. Steadily, my motion sickness calmed. I closed my burning eyes and rested.

After a while, Patrick shook me lightly and said, "Look! We are nearing land!" I got on my feet to witness the docking of our ship. The mighty ship slowly advanced, enjoying its last moment of freedom, teasing the impatient island with its long delay, undulating lightly over the shallow water. The fastidious sea had discarded her dark green costume and reappeared in an azure gown, long and smooth, with slight ruffles of laces. Above her reflected an indulgent sun, his face drunk and beaming with mischief. The sea dazzled me with her new shade as she winked at the sun seductively, while I shielded myself with my rice hat from his hot and impatient breath.

I floated over the surface of reality, free for the last time. As the ship docked, I was yanked out of my beautiful hallucination. The other passengers disembarked while we were held back by the ship officers. In this brief encounter, Anh Tuấn, who was standing closest to Mom, spoke into her ear: "I was able to send a note home through a passenger."

The border patrol mounted the ship.

In my mind I saw Dad running like a rabbit. I visualized myself soon running like a rabbit, and I felt faint.

The wooden plank that linked the ship to the shore groaned under the weight of our group, with the men walking in front, their arms tied behind them, and the rest of us following closely, escorted by the border patrol. The ground met my unsteady steps suddenly, and continued to arch and dip under my feet. I startled when the ship horn blew loudly behind me, sounding its mournful *Dooommm!*

As a sixth grader, I had wasted much of my time compiling pages and pages of fortune-telling into a notebook. Each fortune was marked by a number, which was also printed neatly on a small piece of paper, folded, and stored in a plastic bag. When I asked, "Want to know your fortune?" my friends' eyes widened in excitement. They used to wait in line for me to predict their future.

My book of fortune was in great demand among grownups, too. My mother thought highly of my psychic power. Each time she had company, I would be presented as "my girl . . . she can foresee the future."

All the ladies would gather excitedly around me. Each was focused when picking her number out of the bag. Each kept quiet and intently followed my fingers while I flipped open my book to the corresponding page. I was accorded great respect that made me a little giddy with self-importance as I read the fortunes aloud in a clear and serious voice. Each nod of a head promoted me to a higher pedestal in their admiring eyes. At the end of the fortune-telling, I fascinated the ladies further with a recitation of advice on how to cultivate good fortune or thwart an adverse one.

I, myself, had succumbed to the mystic power of my pages. I kept picking numbers out from the bag and tried to interpret the contradictory meanings of my fortune, using even my dreams to light the foggy mirror of my future. Oh, if my worthy, wise book had suggested to me that at sixteen I would attempt to sail across my country's border in a tiny boat, survive a shipwreck, and suffer a prison term, would I have believed it, or would I have flung it into the closest garbage can, disgusted and frightened by the malediction?

But here we were, escorted into the village through a dusty lane by policemen with long rifles. From their dingy homes, villagers poured out to gawk at us. The little children pointed at us, shouting, "Escapees," and ran off. The adults exchanged their gossip. They seemed to recognize the two fishermen, calling them by their names. The village ended at a dirt lot littered with household trash—rusted cans and broken clay pots, torn rags, discarded fishing nets. Beyond this, we passed through a wooden gate and entered an enclosed compound with raised barracks. They stood like train cars and were supported above ground not by wheels, but by wood columns. The small doors of the inner boxes were closed off, but from the open doors of the peripheral units, many female heads poked out. We were then led into a framed structure serving as the jail office and staff living space. The men were segregated.

One by one, the women of our group were called in. I saw Mom take off her cone hat and leave it on the doorstep before stumbling inside. When she reappeared, she retrieved her hat and gave me a look I knew so well, a look that conveyed clearly: do what I do. How many times she had given me that penetrating, soul-reaching look— when her guests visited our home and I butted in, blabbing away about our family affairs, or when she had taken me downtown for a new dress but had walked away from the shop without buying and I had begged, had insisted? This time, I did not fail Mom. I followed her example to leave my hat outside the door before entering the dark room. A young woman with a firm voice instructed me to follow her into an inner room. There, she told me to take off my clothing. "Everything off."

Then she ordered me to raise my arms high above my head, while she searched through my hair, my ears, peered carefully inside my mouth, probing under my tongue. Next, she demanded, "Jump up and down." Still unsatisfied, she made a last attempt: "Squat!" I quickly obeyed, hoping for nothing worse. Wobbling out on shaky legs, I gathered my hat—*merciful Jesus, we outwitted them this time to safeguard our gold*—and joined the line of women behind a guard. We marched across a dusty courtyard toward the women's cells.

I had never seen a jail even in movies. The mental image that I had constructed from the descriptions in books like *Papillon* and *The Comte de Monte Cristo* was so frightening that when I stepped over the threshold of that simple wooden structure, the transition was to me only subtle—I was hardly aware that upon that step, I had lost my basic rights. Through that simple unbarred door, I became a criminal—a state prisoner. Perhaps the last three years had prepared me for this. I had already lived a caged life, being dictated as to what school I should attend, what subjects I would study, or what thoughts I would utter. Does it matter to a bird where her cage is placed—inside a room or among the foliage of a garden?

It must not have been so simple for Mom. This trip had already divided our family into three groups. Since their relocation to Gò Quao to wait for our departure, we had not heard any mention of the whereabouts of Grandma, Anne, and Michelle. Dad had vanished from our world since that fateful night. And now . . . the last straw. As we were led into our cell, the officer noticed that Patrick, although still a kid, was too old to stay with the women; he was sent to the men's cell.

My brother complied bravely, without shedding a tear. He simply picked up his bag and walked away from us, his small frame bearing his forsaken fortune. Unknowingly, my little cadet had leaped over his adolescent years to cross into manhood. Following him were Mom's eyes, fastening onto the closing door that would sever the umbilical cord to her baby boy. Her favorite son—she kept her eyes on that door, as if by looking long enough, her gaze could penetrate the wooden structure and assist my brother to safety. But no, behind the Red Curtain, there would be neither safe parting nor sound return; and although still childish, although still innocent, the little boy of fourteen would act his role unassisted.

Dinner was announced by the sound of a metal gong—stroked three times from the staff's housing unit. Following the veteran inmates' example, we scurried in our flip-flops to form four lines outside, along the wall of the two female blocks. One by one, we sounded out our number, with number one starting from the person at the front of the lines, until all the prisoners were accounted for. The last person added, "And all," to her number. Then the person at the front sounded her request.

"Present ourselves to the officer-in-duty. Request to go out for dinner."

To this request, a young officer answered from his high post, "Request granted!" and we moved to the kitchen. Each person picked up a bowl—the dried shell of half a coconut. Each prisoner—adult, child, woman, or man—was given an equal portion of food: the equivalent of a compacted bowl of rice and a few granules of coarse sea salt. That bit of glutinous sweet—slowly chewed—served only to tease my appetite, leaving me with a rumbling stomach.

Days followed days and nights yielded to nights. We soon settled into the jail routine. We became part of the community of inmates, sharing one common bamboo platform, moving about as a unit, passing through the days of our long confinement without much thought, just letting them go by.

We turned into seasoned prisoners in a short time. We could manage to bathe ourselves in a running stream, wash our clothes and hang them to dry, with time to spare for callisthenic exercises. Lacking toilet tissue, we became adept at using leaves. The vaulted latrines, raised on top of excavated holes that were refilled periodically, no longer intimidated me—although I still could not bear to look down at the filthy cesspit with its cloud of flies.

After a few weeks, the exposure to sunlight wore out our cotton outfits and caused them to tear easily, like paper. The inmates lent us their needles and taught us to salvage fabric and threads from shirt pockets to mend our clothes. When we ran out of pockets, we cut our sleeves to patch our outfits. After two months, we had turned into the tattered peasants we met on our first day here.

At night, the only incandescent lightbulb was switched off soon after dinner. We tracked the passage of weeks by the changing moonlight through a barred window. Small talks among other ladies continued late into the night, but we kept to ourselves lest we utter something foolish.

Some of the prisoners assumed new identities. Lady Phạm gave herself a new first name, Mrs. Mai. Her daughter Châu called herself Yến. I did not ask the adults for the reasons for their name change. It was impractical—even dangerous—to question or know too much.

We kept our real names.

Mrs. Mai was overprotective of her capricious daughter, who always had some kind of ailment. For no apparent reason, she would roll into a ball and cry from a debilitating stomachache. The devoted mother would spend hours rubbing her daughter's back with heat balm while lamenting, "Oh! Buddha! Have pity on us!" Did they fake this sickness to enjoy certain priorities like more space and less work, or was Yến really afflicted? I never knew. But seeing the amount of attention poured over her, I inwardly wished I would fall sick like her to benefit from all the attention of the mothers.

One morning, Mrs. Mai was summoned to the staff office. We had been warned about the upcoming interviews and had been rehearsing mentally what to declare to gain the state's clemency, or a shorter jail term. Mom was anxious for Mrs. Mai's return. What the lady said to the police could affect our family. They kept her a long time. When she finally reappeared, she was flushed, embarrassed. Mom pressed her for a detailed description of the happenings.

"How many officers are there?" Mom asked. She bombarded Mrs. Mai with more questions: "Did they contact the local police back home for a background check?" and "Do they threaten or beat?" To all these inquiries Mrs. Mai gave negative answers. But when Mom asked her specifically, "So why do you look such? Something bothers you." Mrs. Mai again flushed and admitted softly, "They asked me if I was Mr. Phạm's wife. I said no. I told them I was only his lady friend."

"Why?" My mother was intrigued.

"I don't want to incriminate him. Don't you know they sentence the husbands heavier?"

"How clever of you. You should be proud of your quick wit." Mom beamed.

Mrs. Mai looked sheepish. "They poked fun at me for being . . . promiscuous at my age."

She looked at me and lowered her voice to keep her next sentence private from me, but my ears picked up some words, " . . . compromised lady . . . die of shame."

Mom guffawed. I tried to hide my smile, considering Mrs. Mai in this new light—not as a mother but as a woman. I imagined her scuttling on her short legs after Mr. Phạm to court him. I pictured his humorless face—he looked more a stern professor with formulas in his head than a ladies' man.

We found ways to pass time inside the cell. I made friends with Lục Tần, a Chinese girl of about sixteen but declaring herself thirteen. She had a twin sister living in the adjacent cell. They told the officers they did not know each other. Each time we got out for mealtimes or for a bathroom trip, the two girls would hang on to each other, crying and furtively speaking Chinese, since prisoners were forbidden to converse in a foreign language. I became Lục Tần's Cantonese student. Until this day, I did not forget what she had taught me, a sentence we often repeated: *"Um tchee kaie say tie hue Take Saik?*—I wonder when we will be transferred to Rạch Giá?" A wish we all shared. As a small province, we had learned, Phú-Quốc could hold us only temporarily until a government ship was sent to transfer us to the central jail in Rạch Giá.

Weeks turned into months. We saw Patrick often when the lines of male prisoners passed our cell door. My brother no longer resembled himself in my eyes. He grew taller, squarer, with bony limbs like tree branches. He was no longer the little shrimp I had bossed.

"It's the ocean air." Mom told Mrs. Mai. They both noticed the transformation. I agreed with Mom. Patrick's growth spurt could not be explained otherwise, for we all had been living on starving rations.

The jail menu varied very little. On good days, we had dried bits of fish or diluted vegetable soup with rice. Most of the time, we had only salt. Sometimes, we would even forgo our salt for fear of cracking our teeth on the stones peppered inside it.

Besides our group and the Chinese girls, the other ladies were petty criminals—prostitutes, office frauds, etc. They were incarcerated on this island because they belonged here. Their advantage was that they had the regular visits of their families to bring them extra nutrition in the form of fruits, cakes, and meat. This surplus gave these ladies a higher status in the cell. For the exchange of a banana, for example, they could claim a better corner to sleep in or a larger wall space to hang their belongings.

If the ocean air nourished Patrick, it did nothing to alleviate my regular hunger bouts. With nothing to distract myself from the day's banalities, my senses were oriented to food and easily stimulated. A banana being peeled softly by someone was immediately picked up by my ears—the sweet smell of the fruit wafting into my nostrils, teasing my brain. At times, I hallucinated biting into that soft, yellow flesh. In my longing, I imagined how good it was to chew it slowly and mash it to pulp with my saliva.

I had to literally tear myself off from that base desire that reduced me to no more than a craving dog.

The longest period of the day was between breakfast and lunch, when people with money had snacks brought back to them from the market by the cook—authentic islander snacks, wrapped in banana leaves or floated in a cellophane cup, sweet mung bean suspended in thick coconut milk. Tortured, I had to close my envious eyes to the sight. It took all my willpower to hide my desire for nourishment. But nature betrayed me: I would obviously swallow hard my saliva, the longing would be in my eyes, and my empty stomach would gurgle loudly.

One mid-morning, the cook sent in a cup of sweet to us, the kind that came in layers—the bottom of the cup was layered with a red-bean paste, next to a layer of soft green beans, with a thick topping of coconut milk. I scampered immediately over. But Mom sent the cup back to the kitchen with these words to the cook, "It was a mistake. We did not send any money."

Almost immediately we saw the reappearance of the sweet bean cup in the hands of the old cook, walking barefoot into the doorstep of our cell. His face was the face of most old island man, dark and wrinkled, with missing teeth. All the ladies crowded him curiously. He returned the cup of snack to Mom, saying, "Someone from the male unit paid for the snack. He told me it was for you."

My mother's face lit up. She understood the meaning of this.

Anh Tuấn's message had reached Saigon. Our families had been informed of our capture and had sent over the money to buy us extra food. We would be cared for in the coming months. Mom pushed the snack to me, "Eat! I don't want it." I did not wait for her to say this twice. I tried to savor the treat, to take my time with it, but like a stupid dog I gulped it down with gusto. When I finished, I was twice as hungry for the wonderful sweet taste. Like a drug addict, I dreamed of my next dose.

Mom befriended the local girls by giving them haircuts and reading their palms. Owning an haute coiffure salon was once her girlhood dream. The dream became pragmatic as she became her children's and husband's only hairdresser. Now, this manual skill made her useful within this illiterate female circle. Try as Mom did, she could not get these young Southern girls to relate to her—she behaved too differently, spoke with an outrageous accent, and looked out of place.

But with the trimming of each lock of their hair, the girls became friendlier with "Mama," as they addressed her. We were no longer strangers. Whatever remained of our alienation was abolished by palm reading, something Mom picked up overnight, perhaps from her experience with my fortune book. Inside the four walls of a jail cell, her survival instincts had guided my not-so-diplomatic mother to mold herself into a common psychic reader. By a touch of a hand, she could win the trust of these strangers around us. By sharing and hinting at the affairs of their young hearts, she could wiggle herself into the intimacy of those who were against her, who might hate her—hate her for who she was, for her Northern accent, for her light skin color, for her obvious intelligence and educated mind— reserving thus a safe place for us.

My mother had not remained idle for a moment in her life. Confined in the four walls, she was at first reduced to impotence— daily gazing across to catch a glimpse of Patrick and agonizing about the rest of our family, not knowing what had happened to my father, sisters, and Grandma, having no idea how her older children fared overseas without the usual funding for school, food, and lodging.

Mom never shared her worries with me, but if I was myself besieged with such pessimistic thoughts, I presumed they played out similarly in the busy background of her mind. She was a perpetual worrier even when life was rosier.

But gradually she re-emerged, the mother that I knew, that I feared—a spirited and resourceful woman. She became a sort of healer to the rest of us. This came to her in part instinctively through the years of doctoring her nine children. But she had also learned her diagnostic skills from her professional training and experience as a pharmacist. What she did not know, she improvised.

The prisoners had nothing to lose in trying Mom's healing art. In the absence of medicine, common folks in Vietnam had for generations relied on homemade or natural products to cure themselves of a range of ailments, from bodily aches to bone fractures. Some methods were simply gross: fresh cow dung application to relieve the pain from bee stings, live lizard (or fish) gulped down to clear mucus-clogged lungs, suction cups for cough, cutting and bleeding to extract "poisonous, bad blood"—an endless list.

Inside Phú-Quốc Jail, even these simple remedies were hard to get. But we had some heat balm and eucalyptus oil. These products became our cure-all medicines. Mom became an expert at curing aches. She would apply a small amount of heat balm followed by some kind of rubbing until the site reddened; for migraine and headache, she subsequently pinched the temples and forehead; for flu-like aches, she scratched with a coin along the back and chest to create a fish-bone pattern, following the acupressure points. The soothed person emerged bearing the marks of the treatment: a purple-reddish dot in the middle of her forehead looking like an authentic Hindu or with her back covered with red stripes, as if she was whipped.

I also learned to give a good massage and relieve people's headaches by an even simpler method that does not require the precious heat ointment—by pulling on people's hair until the head skin clacked. The snapping sound was satisfying to both healer and patient.

Then Mom was confronted with the more-challenging cases of stomach cramps caused by menstruation or indigestion. At first, she tried the usual rubbing method. When this failed, she improvised, coupling the rubbing method with her intuitive acupressure knowledge. She told the patient to bare an upper arm. She applied some balm to this arm, then slapped it hard until the part reddened. The patient grimaced.

"Feel better?" Mom asked.

The patient winced and shook her head no.

Slap, slap. The patient twisted her arm in Mom's grip.

"How about now?" Mom again queried.

Slap, slap. Her patient gave a crooked smile. "I'm better. Thank you. Thanks," quickly withdrawing her bruised arm. The improvement could be achieved because the pain in the sufferer's arm had displaced the one in her stomach—or, we never knew for sure, the stimulated acupressure point had indeed sent forth healing energy to the stomach.

The latrine provided rare opportunities to get outdoors. We filed out for a trip to the bathroom like happy school students breaking for recess. Being over-sensitive, I usually waited for someone else to start a line to avoid the humiliating sound-off.

My mother, on the contrary, seemed to enjoy the sordid shout-out. She was normally a loud mother and might have itched to exercise her voice box. I cringed as her voice rose an octave, shattering like broken crystal over the stillness of the compound, "Request to the officer-on-duty, permission for peeing." How I was ashamed of my mother every such time. It was not the coarseness of her language that offended my sensibility—we were ordered to state the exact nature of our request. It was her shameless enthusiasm, her zeal for proving herself to this base world, her effort to blend in that hurt my pride so.

Greatly amused by her Northern accent and by her positive attitude, the guard played deaf to tease her further. Unperturbed, my mother repeated louder, "Request for peeing." My humiliation was beyond all words—to be standing behind this brazen woman sounding aloud her private urgency. Finally, with a chuckle, the officer granted us the permission to get out. Upon return, emboldened by her success, Mom sang out cheerfully, "Request to return." She said "return" using the Northern word, which tickled the young Southern officer like a feather. Humorously, he imitated my mom, causing a general outburst. We became the butt of a joke for the whole camp.

I fumed, more so because I thought she was doing this intentionally to teach me a lesson about being assertive. From that day on, to amuse themselves, the girls always asked Mom to be the line leader. Mom complied without a second thought.

We lived thus as if we had never had another life, splitting our days between mealtime, bath time, and bathroom time, until one evening. Right after dinner, we were ordered to finish our last bathroom trip and retire early. The light was off sooner than usual. We were alarmed by the untypical activities in the staff unit. We sensed changes but could not pinpoint the cause of all these subtle indications. The unknown hung above us as a dark storm over a chicken pen. In this suppressed atmosphere, the women exchanged rumors. One group guessed that the prison was preparing to receive a new batch of inmates. Another group hinted at jailbreak, which seldom happened on this island. There was nowhere to run, except back to the open sea, where anyone would drown without a fishing boat for transport. And no foolish fisherman would transport an escaped prisoner to be intercepted by the police boats that patrolled all seaports.

We hoped it would be a transfer to Rạch Giá, so we packed up and waited. The moon rose high and bright that night, lighting the courtyard with a soft luminescence. We were not fully awake, but drifting in and out of an uneasy sleep, dozing yet conscious of many movements outside—a massive mobilization. The rumbling of trucks was unmistakable now and the sound of flanking rifles. I was fully awake. A wild fear seized me. I had heard of secret mass executions in concentration camps. Could it be?

The sound of many footsteps was distinct, followed by doors being shut and men's voices shouting orders. We bolted up at the sound of heavy boots coming toward our cell. Somebody came with a flashlight. He stopped at our door and aimed the yellow beam into our cell, his voice loud and clear: "At the sound of your name, you must take all your belongings and step out immediately." Mom reached for me and squeezed my hand, clammy with a cold sweat. The names were fired off like bullets; people hastily packed and stepped out like zombies.

"Hoàng Lệ-Quân," Mom gathered her cone hat. As she struggled up on her feet, I heard my name, "Lê Thị Hồng-Mỹ."

My cone hat. My bag. Mom.

Stupefied, we filed out quickly, our thoughts congealed. A mass execution? My heart raced wildly as I looked for a way to escape. Then I saw the caravan of army trucks, their open beds full of male prisoners. A transfer. A transfer, I told myself, half unconvinced, half hopeful.

I tried to locate Patrick in the moonlight. I was not certain he was among the men, although there was a small frame that could be him. We climbed up onto the truck. I held tight to Mom so that we would not be separated by the mass of people. The truck bed was loaded to full capacity. Then the engine roared, discharging diesel smog into the cool night. I sniffed in the dieseled air of long ago, my eyes misted with the memory of our past and its stark contrast with our present.

The trucks wheeled out heavily onto the unpaved roads. Within an hour, we recognized a seaport and a huge ship.

We witnessed the boarding of the men in our group: Patrick, Anh Tuấn, and Mr. Phạm.

22.

Rạch Giá and U-Minh: A Misadventure

Four score and two tens, within that short span of human life,
Talent and Destiny are poised in bitter conflict.
Oceans turn to mulberry fields, a desolate scene!
More gifts, less chance, such is the law of Nature
And the blue sky is known to be
Jealous of rosy cheeks.

(Truyện Kiều by Nguyễn Du)

With my meager knowledge of Vietnamese literature, all I knew of Kiều was her crushing fate; she was believed by Vietnamese to be scorned by a jealous god for her beauty and talent. At sixteen, I was about Kiều's age when she sold herself to save her family. Unlike Kiều, I was endowed with neither great beauty nor exceptional talent. Yet I shared her journey, walking in her delicate and trembling footsteps, tossed indifferently from one master's hand to the next, exchanging one dark cell for another. Like Ms. Kiều, I had lost the control of my own destiny, now guided by unknown forces. Through her innocent eyes, now imbibed with tears, I halted beside Mom in front of the massive iron gate, its black metallic bars like teeth in the cave-mouth of a hideous guardian lion. The monster gaped its jaws to gulp us all down into its sun-deprived bowel—a tiny square, concrete courtyard where we were squeezed in shoulder to shoulder. The gates closed with a heavy clang, sounding the end of our life chapters.

What a contrast was this dungeon to our last prison. There, although confined, we were surrounded by nature, touched by it, soothed by the presence of a gentle Mother who governed over victims and villains by the same laws—to bring us rain when she had oppressed us long enough, to lap at our bound feet with her cooling tongue of stream water, to entertain us with her hymns chorused by crickets and crawlers. There, our bondage was made tolerable by the space around us, by the constant presence of the dome of heaven embroidered with brilliant stars, by the faithful rainbow—a long-ago promise.

But here was a place of gray concrete and black metal. Here, wherever the soaring barbed-wired walls stopped, they were replaced by heavy steel-gauged doors with multiple latches and large padlocks. Here, there was nothing of nature to assuage the agony of freedom lost—gone was the colorful sky with its decorative moon at night and glorious sun during the day. The green foliage bordering the edge of a meandering stream, the flocks of passing birds, straying butterflies—all had been taken from us.

They confiscated our hats before we were even stripped naked at the initial inspection, and with them went Mom's last possession. We had nothing left but our lives to preserve—and preservation was possible only by the grace of God. How our heads spun to cope; each silent prayer was a fragile thread of silk to sustain us through the gales of misfortune. Our life force pulled us through, up for a gasp of reviving air, then our ill fates yanked us down and pushed us into the mud. Again we resurfaced, blue with the want of life, fierce with the desire to live, to return home. Home. Not where our house still stood, but where our family could find one another.

Through a small door, we were disgorged into a zoo of humankind. More than a hundred women of all ages and all walks of life, and little children, poured out from the smaller concrete cells to witness our arrival to the women's quarters. We were akin to two new monkeys being delivered to an enclosure already overpopulated by the same species, where each log, each boulder, each den had already been claimed.

We faced the hundred pallid faces, anemic from the lack of proper nutrition, candidly observing us. Mom broke the silence first: "Hello!" A tirade of unmasked curiosity ensued.

"Where were you caught?"

"What's your name?"

"How old is your daughter?"

We survived the ice-breaker and were led by other women prisoners into a dark, windowless concrete cell, measuring about ten by five feet, with a knee-high, wall-length concrete slab.

"This is where you sleep, eat, and stay."

The current occupants made room for us. With our addition, the total number of dwellers in the cell was increased to ten women. The dark chamber was oppressive and lacking air circulation. *Was it how Papillon felt, in the cellar of his dungeon?* Our voices boomed as if from the bottom of a deep well. Here, we were truly cast off, abandoned by society, cut off from the real world.

Our jail mates explained to us. "This cell is the worst. We'll get the chance to move outside where it's cooler. They release people from here weekly."

Mom pulled up her knees to give me some room to lie down. The cement platform was cold and hard, a rock bed. The exchange between Mom and the other woman went on above me.

"I hope so." Mom sighed. "How long have you been here?"

"Two months. My daughter was out before me. My sister has a small toddler so they let her go early, and she took Lan with her."

"Really? They let her do that?" I could tell my mother's curiosity was piqued.

"Well, we were lucky. Lan was taken for her aunt's underaged daughter. They resemble one another, you see. I did not breathe a word. And my sister did not even realize that Lan was following her. I guess by the time they were both out, my sister realized the mistake but just kept her silence, acting stupid."

A commotion sounded from outside. Our cellmate stood up: "Time for dinner. Come get your ration."

I stepped out, as if from a tomb, into the light-flooded courtyard that had been converted into a prisoner holding place, choked with bodies—lying, sitting, moving, quarreling, milling endlessly. There was no exposed floor for me to walk about. The only way to get back and forth was to trample the bamboo mats that delineated the personal space, stepping over limbs, bumping into people.

My objective was the two balls of rice that I had waited all day long to get my hands on. For these, I elbowed my way through the crowd. For these, I hurried to the metallic door where three aluminum tubs were pushed through, with the rice balls still smoking. I caught our ration from the hand of a cook and discovered in the third tub fish stew. The inmates had lined up their containers to receive this rare treat—holding plastic and aluminum cups, bowls, and plates like the humble tin cans of street beggars.

I was seized with a new panic. I did not have a container with which to receive this bounty. The words spilled out of my mouth before I had time to realize what I had done: "Please, help me, I need to borrow a cup." My downcast eyes avoided the face of the one I addressed. But the stranger slipped a square-shaped plate fashioned from the bottom of a plastic canister into my hand. I looked up to see a pair of sympathetic, black eyes smiling at me.

"You are new here, I know. Soon you will get your own utensils."

The evening meal was consumed and, at my jail mate's suggestion, I was prompted to line up at the only well head to collect water from its circular mouth. It was but a few strides to the far end of the heaving courtyard for this purpose. But the sight of the elevated well, with its head poking up in the middle of a large crowd, struck a deep chord inside me. I had the impression that I was in a play rehearsal, and when a small boy thrust his little cup at me to ask for water, the scene was like that of a biblical time when Jesus met the ill-reputed woman at a well and asked her for a drink. Could it be that I was here to pay for all the sins I had committed—for the vial of

Chanel I had stolen from Grandma, for my headstrong way against Mom, for all the trashy romance novels I had devoured hidden in the bathroom?

The inmates who gathered here daily did so for the same purpose as the biblical congregation of time past—to bathe, to wash, to exchange gossip—and more: to look up at the small square of blue sky and soak up the precious rays of sunlight.

The well was drained of its last drop three times a day during the time of high demand. It was early in the morning when the inmates gathered for their morning wash, but by noon, its replenishment could not keep up with the constant usage. The gallon can that the prisoners threw down to collect their water hit the bottom of the well with a loud ding, and the last drops of water hauled up were milky, no longer potable. Yet, as soon as the shapeless and dented bucket was released from one hand, it was promptly snatched by another. The single line to the mouth of the well was zealously guarded, like the rocky path to a gold mine. It was in this part of the zoo that the female inmates lost the last shred of their humanity and turned into vicious vipers with their necks jabbing, spitting out unkind, poisonous words.

Everywhere else the female prisoners were cows chewing on their cud, cats lying on their side with limbs folded up, rats scurrying about, dogs crouching on their hind legs to defecate. The children playing with each other resembled monkeys, with their same shrieks and laughter, teasing, chasing, poking at one another—monkeys without branches to swing on. When the little ones were tired, they returned to their mothers and fell asleep in their mothers' warmth, and their monkey-mothers combed through their hair searching for lice and lice eggs, popping them into their mouths like nuts.

Like zoo animals, the prisoners were exhibited objects; we slept in the open, bathed in public, and used the bathroom in a group. The only bathroom, better called a "shit room," had a high concrete platform with four holes, beneath which sat four large wooden buckets. There was no plumbing to wash or drain the waste. Instead, our rinsing was done with a small cup of water.

Each morning, a group of women took turns hauling out the full buckets. But the volunteers took up the execrable task for a chance to venture outside. For me, it was a chance to get news of my brother. One morning, I volunteered. Paired with another woman, one of us on each end of a wooden pole, our team carried out the four buckets in a stinky and loud procession, with another woman clearing the way in front of us, shouting, "Buckets through." The path was quickly evacuated allowing the containers—their full contents sloshing and dripping, their faithful horde of flies a moving hive—to clear through. Another group of women followed behind the buckets with canisters of water and bamboo brooms, scratching at the soiled ground as best they could.

Through a small opening, we sounded our request to be let out for janitorial duty. On the other side the latch was lifted, the padlock was keyed, and the heavy door was pulled outward to let us out. I was short of breath from the exertion, and I paid heavily for the small puffs of air with the clinging stench that invaded my lungs. Soon we traversed across a square to the next building. The pole pulled me along with the quick but careful steps of my jail mate. I strained my eyes for any trace of Patrick. But there was no other soul about, and my eyes encountered only the thick concrete walls topped with barbed wire, impenetrable from within and without. It was a futile trip. I related this to Mom, who had waited impatiently to learn the fate of her young son. She averted her tear-brimmed eyes while ordering me in a thick voice to "Go on, wash the laundry while the well is not occupied."

The details of our daily lives kept us busy, kept us going. The sleeping platform was crowded, so Mom suggested that we alternate our sleeping position, to lie down shoulders to feet, thus saving a few precious inches to rotate our bodies. I could not imagine how difficult it might be for that pregnant woman. I watched her with her swollen belly, huge over her emaciated frame. I surveyed her good-looking visage, and pitied her. She never spoke to anyone, and was weighed down by both sadness and her physical burden. Each time she ate, she seemed to eat for her baby's sake, chewing painfully as if tasting the bitterness of her existence inside her mouth.

Every few days, the small door opened to let in a group of new inmates, mostly escapees caught from the local seashores. We met one particular group of women with their faces and arms badly sunburned. They had been fished from the open sea after a shipwreck and spent more than a week in the ocean, miraculously surviving by hanging on to luggage and gallon bottles. Yet, in their eyes, the hunger for freedom was huge, unconquerable. I knew now that, like us, they would try to sail the ocean again—carried out on little baskets, on small boats, on two-liter, three-liter engines, with a few canisters of gasoline, some rice, and a few gallons of water. The fear of perishing would burden their hearts, and the parents would shave their daughter's head and darken her skin to disgust the pirates, and the husbands would make sure that their wives took contraceptive pills so, if they were violated, there would be no lasting consequence. The mothers would feed their infants with sleeping medication, so that the little ones would be drowsy for the whole crossing. But they would go out to the sea, no matter what.

I met many girls whose innocence was ripped apart by not one but ten pirates. I met mothers returning without their babies. None of them cried. Their eyes were dull holes where the spark of life had been extinguished.

Good news and bad news started at the swing of that metallic door that was the barrier to the outside world. New inmates were pushed in weekly through that opening, nameless and exhausted. Since the jail was full beyond capacity, another group of women would be released to make room for the incoming. The mothers and their young kids were always among the first to be released. The period of inmate liberation was an exciting time. We dropped all that occupied us and gathered as close to the little door as possible, craning our necks to hear the names of prisoners being called for release. These formerly nameless individuals gained back their identities on the wings of freedom.

Our eyes followed the departing people and our spirit escorted them into the courtyard. Inwardly, we lit a flicker of hope for ourselves, which wavered, sputtered, and then died as the list of names ended; the officials and the freed people departed. Between the opening and closing of that small door flashed the picture of an exhilarated crowd waiting to leave this dungeon behind.

It was with disbelief that we caught sight of Patrick one day, among the departing. Mom asked me countless times if I had also seen her vision. I could not be sure. Yes, I thought I saw him, a bone-hugging figure that was more the ghost of my little cadet. A figure with the bright eyes of my optimistic father on the gaunt face of a boy-child. But I had also seen him many times in the depth of my sleep, calling me out to play. The whole face of the earth was distorted in my child-eyes. Where we once thought was safety—our home country, our bedrock—had become a place of sorrow, of separation, of condemnation. I did not trust my senses any more than I could trust the power of that boat engine. My passage to freedom had so far been rigged with false promises. My eyes had glimpsed the open ocean, yet here I was locked between thick concrete walls. Could I trust my eyes?

The afternoon left us guessing, and by lunchtime we had abandoned our wild hope. Darkness claimed us inside our cell, and we merged into the blank timelessness of our captivity. My mother and I, who once had not the time to exchange thoughts and bond deeply, became one another's shadow minute to minute. In late afternoon, I woke uneasily from a long, untimely nap. I woke to the commotion of the crowd, to the silent shape of my mother hugging her knees in the dark, to the screeching grind of a metal latch. I woke to the sound of my mother's name being called at the door. She startled. We ran out, hopping like two frogs over the other women, to receive a basketful of fruits and necessities, tagged with our names— in Patrick's handwriting.

Much later, when we were reunited with the rest of the family, we learned that, by observing the process of releasing children, Patrick had formulated a plan for his escape. With these few precious seconds of insight, he befriended a woman on her way out and begged her to take him as her son, promising her a large sum of money. The lady was intrigued by the cunning little fox, who seemed wise beyond his age and spoke as a true businessman. But, unconvinced, she questioned Patrick about the source of the promised money, to which he replied with confidence, "My aunt lives in this city just outside the prison wall, within walking distance. You trust me!" She allowed Patrick to hold on to her. There was no need for lengthy explanation to the guards; an accompanied child was released without any need for paperwork.

Thus, Patrick freed himself. He indeed had made a solemn promise without thinking, but he kept his word. He led the young lady to the house of Ms. Hỷ-Phụng, whom Mom had referred to as Aunt Hỷ Phụng when she had taken him to visit Dad a year or so before. As in a dream he walked, guided by the instinct of a wild fox, sniffing his way around the crowded market of Rạch Giá City. There he found it, Ms. Hỷ-Phụng's house, the concrete steps leading up a timeless door, its paint peeled off. He knocked hard on it, master of his own destiny, trying to camouflage the loud thumping of his racing heartbeat. The lady waited like a docile cat for her treat of tidbits, which the master was about to toss. The door yielded, and the large frame of Ms. Hỷ-Phụng appeared.

"Well, well, well! Who is it that I see at my doorstep? Patrick, son, come in. What a surprise to see you at this time. Where's Mom?"

Patrick explained the situation to Ms. Hỷ-Phụng in a burst of words, brief but coherent and urgent. It was clear to her that the boy was in control of his plan. He needed money to pay for his ransom— now. And he needed more money to send his mom and sister some food. Lastly, he needed money for his ticket home to Saigon. Now. He promised a full refund when he found his family. Ms. Hỷ-Phụng, like the young lady he had walked out of jail with, was speechless in front of the commanding child.

As soon as he related his story to Ms. Hỷ-Phụng, he felt deflated, a small child again in front of an incomprehensible adult. Would she help solely based on the words of his mouth? She should. She must. It was upon her friend's doorstep that Mom had dragged herself with him, full of confidence and trust. Something in Ms. Hỷ-Phụng's

Chinese demeanor had captured Patrick's faith in her that night. But he was alone now. Would she help a mere child?

Ms. Hỷ-Phụng's eyes welled up with tears. She disappeared, leaving the boy in an awkward silence, unsure of what to say to his savior. Had he failed her? Ms. Hỷ-Phụng soon returned with a handful of bills: "Here, Patrick. Do what you deem right." Patrick paid his promised fee to the young lady, who took it with amazement, bidding him goodbye respectfully, as from servant to master.

When all was said and done between the boy and his helper, Ms. Hỷ-Phụng offered to take him into the market to buy provisions for his imprisoned family. Patrick declined her goodwill and asked instead for the necessary information to get there, the current market price for things, and the way to the bus depot. She patiently described the location of various food stalls in the market, gave him the names of a few trusted merchants she knew, and bade him goodbye. He departed for his mission.

After returning to the high forbidden gate of the prison and left with the guards the food bags that he had bought in the market, he left for the bus depot, catching the last bus to Saigon, in search of his father and sisters. Patrick became his family crusader at age fourteen. He left the protective cloak of his childhood behind on that roadside, mounted the steps of the large vehicle—ruler of his own fate. His innocence rolled away from him under the wheels of the bus, back to a distant past, no longer visible.

His next life would meet him head on. He somehow had an inkling that this vehicle would not carry him home. That home was of his past.

* * *

Wait for me, and I'll return
Only wait very hard
Wait when you are filled with sorrow . . .
Wait in the sweltering heat
Wait when the others have stopped waiting,
Forgetting their yesterdays.

Wait even when from afar no letters come to you
Wait even when others are tired of waiting . . .
And when friends sit around the fire,
Drinking to my memory,
Wait, and do not hurry to drink to my memory too.

Wait. For I'll return, defying every death.
And let those who do not wait say that I was lucky.
They will never understand that in the midst of death,
You with you waiting saved me.
Only you and I know how I survived.
It's because you waited, as no one else did.

("Wait for Me" by Konstantin Simonov)

While I was detained with Patrick and Mom in Phú-Quốc, Grandma, Anne, and Michelle waited impatiently in Gò Quao for the return of my father. For what else could they do? The brief reason Dad had provided them to explain why he sent them to Gò Quao—two city girls, aged ten and eleven, and a feeble eighty-year-old lady—was satisfactory at the time but was now no longer plausible. Their weeklong wait to be reunited with my father had turned into unbearable months.

Two months before, Anne and Michelle had arrived in the green lands of Gò Quao escorted by Mr. Thuyết. It was their first trip without our parents. They were charmed immediately by the lush landscape, the majestic surrounding forests, and the innumerable waterways that zigzagged the Mekong provinces of Kiên-Giang. To these two innocent girls, the trip was only the beginning of a marvelous discovery. They absorbed all the new sensations created by the nature around them with mounting interest. Soon they would hop from canoe to canoe expertly. They ceased to worry about the mud that caked their toes and heels. It took them only a few days to darken, transformed from head to toe into local girls. Grandma's arrival completed their notion of a perfect adventure only found in books.

They were at first guests of the family and stayed with the mother of Mr. Thuyết, who was a member of Dad's escape organization. But as the deadline for Dad to return was long overdue, they became a burden to the host, and their dependence turned into a nuisance. The Mekong provinces had flooded heavily that year and the limited source of precious crops to sustain the villagers had dwindled to almost nothing. No one could afford to feed an extra mouth, especially one that does not contribute in kind or deed. The limited source of money Dad had left with Grandma was a reserve for only few weeks. After this, she sold off her gold rings, then whatever else she could.

Two months after their arrival, the threesome was sent packing to a village deep in U-Minh, a region known for its thick woods—an impenetrable haven for Việt-Cộng guerillas but a trap hole to the unguided American forces.

U-Minh means both *darkness* and *light*. I had never visited this region before, but by its name and by my sisters' descriptions, I could imagine a place of changing qualities—full of light and shadow, beautiful yet dangerous, at the same time nurturing to its local inhabitants and treacherous to its foreign invaders.

Michelle never forgot her experience there. Years later, she recounted their adventure turned misadventure in a reminiscing and rambling letter:

> *I experienced the country life for the first time when we descended into Gò-Quao. I really enjoyed that summer, because it was a summer filled with adventures just like the ones I had read in my French books. Uncle Thuyết took us sightseeing at The Black Woman Mountain. There, we encountered real Vietnamese aborigines; they were the images of the Seven Dwarves from the movie, dwarves with dark skin and ugly monkey faces.*
>
> *All of the children had distended bellies due to malnutrition. Many people suffered from hyperthyroid due to lack of iodine.*

Waking at dawn, the men ate large bowls of rice and salted meat. All day long they were up in the mountains cracking boulders into stones. At sundown, they returned home to join the women for early dinner with rice and light vegetable soup and hot tea.

Their pleasure was simple. They talked, gossiped, played a tune on guitar, harmonica, or plucked an ethnic one-string instrument, picked at their teeth, bathed and retired early for the next working day.

Uncle Thuyết's mother, the matron of the house, was upset to see Anne and myself swimming in public. She was even more shocked to discover that I had only my panties on. I did not know that a girl of my age cannot swim naked in the river, but should bathe with her clothes on, hidden in the back of the house.

From the country boys, I learned to cut down banana tree trunks, nailed them together to make into a raft. I learned how to catch fish with worms and baked them in lotus leaves. We slept on straw mats in a large wooden bed. As the flood continued to rise, we had to rely on small boats to get around the house or to church. The church's altar was where the priest's boat parked. The people worshiped in their own family's boat. Goods such as meat, vegetables, fabric, etc., were rowed from house to house to be sold.

With time, our arms and legs were covered with mosquito bites and pustulated blisters from wading in dirty water. Anne and myself were no longer whole, but two wet bags of raw flesh.

When he could no longer wait, Uncle Thuyết left us to go searching for our parents, with whom he had lost contact . . . .

It was during this time that Grandma's delicate health nosedived. When her condition seemed irreversible, brave and penniless cousin Long decided to hitchhike back to Saigon with the bad news. By the time Aunt Linh, Long's mother, and Aunt Sự arrived to U-Minh, Grandma had slipped in and out of a coma. Her kidneys were failing. A swollen chin, where a weeping boil had developed, distorted her thin and almost transparent face.

The two aunts carried Grandma's emaciated body into a hired

boat, followed by my two sisters, limping along on their heavily suppurated legs. Anne told me, "We could hardly walk. Even the bottoms of our feet were full of open blisters." It was a bittersweet reunion with Aunt Linh and Aunt Sự. So much had changed after two months. Michelle added with a sigh, "We had grown so dark. Anne was much taller, too. But Grandma . . . ." It was not easy for Michelle to recount this. Grandma was the only adult left for them to depend on. They did not know what to do.

Michelle admitted, "We were terrified to see Grandma slowly slipping away."

Anne was inconsolable. "We were all so helpless."

During the river crossing, Grandma opened her eyes and recognized her daughter, Sự. She was lucid enough to notice that they were all in a boat. Her countenance relaxed. With a satisfied deep breath, she murmured into my aunt's ears: "Leaving now? Thank God for saving us!" She must have thought the boat was heading toward the ocean, to freedom.

Until this day, Dad has avoided discussing the reasons for his months-long disappearance. There was nothing any of us could do to make sense of this event. Where was Dad when his presence was needed most? The only explanation he provided us was, "I was out looking for Mom."

"Did you finally learn about our capture?" I had insisted on this crucial information from my father.

"Yes, much later," he answered, clearly wanting to escape the probing. "I thought your boat had gotten away and was waiting for your news from abroad. I was trying to finance another boat to bring Grandma and the rest of us along when I received the bad news."

I did not push Dad to talk, for I saw the agony on his face. I mentally put myself into his shoes and walked around in them, wallowing in the depth of his despair.

The sad news of our capture instead of the waited, joyous news of our arrival to Thailand must have numbed my father. From our relatives, he had learned that our home had been appropriated by the local government during our extended absence. How would he explain this to his mother and daughters? How could he tell them the cruel consequence, that they were homeless and penniless?

Knowing my father, I can very well picture his sudden loss of direction. I can see him crushed like a ball of paper, unable to tear himself away from the grip of fear. I can see him being cowed down, unable to respond, prolonging his days in self-denial, vagabonding from countryside to countryside in search of another truth, one that was less painful.

The message from Saigon reached him finally: "Come home. Mom will not last." Yes, it was inevitable. He had no choice but to return home. He admitted to himself, finally, that there was nothing left from this trip to salvage. It was a failure. Half of his family was now locked up. The two youngest daughters were living with their aunt. And his mother was dying.

All of this I can plainly see as if I were my father. Looking back, I watch him as if he were an actor on a movie set, with his face in his hands, his shoulders shaking with heaving sobs.

Grandma had fought bravely to stay alive until the day Dad resurfaced at the doorstep of Aunt Sự's home, a lost soul. Within days of his return, a week before Christmas 1978, Grandma passed away, another family member destroyed prematurely by the lack of proper nutrition and medicine. In one short year, we had lost a lifetime—our grandma, our home, and our parents' entire savings. How does one live on, knowing that one's whole life, the painstaking years of frugal living and earning by the sweat of one's brow, has been wiped out, vanished? Nothing left but thin air?

What words could I use to describe the state of my father's being? I felt inadequate in the face of his desolation. His guilt and grief. How dark and bottomless was his despair? How chaotic was his soul, incommunicable to anyone?

My sisters remained with Aunt Sự's family while Dad barricaded himself inside Aunt Huỳnh's house, an alley away. I followed him there with my mind's eye. What was a poor soul to do in this time, directionless? In the empty abode of his oldest brother, my father must have shrunk down daily, seeking his old, confident self in vain.

In the security of Uncle Huỳnh's house, now occupied by his silent widow, within the shadowy rooms that once had been his brother's schoolhouse, Dad, a child again, must have sought the fatherly protection and guidance of Uncle Huỳnh's soul. He must have felt a certain peace sitting on the same chair where his beloved brother had sat, sharing his deep melancholy, musing philosophically about the meaning of life. Those same books that Uncle Huỳnh had read in solitude must have been opened in Dad's hands. The same authors must have spoken to him, giving him some clues to figure it all out.

How did it all happen? Why did his plan go awry? What was missing? What had he done to his family? Probably nothing made sense any more to my father's methodical mind.

His thoughts must have turned often to my mother. She who, in all her practical wisdom, had begged him to leave, forsaking his last paychecks, even the long-awaited pension from Esso. To leave while it was still possible. I was almost certain that he needed her then more than ever. He needed her plain logic, her blind faith in him, and her assurance. His intellect could not save him. His calculations were all erroneous. His wife, with fire in her lungs and iron in her will, with her plain words and clear practicality, would make sure that he rose daily—like a lark rising, a sun, a cow, a horse, a man—rising to their task, to face the challenges of daily life; but she was gone without a firm date of return.

It was then that Patrick reappeared, a returned prisoner, bringing with him the will to survive. Inadvertently, the prodigal son had stepped into his father's empty shoes to prop up the ruins of his family. Not too long after Patrick's return, my half-family reunited in Aunt Huỳnh's home.

Soon after that, Mom and I were granted freedom.

As in a dream, we sleepwalked out of the double iron gate of Kiên-Giang's Central Prison, blinded by the afternoon light, modern daughters of Jonah vomited from the mouth of the whale. God showed himself in the glorious sunlight. I cried out as if I were being stabbed in the eyes, and covered my face from the powerful brightness of what seemed to be a thousand suns.

I stumbled alongside Mom with a queer sensation—as if I were walking with somebody else's feet, moving in someone else's body. It was as if I had died and my body had been taken over by a strange girl, happy and inebriated with life. Into the vast open space she and I entered into a forgotten time. I was that happy girl fast-stepping through the streets, learning the walking movement again—feet colliding onto pavement, ankles springing back, knees absorbing, thighs swinging forward. What a surprise to discover my limbs could work together on such distance. What a joy to meet the distance and discover that it only led us on to more open space, to additional streets, to different intersections, on and on, forever going toward the next block.

I looked up to encounter other beings who walked about decidedly, who spoke of daily business, who came and went freely. They were not a bit astonished by what was happening. Their feet beat the ground as hammers on an anvil, dead to the sensations, oblivious to the action—self-absorbed, unaware, mechanical.

Was I the only one conscious of a miracle?

The Lê Đăng family with the five older children in the front with Grandpa, Grandma, and Dad, uncle Christopher Bảng, and Mom in the back (circa 1962)

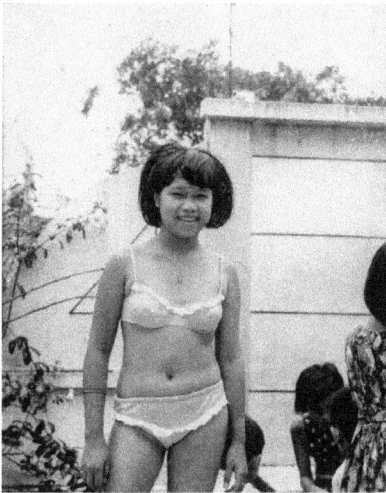

Chị Mai, oldest sister, at home in Tân Sa Châu (circa 1967)

Chị Marie, second oldest sister, by the pool at home (circa 1967)

Anh Khải, third sibling (circa 1964)

Anh Khả (Daniel), fourth sibling (R) and Patrick, seventh sibling at home in Tân Sa Châu (circa 1967)

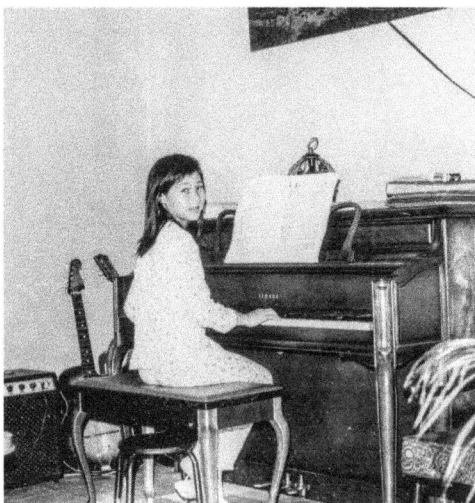

Chị Madeleine, fifth sibling, at the Yamaha piano at home in Tân Sa Châu (circa 1970)

Anne (R) and Michelle (L), the youngest siblings (circa 1970)

A party to celebrate sisters Mai's and Marie's first summer break from Belgium.

L to R: Patrick, sister Mai's friend, Hồng-Mỹ, chị Mai (1970)

Uncle Chấn chauffeur, cousin Mai-Xuân, chauffeur's daughter in the back row (circa 1968)

Anne, Patrick, Hồng-Mỹ (front row)

The Lê family at chị Mai's engagement (1972) without the engaged couple. L to R: uncle Mục, uncle Khôi, uncle Linh, Aunt Kim's husband, Aunt Kim, Mom, Uncle Khôi's wife, Dad at home in Tân Sa Châu

L to R: Patrick on his tricycle, Anne, Michelle, and Mom outside the living room at home in Tân Sa Châu (circa 1970)

Mom and her chickens at home in Tân Sa Châu (circa 1974)

Mom and the red Mazda (circa 1974)

Maternal grandma Hoàng

*Maternal great-grandma,
also called Ancient Grandma*

*Sister Marie and
maternal grandpa
(Paris, circa 1976)*

Aunt Bích and Aunt Hương,
mom's younger sisters
(Paris, circa 1972)

Patrick practicing piano
at Mỹ-Hướng (1979)

Mom on the terrace at
Mỹ-Hướng (circa 1982)

Lê Đăng family celebrating Michelle's confirmation at Dòng Chúa Cứu Thế Church (1981). Hồng-Mỹ was at Dufong Island. L to R (back row): Patrick, uncle Sự, family priest, Dad L to R (front row): Mom, Michelle, cousin Yến-Dung, Anne, friend Phương-Dung

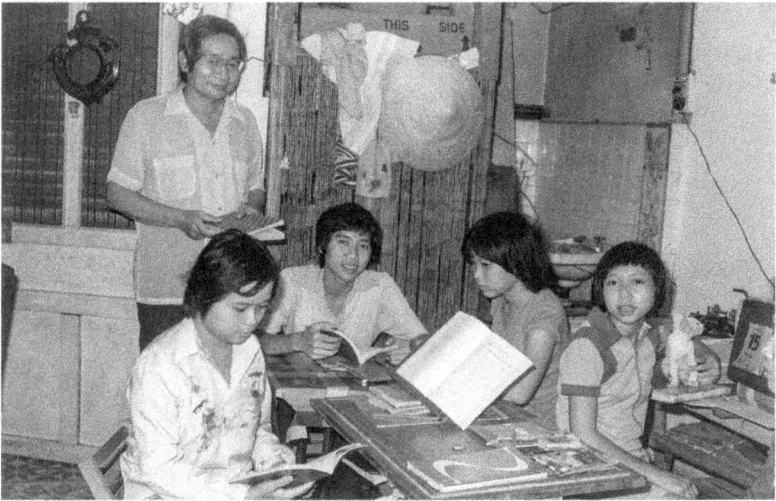

Dad and his homeschooled students in the little study room on the terrace of Mỹ-Hướng (1982)

The four musketeers on the terrace of Mỹ-Hướng (1982)

Parents on the terrace of Mỹ-Hương, taking final pictures before the departure.

Part 2

1979 – 1982

23.

The Noodle Factory

We are to have what we have as if it were loaned to us and not given;
to be without proprietary rights to body or soul,
mind or faculties,
worldly goods or honors,
friends,
relations,
houses,
castles,
or anything else.

(Meister Eckhart)

The year 1979 found us under a new roof in the midst of Trương Minh Giảng Market, beginning from zero in Uncle Huỳnh's home and elementary school, Mỹ-Hướng.

The name means *Toward Beauty*, with "toward" as both a direction and an action—to face, head to, or aim for. Uncle Huỳnh had commissioned the building of his school with the vision of an educator and the longing of a barren man wishing to pass his torch to the next generation.

As a historian and philosopher, Uncle Huỳnh's prime concern was not money, I was told. He could have selected a better location to attract the children of upper-class families. But he had selected this odd corner in the middle of a bustling market to erect his dream school, where it was assailed by the noisy commercial activities around it, where the smells of fish and meat competed with the scents of books and chalk, where like a sentry it stood, guarding the higher purpose of men from the exchange of money and goods below.

He had picked this four-alley corner to lay down his other foundation—not fortified by cement, impossible for engineers to measure, invisible to most eyes and, certainly, resented for many years by the ones who would benefit most from it—for this reason: it was here where the children of the neighborhood would be wandering the alleys without shirts or shoes, idling away the time while their parents were busy making a living. Had it not been for the convenient location of this school, these children would be left to nature, to their games, and then later, to follow the same path trod by their parents: making a living at the nearby market, selling whatever they could.

To the neighborhood's children, Mỹ-Hương was the only hope for a better life. And their education was my uncle's grand solace, for he had placed in the hands of these children, that were not his, the love and ambition he had yearned to give his own—a love well seeded, an ambition expanded by hope. He grew up in poverty and knew firsthand the benefits of a good education.

The spacious building stood in a corner of the quasi-commercial neighborhood of the third district, amidst a jumble of mismatched buildings—low, tin-roofed, drab dwellings consorting with multi-level homes. Soaring above this disjointed neighborhood was Mỹ-Hương, taller by a floor, its windows looking out in all directions for straying children to recruit.

For over a decade, many generations of children had crossed the school's front gates to enter the sunlit building with its inner windows and interconnected archways. There they sat for many hours in front of the teachers and chalkboards, safely tucked away from the lure of the streets, being patiently cultivated, molded, and trained by my uncle's books.

It was not long ago, but so hazy is my recollection. Layers and layers of events had buried the golden years of my childhood. I had been running from the phantoms of my past for so long—for remembering was losing over and over what had been robbed from me. I thought I had forgotten it all, the fine crystals of memories as well as the howling demons. But nothing had been erased. They were all there, waiting like the soft light of a candle on a windowsill, peering out to darkness, vigilant and faithful to the return of a time-worn traveler.

I remember being escorted by the school director, my own uncle, up the stairs to his residence, turning left at the first landing, climbing above the classrooms. Peeping in from the stair banister, I could see a teacher pointing at the large words, white imprints on the black chalkboard. I could hear the children's collective voice, repeating each word read aloud by the teacher—one with mature enunciation, the others like the chirping of hatchlings, together in a chanting duet.

Then the blaring of the school bell reverberating from various corners of the school, the children pouring out, free at last, loud and tumultuous.

Little did I know back then, when I visited my uncle's school and home, that we would return to reside here.

Renamed Hồ Chí Minh City, Saigon was now altered, impoverished, beaten into submission. Once named "The Pearl of the Orient," the city was on her knees to be mummified into a dead man's shape devoid of humanity.

Hồ Chí Minh City. A dead man does not need blood. It sucks up the old metropolis's lifeblood and drains it into its gutters. It haunts. Its decay putrefies the living day and night.

The majority of the city's businesses were closed. The most optimistic merchant was now fearful of his own acts of buying and selling. He was suspicious of himself, on guard of himself. His neighbors and even friends and family members were eyes, ears, knives, guns—enemies. The fear of government scrutiny, the lack of suppliers and money, and the unwritten, contradictory policies were all there to lure him into the concentration camps. Nobody had ever seen such a place and, like hell, it was a place with no return.

All private factories, universities, and local schools were now government owned, some bearing new names. Private homes morphed into schools and schools into hospitals. For an insignificant sum, Mỹ-Hướng Elementary School, the pride and brainchild of my uncle, was replaced by a noodle factory of the same name. The bottom floor of Uncle Huỳnh's home was now owned by the local government, and my aunt continued to live on the upper floors. When we came to her with no other place to stay, Aunt Huỳnh yielded to our family two vacant rooms.

The large rollup front gates would be under the factory's control.

In a way, the new living arrangement suited me just fine. I loved to move around to different settings, and fate had spoiled me with my fancies. We accessed our new home through a small private entrance in the back of the building, barred and locked from intruders by an old metallic slatted gate. We had to acquire a new habit of carrying the house key with us, having no servant at home to open up on our return.

I recall how this small gate shrieked as we pushed it open, pulling at times, sliding it with our stronger right arm so that the tiny metal rollers ground against the metal railings from the lack of lubrication. The sound almost split our eardrums. We struggled through this small opening daily with our bikes, which we rested against a wall at the bottom of a large staircase.

From here, we could follow either the left staircase up or its symmetrical twin on the opposite side. If we all came home at the same time, we would split and race up to see who arrived first to the second floor. Halfway up, on a sort of landing, some half-witted architect had carved out two tiny rooms with ceilings that barely cleared our heads. Small as these rooms were, they had still smaller windows that looked out into the adjacent alley, peering like spies into the closest neighbors' homes. They had perhaps been used for some school purpose, judging from the built-in sinks and cupboards lining the walls. But by the time we came to share the house with our aunt, these rooms were gathering dust.

The two staircases continued to ascend, straddling the center of the building, a sort of hall linking the east and west wings. A peaceful home once for a childless couple, now this spacious and airy floor had become a silent temple for Aunt Huỳnh. The large room she lived in had been the couple's living room, then my uncle's sick ward in the weeks before his death. The adjoining room became an altar room, containing my uncle's portrait. However much I had loved him, the sight of his face staring out from the encasement of a frame spooked me witless.

Behind the altar room was my uncle's library and working space, unoccupied since his demise but still filled with his books. The shadowy hallway linked directly to the last flight of return-stairs. The final riser would sweep a new visitor into the expanse of the open terrace, taking his breath away, his heart still beating fast from the mounting of a long stairs.

Above were only clouds and birds.

Aunt Huỳnh was often found there puttering about her potted garden, amidst the herbs and flowers she planted, the only seeds that ever sprung forth for her. Turning away from this vastness, one faced the last two rooms of the strange house, rooms that might have been added on as if to reclaim the large empty space for practical purposes.

Mỹ-Hương, as described, was more a school than a residence. In this design scheme, it was composed more of rooms devoid of personality and functionality than living space. There seemed to have been no thought for a designated living room, a cozy bedroom, or even a simple kitchen. There were no cupboards or built-in stoves. How the couple conducted their daily affairs, I never knew.

Our two tiny adjoining rooms thankfully were equipped with the convenience of a small bathroom complete with a toilet commode and shower stall. We also had the privilege of using the spacious enclosed balcony, which doubled as another bedroom for our family of six. Under the new rule, our aunt should have reported our extended stay to the local police station but had not done so for our sakes. Dad had indicated to Aunt Huỳnh that we had immediate plans for another escape and, thus, it would be unwise for her to report our presence. Poor Aunt Huỳnh! I am sure if she had her choice guilt-free, she would have preferred to be left alone in her solitude, unburdened by the addition of six law-breaking citizens, to be rid of our noisy, chaotic, youthful coexistence under her roof. Because of her unexpected responsibility, she lived daily in fear of the police, torn between the desire to kick us out and the wish to help. In a way, my father had imposed his family on her. He would not let her say no. He would not make it at all easy for her, would fight for the right to live safely under her roof. All he promised was that we would leave as soon as it was possible. In the meantime, she was to keep our existence a secret.

During the day, we lived quite normally, coming and going as if we were our aunt's visitors. The frenetic activities of the noodle factory covered our coexistence. But by evening, as the factory closed down, and the activities around us subsided, we had to be careful to keep our existence invisible, retreating behind four walls like Anne Frank and her family. We refrained from flushing the toilet, spoke quietly, and tiptoed around. We were the living shadows of my aunt for a few weeks.

Before long, we were reported by a zealous neighbor.

One night, we had just finished our prayers and settled into our sleeping mats when someone shook the back gate and multiple voices shouted "Open up." Dad bolted out of the room as Mom, in an undertone, directed us to lie still, which we did in muted terror. Then I heard my aunt's voice—"Give a minute. Coming"—and the sound of her large bundle of keys retreated down the stairs. The rolling gate screeched.

Things moved very quickly. Soon the light in our room was on. "Who are these people?" demanded a man's voice. As my aunt answered, I mentally prepared myself to be hauled back to jail. But the local police left us where we were and departed—alas, taking Dad with them.

As soon as they were gone, we heard another rapping at the back gate, then Uncle Sự's calls. Again, my aunt was roused by an unannounced visit, although with friendlier purposes. Uncle Sự's energetic exchange of courtesies with Aunt Huỳnh traveled with their footsteps upward. Their conversation in muffled voices became indistinct. They might be discussing our late entanglement with the law.

We were again troublemakers for those around us.

Soon we all gathered in the central hall.

Uncle Sự and his family lived just an alley away from Aunt Huỳnh's place. Their house directly faced the police station, previously a spacious villa whose owner had fled during the last weeks of Saigon. Uncle Sự was short and bald; his compact features and shiny head brought immediate relief to the tension-filled moment. He gathered the essential information about what had happened and promptly departed, promising to return in the morning with Dad. On leaving, he advised us to go back to sleep.

"Tomorrow will be better," he said.

As soon as he was gone, my aunt pulled Mom aside.

"Good Lord! You have to forgive me for saying this. I am somewhat relieved that they found you and the children here tonight." She dabbed her forehead with a white handkerchief. "Uncle Khoa came into my bedroom and hid under my bed. Good heaven! He just tucked himself in under there with his butt sticking up. They spotted him right away. What would people have said of me, a widow, with a man under my bed in the midst of the night? Oh! How awful!"

Despite Uncle Sự's heroic calmness, the event kept us up the whole night. In the early morning, as soon as the sounds of the noodle factory's various activities returned, and the rising steam reached us upstairs, our dear uncle returned beaming, accompanied by an equally smiling Dad. In my uncle's hand was a piece of paper, the official authorization for our family to legally dwell at this address. He said, "It was not easy, not easy! But thank God, I know them well after many months spent monitoring their activities. I know what they want and how to feed their needs. I knew it would come in handy one day. I'm glad! Don't worry about anything. You are in good hands."

24.

The Reynolds Pens

No man was more foolish when he had not a pen in his hand, or more wise when he had.

(Samuel Johnson)

There is a point in time when, turning over the tattered remnants of one's life fabric and musing over one's options, a person has to decide whether to discard it altogether and start anew, or patch it over one last time.

After losing Grandma to perhaps a bad decision—the possibility pierced his heart and salted it raw—after enduring our long separation and realizing what was at stake, Dad felt it was time to pause and reconsider our alternatives. Could it be that the unfolding drama we had tried to flee was destined to be the stark reality of our lives? If so, then we had better hang on to whatever we had left and make the best of it, like this new beginning at Mỹ-Hương.

We gradually settled into a lull, contented with a present devoid of windows to the future. In this cardboard-box home, our dreams no longer flapped their wings in search of light but became lifeless as a moth carcass.

Life at Mỹ-Hướng was cobbled together with the chipped fragments of the Ming vase that was our past. Our initial belongings, besides whatever was saved from our last misadventure, were collected from various homes. Aunt Sự donated her family's best blankets, Aunt Huỳnh shared with us the few pots and pans she could spare, Aunt Linh returned our Sony rice cooker and the dishes that we thought we no longer needed, and we reclaimed the old clothes that were passed on to our cousins before our departure.

Uncle Linh was still detained in some unspecified concentration camp. His family had learned only through the grapevine that he was possibly relocated in the North. Meeting Uncle Linh's family reminded us that even in its gloomiest forecast, our reversed fortune paled against the murky background of Aunt Linh's life stage.

In her youth, Aunt Linh had been Huế's beauty queen. An only daughter gifted with good looks, she was cherished, pampered, and shielded from work, even domestic chores. Married, the mother's princess became her husband's queen. Uncle Linh's military pay and benefits had afforded him the luxury to perpetuate his wife's lifestyle and habits.

Four years into the economic deprivation, while the lack of a steady income might be the universal punishment for South Vietnamese, Uncle Linh's absence wrought onto his family of six more than psychological trauma. It was an economic catastrophe. While other Vietnamese in the same situation had adjusted and scraped out a living with whatever resources they had, Aunt Linh was completely helpless. Her husband's capture had paralyzed her. She was left with four children, without an income, without a notion of what to do to survive, without even the mental strength to fight.

Within months of hearing no news from her husband, Aunt Linh and her children moved in with her mother. They slowly sold off their possessions—first the luxury items, the jewelries, then the fine bedsheets, the better clothes. A fort under siege, they were only holding off the ominous final onslaught.

Although bankrupted, my parents could still depend on their grownup children to help us rebuild. The first parcels of gifts from overseas arrived as soon as my oldest sister, Mai, received news from Vietnam about our failed escape. Clothing arrived, although, to our consternation, with sizes grossly misjudged, perhaps based on my sister's memory of our last reunion in 1970, nine years past. Our parents' first large purchase was three bikes, an indication that we were to settle.

As soon as news of our settlement reached him, Uncle Chấn came for a visit. With no contact besides our cousins down the road, we longed for social stimulation and anticipated his visit with joy. He came, dressed like a beggar, but had in his hand a large bar of Nestlé chocolate for our homecoming gift.

He told us it had come all the way from France.

We took turns sniffling the heavy bar and thought it smelled not only of milk, of cocoa, but also of freedom, of France, of some distant dreams we had long buried.

It had been some time since we had last met Mom's brother at his home, that day before the collapse of Saigon. Subsequently, much had happened. My uncle's escape with Aunt Bích and her husband had landed them all in jail for almost three years. Many lives were destroyed by that one event.

Aunt Bích's only daughter had died. Aunt Bích herself was now in France, separated permanently from her husband, who had severed ties with the rest of the Hòangs. Uncle Chấn's wife and three daughters had left for France when he was in jail. It was understood that they were to save their own lives in order to save him.

In this new circumstance, Uncle Chấn reappeared in our circle a much more admirable individual, with his scraggly beard, his torn jeans, his bachelor's nonchalance and freedom. He looked like a pirate, the terrible Bluebeard of our younger days. Before Mom had the time to pull him elsewhere, away from our indiscreet inquisitions and open comments about his poor appearance, we gathered around.

"Good morning, Uncle." We bowed and greeted him.

It was marvelous to hear my uncle's talk. "Ah! Pain in the butt!

How are you all? Look at Hồng-Mỹ! She's quite a lady. A bit too healthy, are you?"

He jested. "I would not touch this deadly chocolate, if I were you."

He ruffled Patrick's hair. "I need a tennis partner. Will you join me tomorrow?"

Michelle's eyes shone brightly, her nostrils flared with pleasure. "Can I come too, please?"

"Can I come *tooooo*," Uncle Chẩn mimed her but acquiesced without hesitation. "Come along. You can pick up the balls for us."

I followed the motions of his left hand. His fingers were clutching a small package. He satisfied my curiosity by thrusting into my hands a soft, lumpy package, winking his eye. "It is not to be eaten, lady."

I uncovered the wrapping to find a pair of ragged underwear, mended many times over by some awkward seamstress, himself most probably. I blushed after discovering my uncle's shapeless intimate apparel, bashful to witness my elder's careless disregard for his public image. At the same time, I felt privileged to be trusted with this token of his manhood, and proud that he did not doubt my sewing ability. At Mom's criticism of his wife's neglect of him, he indicated that Aunt Danielle did send him brand-new underwear, but he sold it at the black market for money. He seemed to speak with a morbid pride and displayed a sentimental attachment to this disgusting piece of menswear, which he said had seen him through those three brutal years in jail. Addressing me with a tinge of humor, he explained that he wanted the clothing mended and returned without much delay.

"Else . . . ," he danced with his right hand mockingly circling his underwear area and left his sentence hanging.

His directness and outrageous behavior charmed us. His neglected appearance could not efface the vestige of elegance that once pervaded his manners. Meeting my uncle again after the turmoil of our life seemed to lift us for a moment into a time gilded and magical, when there was school in the morning, homework to turn in, friends to call on the telephone, and places to visit in the summertime.

Then Uncle Chấn sat down with my parents inside our bedroom, which was converted to a sort of living area during the daytime, furnished simply with a plastic mat and some pillows thrown pell-mell as seating cushions. They conversed for a long time. When Uncle Chấn left, Dad became extremely agitated. He paced the floor awhile and, finally, mounted his bike to go out. To my inquiry, he simply said, "I'm heading to the Central Post Office to wire Mai a message."

My uncle had presented a very simple idea. We had been receiving goods from oversea to subsist. Why not convert these products into marketable goods that generate profits?

It was a timely tip.

The conversation with Uncle Chấn had changed our parents' fundamental belief that engaging in commerce under communism was plain suicide. On the contrary, the key to financial freedom was already in their hands. All they had to do was to open the lock—to shift from the position of consumers dependent on the continual supply from relatives overseas to that of suppliers, generating survivable income from imported goods.

A strong wind of reform blew through Mỹ-Hướng, until then cloistered in self-penitence. My parents were now active players in a novel and exciting gamble. Their entrepreneurial spirits were revived. Their zest for life was tangible. It shone in their eyes, until then clouded with dark thoughts. It woke them at night like a couple of nighthawks, swooping into the dark to unseen prey.

My parents were again building, laying foundation, measuring. What they erected I could not see, but by their preoccupations I guessed it would be huge. It had to be immense, like freedom, for it had the power to pull Dad away from planning our escape. Later, when the project began to take shape, it was clearer to me that my parents were pouring concrete for a self-sustainable economy, designing a master plan to combat destitution and break away from the shameful dependence on their grown children. It was pride that was re-erected in their hearts, and risks that they carefully measured.

But they could not rebuild alone. We were all involved, especially sister Mai. Dad wrote to her in a heavily coded letter, revealing as best he could what he had in mind without divulging the whole scenario, keeping his plan secret from the ears and eyes of "the system."

From the beginning, sister Mai's support for our continuous demands was unwavering. Mai, whose bitter arguments with my parents in her last summer visiting home still rang loudly in my ears. Mai, Dad's princess and leader of the pack, at twenty-four, had become Trịnh Đình Cương's wife. Therefore traditionally, she was more a member of the Trịnh family than our savior. But Mai, befitting her bubbling personality and daring attitude, had taken the reins of the family chariot and stirred its fractured frame into a bold course full of new perils, yet leading it out of the forsaken plains toward breathtaking vistas.

Since then, Dad never looked back, but Mom was less optimistic. Her faith in my father had suffered and she showed her skepticism in everything he proposed. Seeing the huge amount of goods arriving, she balked. She quarreled with Dad often now, leaving him no peace.

She nagged and nagged, predicting the worst for him. "You'll see. At this rate, Mai will end up with a divorce and bankrupt herself."

"So what do you want me to do, stop and starve our family here?" Dad's voice was unyielding.

Mom sneered, her sentence etched with irritations. "Starve? You spend generously, always giving away money to Aunt Linh and Aunt Sự. No wonder they adore you."

In the end, the urgent need for money prevailed. Mom's resistance weakened when she realized, with each passing day, that my uncle's practical suggestion was blessed by many strokes of luck, opening our door to profiteering. The first shipment of goods sold on Hồ Chí Minh City's black market like hot tea on a rainy day. The subsequent shipments were quickly sold, too. In his vision of new wealth, which he knew could be of brief duration, Dad doubled his efforts to make quick money.

The risk emboldened Dad, a badly defeated knight who had

sheathed his sword from further battles, who had resigned from further adventures. He remembered too often and too vividly the desperate confusion and fear that had gripped him. How he was forcefully pushed through life's many twists, hands groping and head covered in a bag, a prisoner of circumstances, into the grip of living horrors—hard labor, slavery, destitution—where death awaited mercilessly and patiently. Each of his losses seemed a token earned for his enemy.

But by exposing himself again to chance, by trying to beat back the many forms of his mental beast, he began to reclaim not only his means for economic survival but also his fighting spirit. He inadvertently rekindled the pilot flame of the idle furnace that powered his life ship, steering it against the stormy weather, again his family's captain.

With Mom's alliance, Dad's fertile mind shifted to grander ambitions. He began at first wishing only to fatten his pocketbook, but now he had plans for balancing his family's budget on both sides of the Pacific Ocean.

During this period, Hồ Chí Minh City was experiencing a severe shortage of basic essentials due to a combination of an international embargo and a significant decline in local manufacturing. Foreign goods, infiltrating into the city's black markets through the families with ties overseas, filled this void. The most coveted products were antibiotics, soaps, fabrics, jeans, threads, needles, bras, and pens. Knowing this, the communist government quickly adjusted to transform the empty airports as well as seaports into huge import centers. However, keeping up appearances dictated that the new and poor government establish a regulating policy that restricted both the frequency with which a family could receive goods and the amount of goods allowed per shipment.

Immersing himself in this new game of fortune, Dad spent his time drawing flowcharts and writing formulas to maximize our profits. He came up with a system in which we would receive goods under both Mom's and Aunt Sự's names. My aunt readily agreed to this arrangement because she would suffer no loss.

She laughed heartily at the proposal and quipped, "It would be unlikely that Aunt Kim and Diệp, or my two sisters-in-law, would be in a position to assist us. They must be beggars themselves in the U.S."

While Dad was scheming ways to make money, combining his planning skills with Mom's business sense, Mom frequented black markets, researching demands. We started out by selling random merchandise, necessary items that sister Mai sent home to keep us well supplied.

If she sent jeans, we sold jeans. If she sent chocolate; we provided the market with chocolate. We made little profits here and there. We mostly enjoyed the daily marketing: selling and buying, scouring for products to supply and consume, re-establishing a routine that kept us gainfully employed, steering us away from the boredom of home.

As we gained a better business perspective and became adept at maneuvering the various bureaucratic obstacles at the airport, we ordered our merchandise more judiciously. Our parents did their homework carefully, aiming for the market demand but choosing items with minimal freight.

We hit gold when, by chance, a shipment of blue-on-white Reynolds ballpoint pens, elegantly designed and marvelously engineered, arrived. These French pens were in great demand; their small size and weight made the shipping packages less bulky and therefore cheaper for my sister to send and easier for us to pass them through airport customs. Dad thought long about this and pinpointed a strategy for our next grand venture, embarking on large-scale import within the confines of the government restriction. In a way, we had been enjoying conducting business duty free. It took one crook to outdo another crook. Of course, Dad also counted on Mom's ability to bribe her way through the scrutiny of the airport security.

Mom, for a while now wearing her long thin hair in a loose chignon, had been resisting our exposure to risk. With time, though, the family's general ceased her combat with Dad. She devoted her valor and keen sense to help rebuild our economy at home and save Mai's new marriage from collapsing under the weight of six dependents, not counting Mai's additional responsibilities to financially support Daniel and Madeleine through their final college years. Without the money sent from parents, their college funding shortfall could not be offset, even with the contribution from Marie who had started earning a pharmacist's salary.

Dad was most upset each time we received unflattering and discouraging news from Daniel and Madeleine. Distracted by romantic liaisons and other disgraceful fun, both seemed unable to keep up with their studies. They might not graduate on time; or they might never complete their degrees. I could feel my father's mounting frustrations and powerlessness. My devoted parents had been robbed of the ability to bring their wayward children home to be influenced and reformed.

It was the painful thought of her grownup children abandoned overseas that sustained Mom's courage in perilous moments, which increased with each new shipment. She recruited Patrick as her Reynolds peddler. With his charming personality and hot pens, Patrick became instantly popular on the streets around Bến Thành Market.

Like a drunkard who will not surrender his bottle even at the cost of death, Dad feverishly wired Mai for ever bigger and riskier packages. When finally he sent for two thousand Reynolds pens, the system imploded under its own weight. As usual, Mai was prompt in sending us the requested merchandise. Within weeks, we received the coveted yellow "Notice of Shipment" by mail, with a date for us to be at the airport to receive our goods—usually between two and three weeks. Knowing that this particular cargo would carry a high economic stake, our parents rehearsed the many scenarios of what could go wrong.

At four in the morning, Mom, with a haggard face from having slept poorly, roused Patrick, her trusted bodyguard and business associate. I knew their routine by heart, having been in Patrick's place many times myself. By five, they would be at the market's rickshaw station to hail one cyclo to Tân Sơn Nhất Airport. Once there, they would line up to check in through many stations. It usually took three to four hours to clear these lines.

But what is time? What is the value of anything under communism?

At the first station, they would exchange their Notice of Shipment for a unique number. At the next station, they would fill out paperwork. The longest time would be spent waiting in the queue to receive the actual cargo and bring it through the security clearance. They would brace for problems at this last station, holding their breath when the agent would slash open the shipping container with one swift motion, expertly brandishing his sharp razor. The container would be emptied and meticulously scrutinized for smuggled goods: dollar bills hidden skillfully inside shoes or stuffed animals, Western music or books, motion sickness pills (these were on the list of forbidden import because of the popular demand and the implication of this—only people planning to escape by sea would be needing them).

On that particular day, Mom and Patrick watched in horror as the carton was cut and two thousand pens spilled out like forbidden candies from a student's knapsack. The security agent was someone Mom had never seen, although she had been frequenting the airport.

"Security!" the agent shouted before Mom even had time to recompose herself. As the carton of three by three by five feet was hauled away, a procession of people followed it.

"What's in there?" they wondered.

"Did they find gunpowder?" they asked.

Mom was stunned. But she regained her wits quickly enough. She began to wail loudly, crying for her daughter, who must have worked herself to death to send a cargo this size home, a gift for "the good children of Uncle Hồ" in the neighborhood school. As she sobbed and sniffed, Mom inquired about the many ways to make amends with the government for this lapse of her daughter's judgment.

"She was just trying to help rebuild the country," Mom wrung her hands.

The agent in charge saw that Mom understood the inner workings of the system, so he gave her a form on which he had scribbled, "Five hundred common ballpoint pens," purposely omitting to mention the pens' brand name and reducing their numbers to within an acceptable range. He pocketed Mom's bribery of five hundred *đồng* and released the cargo.

It took two cyclos to bring Mom and Patrick home, one for the offensive cargo. Those two thousand pens flushed the starved market and sold at almost three *đồng*s apiece, curing my Dad's feverish thirst for risk and ending the era of the Reynolds pens.

The quick and easy income afforded us a carefree lifestyle, simple yet richly rewarding. We entered a period of relative peace and savored each new day with the detachment of tourists, waiting for the opportune time to depart.

School was a thing of the past. We enjoyed our freedom at the market and at our cousins' home. I enrolled myself in esthetic gymnastic, the new fad, while my younger siblings took drum and guitar lessons and played street soccer every afternoon with our cousin, Yến-Dung. We realized the immediate convenience of living in the heart of a bustling market. As we no longer owned a refrigerator, the market served as our pantry. We cooked all our meals fresh and in consumable quantities.

Each morning, thirteen-year-old Anne took charge of the grocery shopping, bringing home all sorts of street snacks that we had never tasted so freely before. Patrick's new job was to build up the cooking fire in the charcoal stove, and my job was to prepare the daily meals. I remember I often neglected my duty. After spending my morning at the gym, I'd arrive home as Anne was returning from the market with the delicious snacks. We'd eat and then walk over to Aunt Sự's home to mingle with our cousins, chatting the day away. Returning home, I would find Mom cooking, fuming at my lack of responsibility.

I would get vexed at some of her remarks and bury myself in my novels, which Dad and I bought very cheaply from the famous

Calmette Street, the paradise of book lovers. Imagine a block a quarter mile square, full of little kiosks, each piled high and tight with books sorted in no particular order. Internationally acclaimed titles forsaken by private entities were salvaged and displayed amidst torn maps, old magazines, faded paperback novels. Amidst the tomes sat a seller, engrossed in a thick volume, though he missed not a single beat in responding to our many inquiries. With only a glance, this shopkeeper could pull out the exact book we inquired about from the jungle of books he possessed, interrupting his reading only briefly to hand us our item.

We rambled on Calmette Street every week, greedily gathering books. We hesitated in front of the leather-bound and rare editions, possibly looted from the libraries of Saigon, or perhaps taken from the glass-front bookcases of scholarly homes. Dad was always looking for more math books to complete the *Queysanne Revue* series I had inherited from my friend, Thanh-Tâm, before she emigrated to Switzerland.

I purchased all the classics I stumbled upon, guided more by instinct than by any real cognizance. Over time, I read Antoine de Saint Exupéry's *Le Petit Prince*, Marcel Pagnol's *La Gloire de Mon Père*, and *Le Château de Ma Mère*, returning time and again for any novel by Daphne du Maurier, whose writing style I instantly fell in love with after devouring *Ma Cousine Rachel*.

We hungrily snatched up books, books that were sold cheaper than a tube of toothpaste, books that were highly priced a few golden years ago but were now discarded carelessly, bound in bulk with twine to fuel the stoves or to be used as wrapping paper in place of newspapers no longer printed.

Dad's new passion for modern math pulled him away from the temporal lure of business, and Mom and Patrick happily took over. They ventured into other types of goods and, eventually, launched into another hot commodity: corsets. As soon as a new shipment came in, Patrick would roam the market with his samples, scouting for prospective street peddlers. He was soon recognizable by sight and called by name, a respected fellow supplier of the underground market. Once a merchant was located and the deal sealed, Patrick would return on the following morning for the exchange of money and goods. Both parties looked out for the frequent police raids. When this happened, the plastic sheet used to display the merchandise on the sidewalks was magically wrapped into a bundle and gathered under their arms, and the foot merchants evaporated into the crowd.

Not long after embarking into the lingerie market, Patrick visited downtown with a group of friends, youth members of the local church choir. Among the group was a cute thirteen-year-old girl named Phương-Dung, the choir's exceptionally talented vocalist, for whom Patrick had developed a fondness.

More than he would have liked to admit, she was his first crush. She was the reason for his regular church attendance, the only reason he had joined the choir. It was a rare occasion to be in the company of his object of adoration, and Patrick relished each precious minute. He was about to engage her on a more personal topic, when he came face to face with a lady customer, who waved at him excitedly.

"Patrick! Patrick! Any new bras you've got?"

Patrick quickly moved to the opposite side of the street as soon as he recognized the enthusiastic hailer. The lady took off after him, gesticulating wildly. "Patrick! I need some bras today. Have you got any?"

His girl finally noticed the caller. "Patrick! Is somebody calling you?"

Patrick, red with humiliation, was forced to face his buyer with an answer. He promised her a prompt delivery, as his new friends gathered to gawk at this Bra King.

Meanwhile, Mom's reputation at the airport continued to grow with each new cargo. She had manipulated the system to her advantage and had established a reliable network to help her shipments through, to the point where this episode happened:

One day, with finally her very own Notice of Shipment in hand, Aunt Sự arrived to the airport to collect her gift from abroad. To her surprise, the security agent returned the piece of paper she had

handed to them and said, clearly offended, "This belongs to Lê T
Hồng Chi. She must come claim her package in person."

"I am Hồng Chi," my aunt protested.

"No, you are not," the agent replied. "We all know Hồng Chi, and
you are not her. Go home. You can't pick up the shipment for her. She
has to come. It's policy."

25.

The Unexpected Roses of Life

Our new neighborhood stirred alive early each day. When night was still cuddling with dawn in their immense bed, the delivery trucks' loud brakes were heard hissing from where the sprawling market met the busy street, Trương Minh Giảng. At the first streak of dawn, the *coq* chant echoed back and forth, its tremulous *cuckadoodadoo* dying temporarily, to rise up again at intervals. Then, one by one, white neon lights flooded our neighbors' windows. The rolling gates of the noodle factory screamed in protest as they let in the workers and their banter.

But there was no reason for me to wake early. It would be just another insipid, unstructured day, devoted to filling the void of time with activities uncharted toward any goal. The bland and unfermented flour of my youth was of a substance more fit for cattle feed.

I lay on my mat, listening to the cascading chant of roosters until the first morning light filtered through the bamboo blinds. The sunrays danced softly on one corner of my protective net, creating shimmering patterns that progressively lengthened into brighter shafts, then annoying hot probes, reaching far into the room. I rolled onto my stomach and buried my head inside a military blanket, wrapping its black-on-green pattern tightly about me. I could have slept until the next night and day. I wished I could sleep like Sleeping Beauty for thirty-six thousand nights, to wake only at the first kiss of life—life in its true meaning, with some predictability, with plans for the future, goals to attain, not this life of barely surviving, constant hassle, fleeing dangers known and unknown. This was torture, not life.

Often, my morning reveries were interrupted by the sound of Dad's three sharp handclaps, as his voice sounded the reveille, "*La volonté, mes enfants!*"

"*Will*, my children!" was Dad's trademark call, louder than an alarm clock, subtly inducing guilt in the budding conscience of his young children. My lack of motivation wrestled against Dad's expectation. But he had not spent a few years in his youth teaching and tutoring rich children to earn extra income for nothing. He proceeded with the day, giving me time to decide while busying himself with putting away his bedding, all the while singing little happy tunes like "*Frère Jacques, Frère Jacques, dormez-vous?*"—"Are you sleeping?"

Now and then, seeing that his daughter's will was yet to be mustered, he interjected, "Ah! Hồng-Mỹ is getting up. What a fine example to the other three lazy geese. Will, my children. Will is what carries us through."

Surreptitiously, I had been molded by his loving hands into who I am today, always rising to the call of duty—a foot soldier turned captain. In my family, I am always left to carry the flag forward, because of my father's line of long ago: "Will is what carries us through."

* * *

By the time another monsoon returned, with the ting-ting-top symphony of raindrops on the neighbors' tin roofs, I had carved out a schedule that gave, if not a direction, at least a purpose for me to rise at a set time. To be at the gym by six, I had to wake at five and leave home half an hour later, pedaling the distance between Trương Minh Giảng and the sports complex on Phan Đình Phùng. Huddled inside my plastic raincoat, I offered my chilled face to the cold splattering of the deluge, on a self-imposed mission to re-conquer myself, to firm up my slackened body and my disillusioned spirit.

I arrived each morning to a still-deserted track, peopled by only a few disciples of health. To warm up, I fast-walked then broke into a slow jog, grinding the sandy old track and scattering the tiny pebbles. I was a swinging metronome, my steps beating against the rhythmic *pittity-tat* melody of the rain.

I felt the goodness of life. Positive again.

As more people arrived, we, the joggers, moved indoors to the exercise room, located on the second floor of the decrepit gym building. We changed into our home-tailored leotards and headed automatically to our spots, facing a mirrored wall: some to proudly reveal their shapely curves and firm muscles, and some, including myself, to glance with embarrassment at the image of bulging abdomens and thighs the size of an elephant's. I often hid in the back rows to avoid the scrutiny of that damnable mirrored wall.

A volunteer stepped in front of the group to act as coach and model. Our morning exercises began.

"10, 9, 8 . . . 0 and 10, 9, 8 . . . ."

On and on we persevered, rotating the exercises to target different areas of our bodies—upper torso, arms, stomach—ending with floor movements to strengthen our buttocks, thighs, and hamstrings. Because I was naturally introverted and habitually inactive, my exposure to this group of strangers and strenuous activity was simply an act of will. However, with each new week, my reservation receded and my confidence bubbled. I found the wall mirror irresistible, for I was discovering with pleasure my slimmer profile and my improved flexibility. By then, standing erect, I could deftly curve backward and touch the floor with my hands. I could almost do the splits.

As the months stretched, I added other lessons to my schedule, aiming to learn a trade that would be useful in the future, no matter where I would find myself—westbound, or wasting away under this regime. I asked sister Mai to send me embroidery threads and set out to learn the techniques of decorative needlework. My teacher was a girl about my age. After a few introductory lessons, I thought naively that it would be an easily acquired skill. The only requirements were good vision, nimble fingers, and an acute sense of detail and patience.

Twice a week I sat cross-legged with this girl on the cool tiled floor of her home, each of us facing a wooden stand with our embroidery hoops attached at eye level. These hoops were nothing but two tightly nestled bamboo rings—the inner ring was of fixed diameter, varying from three to ten inches. The exterior ring was adjustable to accommodate the various thicknesses of fabrics and could be tightened with a screw. The simplest technique to imprint a desired design onto the fabric was to transfer it with carbon copy from a pattern. Once this was accomplished, the fabric was stretched onto the inner ring with the design facing out and held tautly in place by the outer ring.

The stand was optional but was useful to free our hands for delicate work—the right hand would punch the needle through the imprinted design of the taut fabric, making a lovely *puff* sound. The left hand pulled the needle out under the hoop and fed it back up to the right hand. On and on this went until the design was completely filled with colorful threads.

This was an elaborate process. The embroiderer earns her living thread by thread, sitting bent and cross-legged all day long on cold floors. The prospect of making this my career evaporated quickly. While I was retreating without fanfare from my first career choice, my mother's interest was, ironically, taken by embroidered blouses. After prowling the market and listening to the exchange of opinions at various kiosks, she thought that the market was ripe for fashion demands. There was a new need for more colorful and adorned clothing.

The people had re-emerged from their mourning garb. They were no longer hiding under black, brown, and gray. Four years of cowering under falsehood was enough. The people would deal their cards deftly—to cheat if need be, to lie if required, to pay if fined, to be ruined and again rebuild—as long as the sun still rose, as long as the hunger still gnawed. The people had become fierce and determined to live the best lives they could. They would carve a decent life out of dead wood, if need be.

I became Mom's fashion model. She would bring me downtown to have the embroidered blouses tested on my body, judging the effects of these shirts on me, which colors would be more suitable for my skin, which would render my profile at its best, and which patterns would elongate my height.

"My older girls might be her size," she explained to the merchant. "If the design and color work well on her, they will look good on her sisters."

She would send the selected shirts to my sisters to wear, exposing these exotic shirt pieces to their foreign peers. If people liked what we sent, we would order the products in greater quantity. I was happy enough to acquire a shirt or two, or simply wear them temporarily until the day they would be mailed to my siblings. It was rare to have my mother's confidence. But she seemed to take my advice seriously on linen choice, especially my comments on embroidery quality.

There was one enormous advantage in living in a communist country. Everything was free. Well, free on the surface. The school was free because the teachers were being paid starving salaries. Likewise, we paid little or nothing for our utilities. But the service was not guaranteed. The dirt-cheap products we lined up to purchase from the co-op were of poor quality. Rice was filled with stones. Sugar was hardly crystallized but stayed in its natural form—wet, lumpy, encased with mud.

Who had the time to philosophize in a communist country? We were all constantly tussled by new calamities, our vital functions devoted only to survive. Who had the time to debate and analyze what was good or bad? But our daily struggle turned us into street-smart individuals. Our impoverished circumstances taught us to make do or improvise.

While hunting for a skill to learn, I discovered an acupuncture class offered free of charge by the Buddhist monks. The Buddhist temple was quite far from my home, but I was desperate to make something useful out of myself. The biweekly lessons, unfortunately, were offered very late in the evening and, with the onset of the monsoon rains, this discouraged my regular attendance. I arrived soaked and sat bewildered in a crowded classroom full of adults, listening without much comprehension to the complicated lingo of this ancient art, thinking only of the long way home in the dark, glistening streets. After a few weeks, I gave up the ordeal, abandoning yet another project to develop myself. I began to suspect my ability to learn. Had I not what it took to pursue a long-term goal? Was it too lofty to attempt to pull myself up from this stagnation? The eleventh grade had come and gone without me. Another school year was ending. I had fallen off the track. Was my desire to become productive as out of reach as the Eiffel Tower? Many nights, I tried to conjure Paris in my dreams, convinced that if I could visualize myself standing in front of the tower, I could reach it one day. Alas! Paris was not easily imagined, a place as unreal and farfetched as the afterlife's heaven that would be our final destination—if God overlooked our daily trespasses.

My road to self-discovery led me to a bleak picture of a girl without talent, without will, with minimal motivation. My weekly excursion into town with Mom did not improve my relationship with her. It was a difficult time for all of us, each jostling our personal issues and conflicts, at the same time playing the critical role of a responsible member of the family, struggling to survive in a fluid political landscape. I was at the juncture between childhood and maturity, dependent on my parents' wisdom for any relevant decisions, yet inwardly carrying a different world view and the burgeoning of a passionate individuality.

In fact, here was another reason for my strained association with Mom. She seemed to attach no particular importance to my adolescent sensibility, did not allow me some primordial respect as an individual apart and separate from her, to yield some room, to tolerate my delicate feelings, to understand the complexity of growing up. I almost died of shame that day when, to prevent soiling the white padded seat of a cyclo with her menstruation, she deliberately brought along a large handkerchief and, under the amusing eyes of the rickshaw man, ceremoniously spread her cloth out before ascending her throne. From that day on, I refused to share a cyclo with Mom. She was forced to wait for a bus with me for a ride downtown. As the loaded vehicle lumbered into view and screeched to a halt at the station, and the few passengers, hanging outside the door, jumped out, we would push our way up the bus steps and into the mass, searching for a place to safely lodge ourselves. We would clutch at bars, poles, seat rails, or fellow riders.

There were times when we would have to split up—Mom entering through the front door of the bus while I scurried in through the back to claim a footing. All was not well when the engorged vehicle started, but like coffee beans in a can, we slowly settled into the cracks, precariously hanging but moving toward our destination.

The worst might be over for other passengers but not for me, because as I fought the uncomfortable feeling of breathing into someone else's face or tried to extricate myself from the foul armpit above my head, I would hear my mother's panic bellow from across the bus, "Hồng-Mỹ, Hồng-Mỹ! Are you there?" The passengers all tried to transmit my name, until there was no way for me to escape the humiliation of identifying myself. The daily tension between mother and daughter forked into all other aspects of our crowded habitation—due, perhaps, to dissatisfaction on my part and stress from Mom—and turned my growing-up years into the worst time of my life.

In the midst of all my misery, a happy occasion presented itself, disguised in the familiar shape of Uncle Mục. The same man who had some time ago refused to get involved in my scholastic life had stopped by one evening to share with Dad his latest discovery that could improve our aimless lives.

"Well, if school is no longer an option, why don't you have your children learn music?" Uncle Mục prodded Dad. He talked on, "I happened to learn about the existence of a very old piano. True, it is barely playable but that can be fixed. The owner wants to sell his unused instrument at a throwaway price. What do you think?"

Dad was torn. We did not have a large enough room for an additional piece of furniture. A musical instrument? It was pretentious to think of music in our current situation. But the incentive was high. "The offer is too good to bypass," my uncle said. "The asking sum is minimal, just enough to cover the shipping fee."

"And who's going to arrange for a repairman?" Dad's question showed that he was yielding to the pressure from his excited children.

My uncle's eyes shone brightly. "Let me take over from here. I'll have the piano delivered within one week, repaired and tuned on the same day."

We danced jubilantly around him. "Come on, Dad. We want the piano."

Dad settled quickly lest our continuous hoopla evoke Aunt Huỳnh's dark humor. My aunt had begun showing her impatience with our long stay and tumultuous existence.

The beat-up instrument arrived the next morning. We made room for this precious addition in our little bedroom and, consequently, I relocated my sleeping place into the adjoining balcony, next to Patrick. The piano innards were composed of, as warned my uncle, more straw-like material than wood, hammers all chewed up, strings missing. Its intact frame, however, gave it the robust appearance of a piano; its keyboard was worn but unbroken. The satisfied look on my uncle's face reassured us that the instrument could be properly resurrected. A piano technician promptly arrived and spent half a day tearing the piano apart, changing each broken string, re-felting the hammers, re-adjusting the tension—in short, doing a complete overhaul. Finally, the piano was tuned and its sound tested.

Ah! The racing of the technician's fingers pursued the notes of a scale over different octaves, changing from the bright harmonic majors to the sadder minors, skipping over the keys like two nimble ballet dancers up and down the arpeggios.

Through the open cabinet of the piano, we followed with

fascination the striking movements of the felt hammers in sync with the dancers above the keyboard. The perfect synchronized motions of these parts—of the fingers caressing the ivory, the hammers thronging the coiled steel strings, the spring-back action of each key—captured our attention. It was so nice to have a piano again!

Finally, satisfied with the rich, ringing tones, the old man replaced the various wooden covers, giving the old piano a new dignity. Uncle Mục replaced the man on the piano bench and kept us transfixed with many melodies, from the exquisite "The Blue Danube" that sent us waltzing around, to the heart-wrenching "Return to Sorrento."

We were each transported to a different place, to the past with our childhood home at Tân Sa Châu, to the future, into the realms of dreams, borne on the harmonious wings of these magnificent lyrics. Our souls were lifted to an improbable future when music would again be a part of our lives, when our days would again be normal and predictable, our broken strings restored and retuned. In that future, we would be the owners of our own homes. Homes with rooms connected by lighted corridors. Rooms with children busy at their desks, rooms from which melodious tunes escaped to hasten the steps of a visitor wishing to witness an artist at work. Mom quickly stamped down the exhilaration with, "Shush! You will disturb the whole neighborhood. It is too loud from here." The veracity of her words struck us dumb. We did not want to entice jealousy—not in our situation. So, a rule was established. We could only play the piano with the dampener on, during the time of nine in the morning to four in the afternoon. We agreed to this condition readily. Within one week, we reconnected with our piano teacher, Ái-Minh, and resumed our weekly lessons. Our little world above the noodle factory was again filled with music, for among the four of us, there was always somebody at practice.

* * *

Three times a week, the electricity would be cut off after seven in the evening. During the daytime, this interruption did not affect us in the least. Mỹ-Hương was never deprived of fresh air and sunlight, not with her uncovered ceilings above one of the staircases and the bank of windows opened out to all four sides. We had no appliances and, therefore, suffered little from the lack of power, as we cooked on charcoal stoves, washed our clothes by hand in large tubs, and hung them on clotheslines to air-dry. The ironing was done using a heavy pressing iron filled with hot charcoal. Dirty dishes were piled into a round aluminum tub and scrubbed with a luffa sponge in cold water. The only inconvenience on those blackout days had to do with having to plan our day better. Dad would not hear our excuses of not having enough light to study.

"Finish your study and practice your instrument before sunset," he would boom many times during the course of the day. But we resisted his wisdom and stalled for time until late, then were delightedly delivered from our books by the sudden darkness. At such time, our joy was short-lived, spoiled by Dad's head shake and his ominous reminder, "A boat not rowed against the current is a retreating boat."

Our piano teacher, like Dad, did not care whether we had electricity or not—the lesson came due when it was due. We learned to work around the available daylight. Those who went out sought to return home before the whole city plunged into pitch darkness, when it would be treacherous or even impossible for anyone to navigate about safely.

Interestingly enough, we began to anticipate these blackout nights. By twilight, Anne and Michelle had managed to gather all the kerosene lanterns and hung them at various corners of the house. Candles were allowed only for short trips to the bathroom because using them was unsafe and expensive.

We would gather on the terrace, Mom and I in our respective and preferred cotton hammocks, Dad sitting safely on a low stool. Patrick and Michelle joined us with their guitars, and Anne settled down with her pet cat, Mimi, on her lap.

Above the cave-like city was a diamond-studded night sky, twinkling. Below us lay the city, congealed in a thick ink, pierced by the illuminating movements of small lanterns in someone's hand, flicking like fireflies. We had nothing to lose: no future, no possessions, no freedom, no home, scarcely a life. But with each heartbeat, we appreciated this beautiful moment when life and time stood still. Our visions were dimmed by the lack of artificial lighting, but inside us shone the love of things we could not pinpoint. This mysterious darkness, this unnatural quietness, had forced us to meditate upon the meaning of our existence, to appreciate the fragility of this moment, for it could easily be taken from us.

Our family talked about everything and nothing.

Mom, who was always preoccupied, hummed delicately. She mouthed the words when the lyrics returned to her, "*Hồng, hồng, tuyết, aaaa, tuyết . . . ,*" mourning the passage of time, in a thin, high timbre. At the time, I did not delve much into the meaning of her strange, operatic cantabile. It was enough to hear her soul in exaltation.

But the lyrics return to me in their full meaning as I write this chapter. For I am now almost at the same age as Mom when she swung lightly in her hammock, softly singing:

> *Rose, rose, snow, snow.*
> *Once I did not know anything,*
> *Fifteen years flashed by, wow!*
> *I look back and realize my prime was fleeting.*

If only I could be back for just one last glimpse. On that tormented stage was my mother in flesh and blood. And now, and here, delivered from our nightmare, I no longer have her. Such is the irony of life.

It is painful to revisit the place where one has suffered, but without coming back to the site of a ruin, how would one lift out, from the ashes, the perfect picture of a loved one?

I did not expect to find her essence here, in the dark, sitting with us and swinging lightly on her hammock, peering into our faces, listening absentmindedly to our soft chattering.

The sudden laughter of a passerby would rise in the air to where we were assembled, keeping company with our family time. Now and then, a young, excited dog barged into the alleyways and shattered the diffused peace with its furious barks. Patrick plucked on his acoustic guitar the sweet melodies of some old tunes, while little Michelle strummed out the chords. I closed my eyes and crooned.

Then Dad recited Ronsard's sonnets for Helene:

> *Vivez, si m'en croyez, n'attendez à demain*
> *Cueillez dès aujourd'hui les roses de la vie.*

Simply translated, it says: "Live, believe me, do not wait until tomorrow. Pick today the roses of life."

Was this not what we were doing, although unknowingly, the six of us trapped together at the bottom of a well, nonetheless savoring, nonetheless sucking hungrily on the sweetness of life's fruits?

We plucked life's offerings in the form of starry nights; in the mystical, hallucinating lantern shadows; in the abandoned, lazy swinging of hammocks; in the jasmine-scented breeze. We were together as a family. And we were all young and healthy.

Years after, at the pinnacle of our individual lives, after many of us had globe-trotted and collected enough bounties, satisfied with our successes, we often looked back at these moments to ask ourselves, "If she knew her prayers would be answered with a seal of death, would Mom still ask?"

She would. She would not be Mom if she had chosen otherwise.

26.

A Wreck

Jeanne Trần Bắc took me by surprise when she appeared, one day, on the other side of Mỹ-Hướng's narrow gate. She was my eighth grade friend, and it had been years since we last met, during which time the adversities of my life had precipitated me into an early cynicism.

The many storms that had swept me from the familiar landscape of my childhood had turned this once amicable, sociable girl into a detached, cold, needing-no-one individual. I had discarded to the four winds the last shreds of my former life, had ceased investing in friendships, and rested my belief only in God and my immediate family. I deliberately isolated myself even from my closest friends, figuring that I had been taken too far away from my friends' scholastic lives to be understood or included. Their circle of friends had undoubtedly widened with each school year, while I had lost touch with a normal adolescence.

My friends would undoubtedly have other worries besides daily homework. There would be boys, broken hearts, and, perhaps, ambitions grander than the immediate gratification of good grades. My peers were moving along another path and progressing toward different goals, and I, who was fleeing the past, had chosen to stay in a corner of their memory.

Jeanne's sudden appearance was a reminder of how much I had lost. Her large grin deepened the dimples on her slim face. With one foot on the ground, one foot resting on her bike pedal, her front wheel wedged into the slats of my aunt's gate, she gazed amusingly, in silence, at my stunned face.

I was about to pull the gate open to let her through when she stopped me, saying simply, "I've come to say goodbye."

I was stricken. "Where to? You don't mean—"

"Yes, I do. France. We got the visas to leave in three weeks."

Somehow, the idea of Jeanne's departure did not take root easily in my mind. Her family, like most Chinese ethnics living in Vietnam, had no real reason to flee the new communist government. They had been settled in Vietnam for generations but considered themselves Chinese, adhering to Chinese customs and barely speaking our language. Mostly businesspeople, they were quite indifferent to our war of ideology, as long as it did not conflict with their money-making machine. The native Vietnamese thought the Chinese were immune to the change of leadership in the South.

Initially, they thought so, too. Chợ Lớn, the Chinese Quarter, was teeming with business—buying, selling, investing. The Vietnamese needed gold to escape and were provided with gold by the crafty Chinese dealers. Their confidence in a cooperative government did not wane even after each new gripping policy: abolishment of the old *đồng*s in exchange for the limited new cash, cracking down on business owners, and another monetary revision that eliminated any accumulated wealth.

They were savvy. They would survive the changeover and again would prosper. Money would finally rule, as it always did. But things had changed. People like them, who once had vowed to stay, left hurriedly, leaving everything behind, telling no one of their plans.

I had never heard Jeanne mentioning her family's desire to leave, however. In fact, they had recently sold their large villa in the Third District and moved back to the Chinese Quarter, where her father owned a packaging business. When I last met her, Jeanne was enrolled in an art class after school, learning to draw still lifes and cartoons. Her room was full of comic figures in bright colors.

"Well, so long," Jeanne said and dislodged her front wheel from the grip of the metal slats, her words skimming the surface of my inner turmoil. I coerced an artificial smile to wish my friend a safe trip. My face was like a piece of dried-out leather. I was the one who was supposed to say goodbye to Jeanne. Dear Jeanne, I envy you greatly, were the words I wished to verbalize. I felt abandoned, cheated. It had not occurred to me that I would suffer this terrible fate alone. I had always thought that I would be among the first to get out of Saigon, and until I did, my friends would stay with me and wither with me. Instead, one by one, they had acquired wings and flown away to better skies.

"Only I will stay," I thought bitterly.

We did not hug for the last time. I did not follow Jeanne out to the alley as I should have, as she pedaled out of my life.

I stumbled upstairs, grieving, not for our separation but for my future. I felt a need to be by myself to sort out the conflicting emotions within me. I despaired for an immediate change. My whole being cried out for swift action, but . . . . I did not forget the months I had spent behind bars. What sort of change would life bring us? I did not wish for the rupture of that fragile cable that had kept us dangling atop the abyss. Would it hold if we stayed still? Or would it loosen its hold of us, and its final rupture would be a matter of time? I stalled for time. Yet, impatiently, I wished for the final plummet, to get the suspense over with.

I wrangled with Fate for change, then ambiguously wished she had granted me peace, thankful just to be alive. Oh! What did I truly desire? For the moment, all I needed was a place to be by myself.

Upstairs, I found the main floor fully occupied. Mom and Aunt Sự conversed across the dining table. From their low tone and concerned looks, I gathered that their conversation crisscrossed between the household economies, the general news of the Lê family, and the latest rumors about who had successfully escaped the country, who had failed and returned, and who had been caught and jailed, or perished.

Through the open door of our bedroom, I could see Dad at his desk, bending over his math book and scribbling notes to himself, clearing his throat now and then per habit. The behemoth bureau was of heavy oak, in dark maroon, built to the owner's specifications to include a three-sided hutch, tall and thick like a wall, perhaps to isolate the scholar at work. If life had not been so cruel to plunge South Vietnam into the hands of the Vietnamese communists, my uncle would still have been sitting at this desk, focused on preparing his history lecture for the next day. Instead, here was Dad, desperately aiming the beam of his rusty intellect on theoretical math. How would it be useful to him at the age of fifty-seven? Wasn't it a little late?

I stole away to the top floor with my diary. There, I found Aunt Huỳnh bending among her flowerpots, a mute figure in white, lost in her own world. I escaped into one of the vacant rooms where, finally, I could be alone. I slumped onto the white surface of a large, built-in plywood plank that served as a writing table. Many times before I had come here to pore over the books left on the hutch, some belonging to Uncle Mục, fully annotated. A thick Vietnamese-Nôm dictionary had on its front page the inscription of his name and address.

What happened to Uncle Mục and his family? He must have sought sanctuary here, and now the only thing left was his essence, lingering on each crinkled turned page. Would someone else find my diary here, long after I was gone, and commiserate with my dark moods?

I wrote in my notebook these lines: "So long, Jeanne! When you see other old friends in France, give them my regards. Tell them I miss them. Write soon and describe for me life in Paris. I do love to have Paris invoked in pages, to help me congeal the words into images and images to reality. I am afraid that I will end up like Anne Frank, one day taken away to never return. How horrible to not return, ever, to this outstretching life, at seventeen."

That night I prayed fervently, conveying to Saint Martin de Porres the depth of my misery. Was it coincidental, or did the divine answer my call? For within weeks, we were stirred into action. Dad pushed away his books and started to receive visitors who came and went throughout the day. The continuous ringing of the doorbell and new faces walking up the stairs brought excitement into our hearts. We knew what this meant.

Dad introduced each of his guests to us. They were mostly men—one round-bellied man, one thin-like-a-stick man, a man with a mustache, and many clean-shaven ones. The one called Nam was the youngest and most handsome, an ex-army captain. Captain Nam's sinewy limbs and angular face caught my fancy.

Of course, he was an older man, and I should not have let my mind wander. Oh, does age matter? When one's heart beats with passion, it sits dreamily on top of the world and focuses only on the possibilities of love.

For the first time, I let myself fantasize about an older man, a married man. I let my heart flutter free of restraint. I imagined all kinds of love affairs in which I could include my hero and his boat, many with tragic endings, some with sunken boats and departed love, others with smitten captains but resolute maidens and final farewells.

I felt safe in my impossible dream. Inside the fortress of my mind, I allowed life to blossom, a future to take shape, desires to be fulfilled. My imaginative world consoled me in my bitter reality. I felt honored by my poetic love for this man who already belonged to a different age, to another woman, who could never be mine. I was not humiliated and tainted, as when Patrick tattled to my parents that a working boy in the noodle factory wanted to marry me.

"He shouts that he loves her," Patrick declared to our parents, almost proud for me. And I was stricken by shame. How dared he lower me to this worker's level, someone who might not even have the least rudimentary education?

Ah! What tenderness I feel now for that pure and innocent girl's heart. Love to her was sacred, mythical, and powerful. She thought only of hands hesitantly placed, like a cat nestled in warm palms. She dreamed only of eyes in exquisite contemplation of a beloved face. Love, then, was abstract, vaguely associated with joined minds, mutual yearnings, and the hope to have one's heart answered, knowing not what lay ahead.

My prince might have an attractive appearance—an intelligent face on tall, healthy limbs—but that was not important. What counted most was his inner beauty—his thoughtful mind, his artistic talents, his chivalry. He ought to play an instrument and must love literature and my family.

Then Captain Nam stopped coming. My love dream was dashed, and reality returned. Time passed; waiting for deliverance was interminable. I had been quite sure we would leave on my captain's boat. And if he could not bring me love, he would at least deliver me to freedom.

I did not risk mentioning to my parents the ideas that were nursed in my head: the escape, the handsome captain, my future. I understood their predicament. Whatever they could do to get us out of Vietnam, to bring our lives back on track, they would do. I need not trouble them. My fear of one day falling into the hands of a common boy was also their torture. I saw it in Mom's eyes each time she looked at me.

One afternoon, Mom came home followed by a lady visitor. They came into our bedroom and, seeing the four of us children, Mom ordered us outside. But we lingered, risking her temper to satisfy our curiosity about the stranger. Mom threw us an angry look but kept her silence and sat down on the mat opposite her visitor. By her restraint, we understood that this was serious business—important enough for her to ignore our pesky meddling.

Without a word, the two ladies began exchanging little packets. The stranger unwrapped hers to pull out a stack of paper bills and started counting expertly, flipping the currency like a card dealer, licking her index finger to moisten it every so often. Mom pulled back the red tissue in her palm to unveil leaflets of gold, each the size of a large barrette. We gathered in awe, bent on our knees, and she let us feel the soft, glowing gold and told us that they were 24-carat quality. The gold was paper thin but weighty when I held it.

The purchase of gold meant to us only one thing: our next

adventure was drawing near.

Soon after, we departed from Mỹ-Hương, each with our little bundle. I wore two layers of shirts, the inner one with large pockets that Mom had sewn to hide the gold bars. This time, our first stop was at the main zoo, which had been my favorite childhood place to visit during the summer. I was last driven past here in our red Mazda on our way home from Saint Grall Hospital, a few days after Saigon was lost to the communists. Now, the cages, devoid of animals, looked desolate and out of place.

I wandered around and found myself back on the grounds of the famous botanical garden inside the zoo, tracing my steps amidst foliage, passing the same large copper vases and bells in display, confused. I felt disoriented, assailed by conflicting visions: the endearing remembrance of my past excursions pulled me into a warm embrace while a terrifying premonition seemed to foretell the consequence of my presence here. Why was I in this timeless place, associated with sweet childhood memories, on a dangerous mission to save my future?

In all this beauty, I felt more trapped and terrified than an exhibited animal. I was told to wait here and had not asked for further details, while the hours passed endlessly. I spent a long time in this situation, not knowing what to expect, lurking about frantically like a criminal about to be caught. The heavy gold made it impossible for me to appear casual, weighing down on me like iron chains. Anxiously watching my shortening shadow on the ground, I began to panic, fearing that I had not understood the instructions well and was forgotten by my family.

Toward midmorning, I spotted Mom, reappearing as if she had only been hiding from my sight, with all my siblings crowding her steps. She gave me a quick nod that I interpreted as, "Follow us," and promptly complied.

We left the zoo through its side gate and regrouped with Dad and another group of passengers. All of us boarded a Lambretta, or *xe lam*. Our adventure had started out in an odd setting and seemed to stretch into a stranger shape as we clambering atop this noisy, three-wheeled vehicle, designed only for inner-city transit.

Normally, this oddball crossbreed of a scooter and a minivan would carry about ten passengers in the back carriage—not counting children on laps—sitting in opposite rows, and three people squeezing in the front cabin, with the driver steering in the middle.

That day, an extra bench had been inserted in the middle of the back carriage to allow room for eighteen passengers, fifteen in the back.

Thus burdened, the vehicle rolled slowly out of the main city and soon merged onto Highway One. How long ago had we traveled the same route in our Ford minivan, packed to the brim with briefcases, food, and toys, heading to the beach town, Vũng Tàu, for the week-long summer vacation? This trip was beginning to take on the appearance of a game of illusion, with my family transported as if by some magic to the idyllic scenes of my childhood, only to discover that they were all smoke, yielding to the touch, dissipating to reveal the ugly truth: the road leading to the sea would bring us to danger, to the border police, to jail, or—beyond our shores—the angry seas, the spying pirates . . . to the edge of death.

If I had been a little less passive and had not accepted my parents' wisdom so readily, I would have had many questions for them. Why did we board this tiny vehicle to get outside Saigon? Where were we actually heading? Were we planning to escape from Vũng Tàu, the most obvious escape route that, since 1975, was well guarded? If we were, why? We would obviously be picked up by the border police. But I had learned to keep my thoughts to myself, mute and dumb. I used my heightened senses instead to register what went on around me.

The Lambretta traveled slowly at first but picked up speed once on the highway. I felt less claustrophobic in the compact car with the wind on my neck and back. I sat on the padded bench with my back pressed against the metal frame of the open car. In front of me sat Michelle, her hip between my legs.

When the vehicle slowed down, I thought we were reaching our destination. But no, the driver pressed his gas pedal and zoomed forward, leaving the road behind once more. Not long after, he again relaxed the speed, cruising, then again made up his mind and sped up.

More than a few hours into the trip, the car made a U-turn and headed the opposite way as if it had overshot its destination. Hours later, we again reversed course to chase the road forward. I had the impression that the driver was either lost or killing time until the rendezvous could be established.

With the disappearing sun, the sky grew dark.

The air had cooled down considerably. I recalled saying to myself, "Thank God it's crowded in here. I am so chilled." Suddenly, at full speed, a terrible screech; the car swerved, careened sharply, and then came the impact. A heavy blow in the back of my head. Flashes.

Darkness. I must have passed out for a second. Then the sensations began to return. I rose from the blackness, resurfacing slowly like a diver pushed up by the body of water. I was on my back, with something pressing heavily on my chest. My first thought was: "Did I die?" Then, somehow, I knew I was not dead but, perhaps, pinned underneath the car.

I am about to die, I told myself. I did not panic but lay there, impotent. How silly it was to die pinned under a car. My next thought veered sharply toward my family. Where is everyone? Where is Michelle? She was last sitting in front of me. Oh! Merciful God! She was that heavy object on me, not the car.

We had to get out of there.

"Michelle, get up. Get off me."

We climbed out of the wreckage, all of us in one piece. Someone's child came out screaming with a broken arm dangling by his side. Dad was covered with blood. Thank goodness, it was his arm, scraped badly but not broken. It was dark. The stars twinkled above. It was windy. Someone whimpered, more like moaning.

Dad's voice was urgent, but calm: "Cross the street. Quân, children! Follow me."

We reached the opposite side of the street and ran into the open field beyond it. In the darkness we stumbled but followed each other closely.

Dad said, "Stay low. Keep still. They may be out looking for us."

We understood. It would be jail. The shirt I had on shone brightly under the moonlight. I was so conspicuous. I told myself: remember to wear dark next time. No more flowery clothes.

After a long time, the silence returned, save for the singing of crickets. The highway was empty. It seemed that they had cleared the accident scene. Finally, Dad told us, "Let's go back. We'll catch a bus home."

We returned home early in the morning, before the market's opening time. Only a full day had passed, but what an eternity of difference. We could have been dead on that road. We could have been sailing toward Thailand. We could have returned without a limb, or to bury one of us. But to the world, we were there as always, waiting for the beginning of another day.

27.

A New Year Tradition

The years kneaded me into a little woman but, mindlessly, had kept my knowledge of the world primitive. With much prodding from Dad I desperately hung on to the clever girl that I once was, but it was a losing battle. I steadily became a simple-minded creature not much different from our young maidservants of time past, or worse, content like an ox satisfied by daily feedings. The evolving world was beyond my myopic confinement. Like my maids, I grew up acquiring only domestic skills. I went to the market each morning on a food-gathering mission, and my goal was simple: to bring home the freshest culinary products at minimum cost. My concern was no more than that of roaming beasts and crawling insects. I was not much above a bee attracted by the red of tomatoes and when with both my hands in the pile of muddy onions, digging for the best bulbs, not unlike a dog searching for bones. When my eyes fell on the limp bodies of fish, there was no other judgment in me as to why these creatures had to die and in which painful manner except my hunger for tasty meat.

I was raised to be a polite and soft-spoken girl. But that girl had to learn now to bargain ruthlessly until her voice grew hoarse, pushing her limits with cunning tricks for an ultimate low price, such as feigning to walk away to be invited back for a sweeter deal. Her emotions were visible, her cheeks hot and humiliated from being rudely cut in line by an impatient, uneducated, loud-mouthed housewife. How her heart beat when she thought she had forgotten the money after concluding her first bargain of the morning, searching feverishly in all her pockets in front of the expectant shopkeeper. With those no-nonsense thin lips and devouring eyes, the lady merchant looked mean enough. She would shred her first customer's dignity to pieces with virulent curses if she failed to conclude the deal with money, ruining her day's luck.

Lips trembling from anticipation of verbal abuse, I sighed long and hard as I found the roll of cash inside my bamboo tote instead of in my shirt's lower pocket.

In those market days, I was like a poor cat once well sheltered and fed by gentle keepers but that now could not find her way out of the frightful alleys, neither smart enough to steal food from the streets nor dumb enough to ignore the doors and windows propped ajar on her path. The clumsy feline would sneak in, only to be cornered by a furious owner who would chase her down with a broomstick and banging pots. I was like half-brewed stock brought to the table steaming hot but tasting like boiled water, shaming the new housewife.

I was neither refined enough to be a princess, isolated in her high chamber, nor crude enough to survive the daily abrasion of ruthless merchants. I had learned to negotiate for my own gain but never had gotten used to profiting from another's loss, nor had I accustomed myself to the mercantile cruelty. After a few affronting episodes that made me wince and avoid this and that corner of the market until I was forced to pay a higher price for less quantity to the manipulative, sweet-talking merchants, I yielded my grocery-shopping role to little Anne, whose natural obstinacy made her a better candidate to confront the hostile market.

Her shopping trips stripped her of her cocoon, loosening her tongue and flaming her eyes, transforming her from a reticent, gloomy child into an invigorated bull full of a new ardor for the fight. Triumphantly, she pulled out a whole stalk of fresh cilantro, gorgeously crisp bok choy, round, red tomatoes as big as her fist, and a thick slab of pork meat, and asked us in a confident voice, "Guess how much I spent for all this?"

She shelled out only half of what I used to spend for all those goods. And that was not all, she declared: "Big sister, remember that devil of a woman who wagged her tongue at you for asking a lesser price for two papayas?"

Anne was beyond herself with joy. "She yielded these to me after I showed her what I'd got from her competitor." In my sister's robust hands were two plump papayas, ripe to saffron color, thick as two baby's thighs.

Little Anne brought home to us her vivid descriptions of a January market in preparation for Tết, our lunar New Year. The fruit section held blooming pyramids of colorful exotic fruits, each topped with mouth-watering samples: wedges of well-waxed green oranges, purple mangosteens revealing their virgin-white globules, hairy rambutans with their bright red tops lifted off, and, of all fruits, the symbols of New Year: the "must-have" watermelons. One or two of these giant melons had their thick exterior rind skillfully carved for the fruit peddler to showcase their red, juicy flesh, cut in large cube samples. The horrific vision of splitting an unripe, green and fibrous watermelon in front of the whole clan on New Year's Day is, to many Vietnamese, cause for ultra-cautious melon selection, relying on a combination of skill, luck, and merchant honesty. Many vendors took the extra step to dye their melon's interior red at a specific place where, when requested, they would wedge out a small sample, bloody red, tightly textured, and sweet in the mouth. Anne was boasting now. "Michelle, you have to come with me to see. One completely new section is now reserved for the display of dwarf kumquats, blooming branches of yellow mai blossoms, and other spring flowers. They are gorgeous, wonderful."

She avoided mentioning the meat and fish stalls, for they still reeked with a heavy, repugnant odor, New Year or not. It did not mean that she had avoided this infamous section; it only showed she had enough sense to select what scenery to describe to entice our interest and what to keep as her own business, buried as her childhood memories of Vietnam. I still shuddered from the recollection: the unhygienic display of live flesh, slabs of discolored meat adorned with buzzing black flies, fish long dead, their turbid eyes staring at the crowd.

Our animated conversation and untamed commotion in the weeks before the New Year were not lost to Dad's eyes. He had his head buried in the books but his heart might have wandered in our direction. He constantly asked me, "Do you want to celebrate New Year this year?" When my answers did not vary from the initial, eager "Yes," and the flame in my eyes lit up at his next probing, "Do you think I should give out the red envelopes?" Dad came to Mom with an unusual request: "Quân! Will you make us *bánh chưng* this year? I don't want the kids to forget this tradition."

Oh, yes! How could I forget Mom's best rice cakes? Even little Michelle still remembered how they looked and tasted. It had been four years since Mom had abandoned her annual ritual. Now that we insisted on its reenactment, she pondered the possibility. "I would need a large pot and a stove," Mom said. How would she cook her special cakes without a gas stove that would keep the pot boiling for seven to eight hours? "We don't even have a kitchen, for heaven's sake," she refuted.

Dad continued to nudge Mom toward the objects of his craving. "My deprived children," he said. "They will soon leave Vietnam without remembering our tradition."

She was not convinced until Dad added in his caressing voice, "No one can make those cakes the way my wife makes them. Will you, *chérie?*"

Quietly, my fiery mother brought home the necessary ingredients for her special recipe, starting with the procurement of a kerosene stove, a fifty-gallon drum as cooking pot, then the fresh products: banana and coconut leaves which formed a package to wrap each cake, sweet rice grains, mung beans, coconuts, and finally, pork meat.

I was not unfamiliar with the tedious procedure of making rice cakes. My mother used to spend weeks preparing for the three-day labor, gathering materials and soliciting help from household staff as well as relatives. It was hard work, messy and intensive. In years past, the lengthy process of preparing the house for the large gathering— clearing enough space in the refrigerator for the marinated meat, soaking large vats of beans and rice, cleaning by hand each banana leaf, making the coconut-leaf frames in which to form the cakes— was mind boggling, the logistics insane. But it brought the whole clan together under one roof, resulting in three fun, gossipy, bonding days that were unforgettable. The dining furniture had to be cleared away and the floor covered with bamboo mats. All the aunties would sit together, cross-legged, the working materials spread around them, joking and laughing as if they were again little girls. The fan-like coconut fronds were sheared into long strips. Each strip was then bent into twelve-inch squares and secured at one corner with a bamboo toothpick, forming a frame. After the large banana leaves were washed and wiped, they would be placed inside the frame to form a container into which went all the prepared ingredients, carefully layered: soaked rice, sweetened mung-bean paste, and two large morsels of pork meat—especially chosen to be thick with lard, cut to palm-size and marinated in a mixture of fish sauce, extract of garlic, shallots, and brown sugar. The precious package was secured with nylon twine and piled away. The cakes were loaded into a fifty-gallon steel drum filled with pre-boiled water. The cooking fire was kept constant between eighteen and twenty-four hours. When the cooking time had almost elapsed, Mom took out one rice cake from the topmost and poked it with a sharp bamboo skewer. She inspected the skewer for signs of a sticky substance, which she explained resulted from the cooked sweet rice. Once satisfied, she fished out a cake from the top of the pile and cut it out for sampling. The maid would kill the fire and empty out the batch of steaming, square packages.

Then it would be time to bring the gifts to our grandparents on both sides of the family to honor them, and to the rest of the relatives, she sent each family two cakes. My Auntie Diep, who was single and lived with Grandma, was skipped. She could share with Grandma. In all, forty cakes were distributed and ten kept for our family.

Life with all its glory and comfort had passed us by. The old ways of celebrating with presents and food or dressing up for special occasions were long forgotten. We had adjusted to matching our expectations to the cruel reality and did not want to look back, to rekindle memories that were painful. It was not just another year but a struggling year, another year of growing older without the ability to build up, to secure, to reach higher, to put aside savings, to acquire new wealth or knowledge. In the end, the call of duty again claimed my mother's heart. Dad was nostalgic for the old time, and Mom's children were longing for normalcy. The bustling activities of our market were too much to be ignored. It was silly to celebrate, but we wanted festivities. We wanted to commemorate another year past and mark the arrival of a new beginning. We needed a new beginning.

Mom set out to gather her rice cake ingredients as years before. She would bend the circumstance to match the demand of her family. She had found enough eggs, butter, and flour to bake us a cake with frosting that Christmas when Dad was imprisoned, had she not? Love's way was Mom's way. The desire to provide for her family was strong in her breast. And she would not cease her quest for its fulfillment, spurred on by hope, verging on madness. The day before New Year, Mom assembled a sort of support made with construction bricks for her large container to sit on, then we rolled out bamboo mats and invited our aunts over. It was not a large gathering, but we did sit together and talk as if nothing else mattered. New Year's Eve! The six of us gathered around the simmering drum, taking turns to shield our stove from a strong wind, using now our body, now a large sheet of steel, then both, fighting the blowing air. We were all anxious for our precious pot of rice cakes, knowing that if the fire did not keep the water boiling at high temperature, its contents would be half-cooked, and our efforts to have the traditional cakes this year would be wasted. Mom's eyes flashed in the flickering firelight, whose flames leaped and swerved, then dimmed and brightened again—

like hope. Like love. Without warning, flames burst above us in the night sky in myriad patterns. Spectacular fireworks. Flaming rose petals slowly uncurled—then dropped, dropped, dropped— followed by cotton balls which the flying wind dispersed, chased by the burning stars. *Boom, boom, bang, whiz.* The explosions were deafening, reminding us of the bombing of Saigon.

It was then that we realized: the war was really over. It had ended in our defeat. There would be no more gunshots, only the popping of hellfire, the sizzle of the flesh of our future, and black magic powder thrown by the devil. It was a sad departure of the Year of the Goat. But was there any hope for our family to bid goodbye to precipitous slopes, butting against unyielding painful reality, only to be herded back behind fences?

Upon us came the cunning, mischievous troublemaker, the Year of the Monkey: 1980.

28.

Boat 179

The fifth annual celebration of the victory of Vietnam over the American imperialists, Đế Quốc Mỹ, was elaborately staged in Hồ Chí Minh City. Where could we go to escape its red banners like bloodthirsty tongues, snapping and flicking in the streets, lolling at every pole? There was no way to avoid the blood-colored flags: red like pig guts, spilling from the butcher's hand; the red of debauched lips, smearing rouge on our presidential palace. The red on all our government buildings filled us with shame.

Oh, our "Pearl of the Orient," I cried out for you. Beloved city of my birth! Your dignity was no more. Your classic beauty that once had captured the world's admiration was fading, ravaged by starvation—your soul oppressed, your limbs heavily shackled. But you laughed! That was terrible and heartbreaking, to hear from your dry, bloodless lips the forceful sound of broken china, the mirthless cackles of wrath, the rusty tones of cheap chimes. There was everything but joy in your whimpering laughter—your nerve-wrecking, crow-like khaw, khaw—or the well-rehearsed, tremulous, ear-splitting merriment of your vocal cords. You sounded hollow, forced, drunk. Pitiful, like a child bride. As lost as a girl sold out to be an octogenarian's life partner. The eruption of sound that you portrayed as laughter was only the final rupture of your lungs, and with it, your last breath.

The forced reminder of that "Black April" month and the passing years, combined with the quick deterioration of our relationship with Aunt Huỳnh, seemed to unleash unpredictable behavior from Dad, who was normally composed and forgiving. He would lash out at us for no particular reason. Looking up from his book and catching us idling about, he would roar, "What are you doing there? Don't you ever study?"

Aunt Huỳnh no longer hid from us her irritation. She was fed up with "these kids . . . running up and down the stairs all day long." She said she needed quiet time to pray, and with the piano practice and our family's constant barging in and out, it was a living hell to her. Our clothes hanging out to dry on the terrace had taken all the available space on *her* rope, and she was livid when she finally blurted out, "I had to walk under your girls' and wife's underwear. Don't you all have the decency, the courtesy, the, the . . . ." She did not find the right word to express what she thought we lacked.

It did not take long for Aunt Huỳnh to disclose what was in her mind. She was considering selling the room that had been our home for over a year. She needed the money. Dad, whom I never saw haggle with anybody, bargained with her for time.

"One more month, until we can find a boat," he said. "We'll pay you monthly rent."

My aunt did not give Dad any definite word of assurance, but she dangled some hope in his face by her silence, which virtually unhinged his jaws and relaxed the muscles that had kept his shoulders taut like a board. For the next few days, Dad abandoned his math formulas in pursuit of some new ideas. He sat for hours with a hand on his mouth as if he feared his thought would spill out in words before he had the time to link them up properly into sentences. The cusp of his palm formed a stand with his left elbow to support his chin in these hours of contemplation, his eyes staring in the distance like owl eyes in the daylight, blind but wide open.

Now and then, Dad snapped out of his soul-traveling moments and discussed his plan with Mom. He told her, "If *the witch* wants to sell out her house, then we'd rather buy it. With her, we will never know. What if she finds a buyer tomorrow?"

We were ecstatic: a home of our own. Then I could have my own room. I was already making plans.

Mom disagreed. "We need all the money to buy a boat passage. We hardly have enough."

Dad said, deflated. "We'll ask Mai to send us more things to sell." He added, like an afterthought, sounding apologetic, "It's not such a foolish idea, Quân. Think what will happen if Aunt Huỳnh sells this house before we leave. Where will we stay?"

Mom nodded sadly. "Anyone thinking of buying a home would snatch it at this ludicrously low price she is asking."

She waved the dark prospect away with a movement of her hand. "Let's bide our time. I'll go down to Aunt Sự to see if she can suggest anything else."

She looked up sharply. "What happened to Captain Nam? You both have discussed the possibility of a boat."

My heart. Oh, how it beat. I thought the old plan was scrapped, that somehow the boat and its captain had left without us. What Dad said next lit joy in my face. "We are still working out the details. It's a safe voyage, sponsored by the government. Expensive, but guaranteed. We just have to wait until he sends us word."

Meanwhile, the torture of being at someone's mercy wrung Dad day and night. He was like a bird I once saw, with a broken wing, flapping wildly with the remaining good wing and jerking its fragile legs. With time, the desperate movements of this injured creature slowed, until it hardly moved and, within a few days, died. I understood Dad's fear. Aunt Huỳnh had once before mentioned her plan of selling off the large home she did not need, one room at a time, until she could no longer afford to live by herself. Then she would cash out and move into a convent. Dad, of course, was horrified at her plan. The house had been his dear brother's brainchild.

Even in the depression years of the '30s, when grandparents had to mortgage their land parcel by parcel to buy food, his family would find ways to cling to the home they grew up in.

Normally, Dad avoided the streets for fear of being abducted. Aunt Trọng's brother, a medical doctor, had vanished in that manner, kidnapped from his bike into a taxi and never heard from again. However, what is a snared hog to do but pull, even though doing so would only tighten the noose? Dad took his bike on long excursions, sometimes to see his friends, other times just to be out, airing his sour moods.

He returned one day with a few vials, his eyes twinkling, quick steps moving to and fro as if his burden had been lifted. When I asked him what he planned to do with the vials, he showed the little bottles to me, saying, "They're sold in the streets. Do you know their use?" I nodded. I had seen these around. The label stated plainly "Elephant Fluid Eraser."

That same afternoon, Dad launched into a new project. First, he brought our birth certificates downtown to have them copied. He laid out these duplicated certificates and painted the clear liquid over some of the vowels, erasing the "E" in our last name, then typing in its place an "O." Painstakingly, he worked, replacing letters. Finally, to my dismay, he proudly presented me the updated version of my birth certificate. The first two words of my name, "Lê Thị," had become "Lỗ Thu". I must have looked baffled, because without waiting for my questions, Dad explained softly, "This is now your name."

As soon as he finished fudging, Dad said, "Can you laminate these to make them look more official?"

Could I laminate the documents myself? The request sounded similar to one Aunt Bích had proposed years ago before her departure from Vietnam, after I had shown her my collection of homemade stamps. "Hồng-Mỹ! Can you turn your erasers into official stamps, too?" It was a crazy time, when the adults began to take my plaything for real-life application. But I was a vain child and I stood tall when challenged. "Sure," I said to Dad and began gathering some simple tools: a clothes iron, a metallic pants zipper, and plastic bags. I had done this. I had done many creative projects before, tinkering with various household objects to fashion toys, gadgets, purses. However,

I was concerned this time. Dad had always trusted my ability to perform well in whatever I did, and now I doubted his over-confidence. But I proceeded with the task at hand, my head filled with the question: What are these papers for?

I inserted each record of birth into a recycled plastic bag, brittle and yellowish, unlike the clear and thick laminate film used by the professionals. Atop a fastened-up pants zipper I placed the plastic cover with the birth certificate inside. A newspaper page separated the plastic-covered document and the hot iron which, when pressed down, embossed the zipper shapes onto the melted plastic, forming a neat sealed edge. The acrid smell of the burnt plastic stunk the air.

Dad kept exclaiming, "How genius!"

With a pair of scissors, I trimmed off the excess plastic and finished my job. Dad followed my movement, clearly amazed. "Outstanding," he murmured, as he examined the final products. "This ought to do."

I could no longer hold my curiosity. "What are they for, Dad?"

"Wait for Mom" was his enigmatic response. Once she rejoined us, he explained his latest escape scheme to the whole family. The communist government had begun to allow anyone with Chinese-sounding names on his birth certificate to leave Vietnam in an "orderly departure program" at the cost of five to seven gold leaflets per head. These Chinese ethnics were called *người Việt gốc Hoa*, Vietnamese of Chinese origin. We did not know it at the time, but Vietnam was in a period of economic desperation. Stalinist socialism, with its marvelous system of centralized planning and principle of collectivity, had devastated the South's economy. All decisions were made by Hanoi and handed down to the far regions controlled by the local governments. The lands and crops were collectively owned by the farmers and the government. The central government supplied the farmers with tools and materials. The farmers worked the lands and produced the crops, and the government collected and distributed the surplus products.

It started well in the early days of 1975. The farmers were innocent in the way of the Party. They were happy to be one hundred percent subsidized and were, in the new partnership, the "owners." Over the years, the truth emerged. The farmers realized that being owners of their lands did not give them the sole right to distribute their products for profit. The aforementioned "surplus" was everything beyond an individual's consumption level. The rest was bought by the state at bottom price and redistributed centrally, eliminating all competition and profit. What a wake-up knock on the head!

Once they understood this clearly, the hardy farmers lost the zeal to work. They'd rather sit at home collecting their share of rice from the cooperative than labor for the general interest. This refusal by the disillusioned farmers to be part of the system created a domino effect: poor agricultural production, declining national budget, collapsed factories, and corruption. In the spirit of collectivity, the central planner quickly sent out the rice to the hungry regions. On the way to the needy, the precious grains were diverted into greedy hands instead, and rice that was supposed to feed the farmers so they could work was forged into gold to buy bigger homes for secondary officials in the far towns.

Corruption was rampant at all government levels. Starvation had begun in the countryside. It did not help that Vietnam's invasion of Cambodia at the end of 1978 had stirred up the ancient animosity with Big Brother China. Destitute, a Stone Age Vietnam used what it had left in hand to fight: a simple stone to kill both birds. It promised Big Brother the immediate release of all ethnic Chinese from its borders, and it promised the Chinese in Vietnam the right to move out in exchange for gold. *Phew!* The young socialist republic breathed with relief. It had found the solution to its problems. To Vietnamese families like us, the new stopgap measure sprung a leak in the impassable dam through which to find escape. We were only small fish in the government's plan—but resourceful. If the scorpion fish dwelling in coral reefs could make themselves look like rocks to fool their predators, then we could modify our names to become Chinese and escape our enemies.

It explained why our very authentic Vietnamese name, Lê, was morphed into a ridiculous Chinese-sounding Lỗ. Mom's name, Hoàng Lệ-Quân, could already be mistaken for Chinese. Many Wangs were entered as Hoàng by Vietnamese officials at the entry ports. It worked out even better for Mom, for Grandpa had named his daughter after a Chinese character. She was the lucky daughter of Fate.

And we were the imposters, wearing our camouflage for survival.

Playing on words, Dad jested, "We are now *người Việt gốc cây*, Vietnamese of gold origin, my dear wife and children."

Pay up, fudge up, and the communists would consider us Chinese and let us go. Convinced by the foolproof plan, other members of the larger Lê clan saved up and joined us. Our family left Saigon in early May 1980, the first Lês to arrive in Vĩnh-Long. We moved into the sea town reserved for departing Chinese and boarded in a three-level, tin-roofed home.

From the balcony of our rental, I discovered the neighborhood that had boomed overnight. All the private homes along the small street were now rented out to people like us—gold-laden Chinese ready to spend the last of their Vietnamese *đồng*. The street below was always festive and busy with foot traffic. Most of the pedestrians were city people, easily recognizable with their fair skin, city clothes, and urban behaviors. There was no need to disguise our purpose. People streamed through the dirt lane dragging their large suitcases, hollering in Mandarin or Cantonese. The men were tall, fair-skinned, and well fed, sporting heavy gold chains with jade amulets between their large dark nipples. They would have been good-looking if they had their shirts on.

I spied children playing on the balcony next door. Their features and accents indicated to me that they were authentic Chinese. Many times they tossed inquiries at me, which I did not understand but thought might mean, "Where you from?" I ignored them and went indoors, hiding the fact that I was not one of their people, here to repatriate.

Within a week, Aunt Sự came down with her two sons, Hùng and

Cường. Then my Tenth Uncle and his wife joined us. She came down to send him off and would follow him with their five small children once his safe arrival was confirmed. It was, to desperate Vietnamese, a less risky attempt: save their men and their families would be saved. Only, the jealous Sea God often drowned their heroes. Or sometimes she folded her long tentacles and spared the men but took the wife and children, leaving the men stranded in foreign lands without a family, devoid of their purpose. When the Vietnamese left home to follow their destiny, they knew in their hearts the consequences of their choice. We offered ourselves up to God before we embarked on each of our harrowing journeys, leaving the horizon where the sun would rise, to enter the "Valley of the Shadow." Our parents brought us with them "to live or die together." Even *that* was delusional, for many parents who traveled with their brood were left childless at the end of the journey; and children who had held hands with their father and mother would see them disappear forever when the boat capsized, as if it was the ultimate sacrifice demanded of them, as if it was the children's worst mistake—to let go from their too-small hands the dearest lives.

Regardless, our journey of thousands of steps, once begun, was to be followed one step at a time. The first step was always hopeful. The adventure was beckoning our young souls. And so it was with this trip.

With so many of us under one roof, talking and eating was endless. The house was buzzing with excitement but so hot. We sweated buckets and craved ice cubes, which were not easily found in this part of town. The hosts made up for the climatic deficiency of their home by cooking for us the best of meals. The food was unique to this region: every dish was laden with coconut milk and fish. We ate lots of seafood and tasted some strange meats: eels, snakes, and even frogs. In the month of May, the market had abundant mangos. Dad ordered Aunt Sự to feed us sackfuls of mangos because, he reasoned, "This would be their last chance to taste these equatorial fruits. Have them eat enough to last a lifetime." We consumed so many of these fruits that our faces were full of pimples, and our mouths developed painful sores.

One afternoon, Dad offered to take us to the pier to visit "our boat." We walked the dirt lane to the small pier, and met many people walking back from it, swaying their hands and feet as if they owned the street, conversing in loud, happy voices. And there she was, boat Number 179. She bobbed gently on the undulating water, her hull round and solid. She looked like the giant whale of my imagination. Dad proudly led us across the thin, rickety plank onto the bow. We bent our heads as we went below through the hatch into the bilge, smelling the new paint, caressing the wood, already seeing ourselves swinging in hammocks in our preferred corner of the bulkheads.

Dad looked at us brightly. "What do you think?"

Mom's eyes were like two shiny betel nuts. Patrick ran back and forth, testing his balance, exclaiming every so often, "It's swell, Dad! I can't wait till we depart."

We returned to our rental home with a warm feeling, all holding hands, down the dirt lane, Anne and Michelle swinging Mom's and Dad's hands like a rope and skipping high, heaving so heavily on them that Mom let out a loud, "Ouch!" and yanked back her hand. Patrick was still walking as if on a thin plank, putting one foot in front of the other and balancing himself with his arms outstretched. I wanted to shout with joy, still feeling the cool caress of the marine wind on my long hair and at the nape of my neck. A wild hope nestled in my heart. Soon, we would be free.

The hope kept my thoughts awake in the night. Patrick, too, kept tossing and turning. I heard the working of my aunt's hand fan to cool down Tenth Uncle, who lay shamelessly in the crook of his wife's arm. The night was muggy. The room was overcrowded with all our family members, lying like corpses under the weight of immovable air. Hùng and Cường spread out under the clothesline—one with his mouth gaping wide, the other on his back, like a swimmer. The host family slept downstairs.

Three weeks flew by without any event. Then the rumors gathered, forming dark clouds on top of all the roofs, emptying the one-lane dirt road, and quieting the nights. From different sources came the terrible tale that there was trouble brewing between the local organizers and the county police—some dispute about legalities and money distribution. We were instructed to be ready to roll. To roll where? What to expect?

Anywhere. Anything might happen, was the reply.

That night I had trouble falling asleep. The atmosphere was heavy with unknown forces. The impression was like before a storm. It was so hot. The clouds had to burst soon, I thought. There were noises in the street below, footsteps late into the night, the throaty sound of whisperings. I heard running steps in my heavy slumber, and soon the sound of loud voices.

"The cops are coming. Leave," someone alerted the neighborhood from the street. I bolted up. The household was deep asleep. My parents had not returned from their late-night visit to the boat.

"Hùng, Cường! Trouble. Wake up. The cops are coming."

My two cousins awoke in the confusion of everybody darting left and right, evacuating in haste. Most of the older people had poured out into the large cemetery in the back of the house when my parents ran in from the street. Our family joined the running crowds in the street and headed in all directions. Gunshots were heard in the vicinity. "To the bus depot," Dad screamed. "Hurry, hurry."

Once there, we lay down quietly, joining the sleeping passengers on the cold dirt floor, in the darkness. *Pow, pow* was heard from the far end of town.

The six of us were together. Our parents looked grim. Where were the others?

The next day, order returned as suddenly as it had been destroyed. By noon, we received word to come back to our rental home. One by one, our relatives showed up.

Tenth Uncle was disheveled and wild-eyed. "I saw ghosts last night in the cemetery. They flickered on and off, on and off."

Aunt Sự shuddered. "Shush! Don't talk nonsense. They were fireflies."

Hùng and Cường came in, one bare-chested, the other wearing a lady's undershirt, white cotton with crocheted lace. I pointed it out to Cường, who blushed in embarrassment and hastily disrobed, mumbling, "I cannot see a thing in the dark. Just grasped at the closest piece of cloth from the line and ran."

The turbulence of that night was only lightning and thunder to the raging storm ahead of us and had served only, in comparison, as rehearsal for what was to come.

A few nights later, officials going door to door roused us and told us to head without delay to the boat. "The captain is pulling up anchor," was the message shouted at each house.

People still in their nightclothes poured out of the houses, dragging their belongings and children.

"What happened?" they asked each other, bewildered.

The answer came from different mouths, in different tongues. We vaguely understood that, like the previous time, a government dispute had erupted, and the county police, dissatisfied with being left out of the gold deal, were heading their patrol boat down to arrest all boats found on their water.

The boat had to leave. The crew was frantically loading passengers and supplies. And they would leave on the first notice, waiting for no one. The first passengers to embark might be the only ones to depart. The rest . . . .

No one dared to linger. It was as if the whole town was on fire. The one-lane dirt road was choked with the frantic race to the boat, with officials pounding on more houses down the lane.

The night was pitch-dark and chilly, with a slight drizzle.

We remembered where the ship was moored. We followed the crowds in the direction of the pier, at first huddling together in one march like lost apes, but the closer we got to the end of the lane, the more we dispersed in loud discord, running toward the pier like baby turtles after their hatch, instinctively, urgently, following the shimmery water, or maybe the stars.

We arrived while many more were still running out from the road in one army of lost soldiers, their footsteps slapping the dirt road where needles of rain had pierced the earth and loosened the compacted dirt into muddy lava. The chocolate mud adhered to the flimsy flip-flops and cheap sandals. The sweating earth revolted against the fleeing army for abandoning it to embrace the yielding sea. *Let go*, the beating footsteps seemed to beg, but the earth was angry and splattered them, yanking hard on the slippery soles, toppling the unfaithful fleeing crowd.

"Ma, ma!" the little ones screamed.

"Run, my son." The frail woman pulled harder. The road slipped beneath her. "Your father is ahead, he's far ahead. Run, my son, or we'll lose him." She staggered under the weight of her own bag, but she did not let go of the frightened boy, who was her own flesh, her own life. The drumming of fleeing steps, the sobbing of the sky, the bawling of small children being dragged, being separated, being pushed away and trampled by bigger forms—a requiem.

But ignoring all that, the crowd was intent on escaping until it came to the deep drop into the ocean and froze, confused by the gulf between the shore and the boat. It was then and there that the jumble of people melted into a background of dark silhouettes and riotous sounds.

From afar, ebbing gently, the ship was bright with light. Its diesel engine was humming. The crowded front harbor was a haze of sounds and figures, all jumbled in a maddening chaos. There was the panicky hollering of names from the ship and shouts of frustration and fear coming faintly from various parts of the shore, like hunted animals' cries, tearing at the mist. The pier was covered in mud. Mud caked on the narrow wooden plank and made the crossing to the boat very slippery. One skid and we would be in the waves below. Our parents had boarded first, bringing with them my younger sisters. The local police were directing the confused passengers to quickly board—*run this way, no, this way, not that way, over here.* I clung to Patrick as we clambered across on hands and feet, our useless flip-flops hooked on our index fingers. I slipped and Patrick slid, but we both somehow managed to tumble into the interior of Boat 179 and were reunited with our family. "Where are Hùng and Cường?" our parents asked in unison.

"They were just with us," Patrick and I answered.

"Hùng, Cường," my parents called out.

"Too late, the plank is withdrawn. The boat is leaving," someone indicated.

My heart skipped a beat at the thought that Patrick and I could have been left behind on shore if we had been delayed a tad longer. Water lapped the sides of our vessel, now fully occupied. The ship bore us forwards, lunging. What a feeling, to be inside such a magnificent vessel, to be swinging like the ship's lightbulbs with the rolling waves, to be surrounded by fellow beings, all with the same purpose. What craftsmanship! We admired the sturdy wood beams, their transverse frames interconnected, their planks joining neatly, knowing that the wood was all that separated us from the depthless ocean.

An hour into the crossing, the first good news reached us. The boat would stop to pick up some passengers that had been left behind and taxied out. Finally, our two male cousins showed up. All together, Boat 179 carried two hundred passengers—she was safely designed for seventy-five.

Three hours into the crossing, the first daylight shone through the square opening of the hatch above us. The crew was doling out the first meal of the day, and we waited patiently for our portion. Mom had left to walk to the captain's cabin, "get some news, and use the bucket." We hung up our hammocks. Breakfast came to us, and we attacked our meal as if we had not eaten for years. Mom returned and said to Dad, "All is well. We'll be heading out to the open sea in a few hours." She fumbled inside her bag and got out some biscuits to distribute among our group. Light danced in her brown eyes. She sat down next to Dad. "Captain Nam said hi."

Seven hours into the crossing, the swinging lightbulb above us shook violently. I had my eyes on it, then on my mother's tense countenance. The brown of her eyes had darkened, her irises constricted. Lines appeared on her forehead. Her lips were pressed together.

The wide ship labored over the waves now, like an elephant put to sea. She groaned and creaked from all her joints, beams, and floorboards.

"Dad," I said, "is it normal?"

"Pet, we're in the open ocean. The waves are larger here. It will get calmer in deep water."

Inside, the passengers began experiencing motion sickness. Some became sick, vomiting violently. I resisted the urge, then bolted up and asked for a bag. "*Urg* . . . ." Just in time.

It was Patrick's turn now. His face was pale, his eyes huge. The sound of people vomiting caused the ones still holding out to reach quickly for a bag. The whole ship reeked with the mixed odor of sour digestive juice, sweat, and eucalyptus oil. The muscular teenage boys were in fits of seizure. Prayers broke out tumultuously, causing a general state of panic. In our group, Mom was the only one still immune from the motion sickness. She offered her lap to little Anne. Leaning on Anne was Michelle, limp like a dead fish. A white substance caked her lips.

"Hail Mary, full of grace, the Lord is with thee . . . ," Dad began, and Mom's tears rolled down her ashen cheeks. She recited with Dad, "Blessed art thou amongst women, and blessed is the fruit of thy womb, Jesus . . . ."

"Holy Mary, Mother of God, pray for us sinners, now and at the hour of our death. Amen," Tenth Uncle joined, his voice low and shaken.

I closed my eyes to block out the specters of death.

Each roll of the sea seemed to be the last, but the boat continued to fight. At nightfall, we were all soaked from a leak that appeared to be worsening. The prayers were now loud, competing with the sound of the waves and the groaning of the wounded vessel. The Buddhists were chanting, full of despair. Could it be their prayer for the dying?

May all beings have happiness
and be the causes of happiness;
May all be free from sorrow
and the causes of sorrow;

May all never be separated
from the sacred happiness
which is sorrowless;
And may all live in equanimity,
without too much attachment
and too much aversion,
And live believing in the equality
of all that lives.

(Traditional Buddhist prayer)

"Do not panic, my boy!" a woman cried, stroking a teenage boy's head. He was screaming, foaming from his mouth, his eyes rolling.

Empty plastic containers were passed to us along with the order to "Scoop up and pass." Although the filled containers traveled swiftly from hand to hand in the human chain, the water level rose quickly to our waists.

Running footsteps were heard thudding above our heads. Dad raised his voice and spoke to the whole boat, "Please do not panic. Stay where you are until the captain gives the order to abandon ship. Else the boat will capsize prematurely."

Finally, we received the order. The brave captain had brought the boat into Long-Hải, around 92 nautical miles from Vĩnh-Long where we had started, and we were heading closer to the shore. The men had worked frantically to empty the water from the boat. They abandoned that task now and thrust the plastic containers into the hands of all the children, instructing, "Jump and swim to shore. Go now," pushing the resisting ones onto the deck and dropping them into the ocean, assuring them that it was safe.

"The waves will carry you toward shore; just hang on tight to your container."

Knowing how to float and somewhat able to swim, I was not at all afraid when I took the jug, but when I looked down into the dark water, its depth unfathomable, my boldness retreated at once. It would be a steep drop.

"No! Please." I backed up, filled with dread. My three siblings plunged. They were gone with the waves. I closed my eyes and let go. Soon, my feet touched the bottom, and I dragged myself to shore. It was then that the sea reclaimed me. I was pushed head first into the sand and the water crashed on me, filling my lungs with brine. I lifted my head, and another wave crashed in, tumbling me down. In the third attempt, I cleared out of the current and stood up. My feet felt like lead. The ground swayed under me. I screamed for my brother and sisters as I dragged my feet over the wet sand, trying to pierce the dark with my stinging eyes. Three little forms came to me, holding on to one another.

Patrick screamed into my face, "Where are Mom and Dad?" I shook my head, telling him the adults were not allowed to leave the boat until all the children had left.

Patrick pulled back his hand from my grasp. "I am going back out. I need to go rescue them."

My voice was weak and cracking but firm. "You are not. You stay right here with us until they come. They will come."

We waited on the shore, all the while calling out to the ocean for our parents. Then we saw them, their shadows against the luminescent moon, Dad pulling Mom. We ran toward them, a family reunited in the face of death.

Seeing me, Mom asked at once, "Do you still have the gold?"

I started. "No! It was heavy. I . . . ." I had taken the cotton belt off somewhere or gave it for somebody to hold. Had forgotten about it until Mom asked. How could I be so careless?

Mom looked very sad. She did not say much. Her silence tortured my conscience. I should have kept that gold with me, no matter what. I reproached myself. She was right about me. I was not a responsible person. I was weak, selfish, and easily spooked. A sudden cough shook me. My chest burned. I could feel the rising of a delirious fever.

We ran toward the foot of a deserted building and cowed under some solid structure, trying to shield ourselves from the strong ocean wind. But the wind found us there and whipped its cold lash at us. Mom bent her head over me, blocking out the icy draft for a moment.

Her hand was a cold fish on my forehead and I shook it away, babbling incoherently, "No! I don't want to jump. No!"

Dad scooped me up from the sand. For a second, it was so still. I was that little girl again being carried upstairs in the arms of my father, back to my bed from a late TV show. The heat glowed within me, burning my cheeks and roasting my eyes like a furnace fire, wrapping around me like a fur coat and comforting me. Then I knew no more.

I woke the next morning to find out that we had taken shelter inside the abandoned basement of the Grand Hotel. We stayed there for a day until I was strong enough to walk. Then we boarded the bus back to Hồ Chí Minh City.

Once more, we shed the carcass of another abortive hope, our resilience as ancient and deep-rooted as the courage of the first cavemen digging out a life among beasts and harsh nature.

29.

A Troubling Marriage

We had been scattered into the waves and gathered by the rising tides like sands on the beach. Our lives depended on that moon above. We had been washed to shore like seaweed, clinging to plastic jugs. Who had been with us that night in the forlorn basement of that abandoned hotel, and who had run headlong into the wind, out to the highway, confused and scared? I did not remember the ride home. When and how had I climbed the stairway of Mỹ-Hướng to collapse again on my floor mat? I did not remember.

The humming of the moving sea still echoed, transporting me back to that groaning boat, where hundreds of bodies cried out their anguish to their gods, offering their souls. I wavered in and out of reality, seeing alternately the familiar walls and ceiling of our bedroom, then the deep bottom of the sea closing in—obliterating time and space, flattening all dimensions, leaving only darkness.

I recoiled to think that our life's chronicles could have ended on that May Day, not far from the seacoast of a war-torn country that was once our paradise but was now hell-bound—we had ventured into the rush of ocean surges in a *riverboat*.

As my health slowly returned and my days and nights resumed their respective cycles, the awful meaning of our adventures took root in my conscience. I relived every minute of my ordeal. In my mental vision I saw that beautiful wooden vessel for the first time in a different light, built more as a giant coffin for two hundred lives by some unscrupulous monster, thirsty for blood-tainted gold. How many hoaxes had we survived and how many more were to come? Would I ever have the courage to board another boat, knowing now the full meaning of this fateful step forward? And yet to stay back was to attain only the illusion of life in terms of hope, future, safety. There would be no life if hope was already buried, if tomorrow was laid bare, if safety was forfeited.

Some nights, I heard Mom waking Dad from recurring nightmares. He was jerking and kicking wildly, emitting incoherent shouts. This had happened intermittently. Dad had been bitten by a dog once in his youth and, ever since, when exhausted or traumatized, he would feel in his sleep that same dog snapping at his leg.

Fear seized us, and time was against us. There was no safe season to go out into the sea, for, besides the wrath of nature, the boat people were facing the greatest evils: sea pirates. These Thai-born criminals had discovered their easy targets: tiny boats loaded with exhausted refugees, their gold almost warm with life, and underneath that layer of richness, their marble flesh—their true value. Although unsought, the truth came forcefully. Our parents had chosen the bliss of ignorance, but their last broach with danger had force opened their eyes to the sight of evils.

At night, Dad leaned close to a radio Khải sent us, its "rabbit ears" up, catching the news from Voice of America or BBC. What he learned he did not share with us children. It was grim news: "Pirates patrolling the high seas, ransacking and killing boat people," and softly, in a voice reserved only for adults' ears, "raping women and girls."

I saw Aunt Sự's blood-drained face and picked up from her conversation with Mom the bits of information that I did not fully understand. She said, "Mrs. Hoành's daughter—you remember, the youngest one—was raped and captured. She got the news this morning from some surviving members."

Desperate to leave, our parents had ignored all the bad news and surrendered to circumstance and fate. It began to dawn on them that death would be the better solution compared with losing their daughters to the pirates.

"If we leave again, I'll cut your hair short and blacken your face," Mom warned me.

We had lost a large amount of gold to the sea. It was a huge loss. Many times, I caught my mother letting out long, deep sighs. Her eyes were often distracted in her vacant face. To get her complete attention, we had to physically turn her chin toward us and repeat our words, which she impatiently waved off, painfully saying, "Do as you wish, I am occupied."

The "four musketeers" visited Aunt Sự's family to get away from the heavy atmosphere at home. With eleven members in her household, someone was always home to entertain us. Also, my aunt was a generous host. Her way to welcome us was to wave in a food peddler to her front door and treat us with a snack.

We stepped through my cousins' front door in search of warmth, food, and a laissez-faire atmosphere. We were given love, a shared meal, and a sense of belonging—a home away from home. All we needed to do was to shout, "Anybody home?" and the blind old maid would step out of her dark kitchen, shouting back, "Sisters and brothers, spare my old ears. I cannot see you well, but I can hear you, without your bellowing." She spoke with a small slur, with a heavy Northern accent, in the manner of country folks. We could not detect blindness from looking at her eyes. She did not have the damaged pupils of the blind beggar nor the empty sockets of the army veteran down the alley. When we told her so, doubting her self-diagnosis, she showed her rows of black teeth in a hearty laugh, then, staring at us, she said, "Ah! What good are my eyes? They were eaten by smoke and veiled with age." She was glad for our visit.

Bicycles filled one corner of the living room, leaning in one mass against the patio-sized doorframe. We bowed to our cousins' paternal grandma, whose shape, size, costume, and headgear reminded us keenly of our own grandmother, that same frail frame,

those teeth dyed black, those eyes fading to silver. Around the dining
table sat the rest of the family, chatting with one another. In the
mornings, our two youngest cousins, aged seventeen and thirteen,
attended school. The two older sisters, Điệp and Nga, had found a
teaching position in the suburbs, which did not pay much but kept
them decently occupied. Hùng and Cường, the two boys who had
been sent off with our family, returned to their idle lives inside the
home, periodically catching some quick business selling perfume or
watches or whatever else came their way. Their sons' failure to
escape the country disappointed my aunt's family. Like us, they had
lost a large sum to purchase a boat passage to freedom; but the boys'
safe return was their ultimate solace. Our youngest cousin, Yến-
Dung, was, of course, thrilled to see our faces again. Without her dear
partners in play, all her games would be pointless. What would she
do with her soccer ball if she were all alone, and who would be in her
newly formed rock-and-roll band? More important, who would chat
daily with her? With whom would she fib about having her laundry
done by the old maid, when in reality she was the one who bent
laboriously over the sudsy basin each afternoon? Once we found her
squatting, trying to mend the torn bottom of her pants while wearing
them. When asked, she coolly said, "I find it much easier to sew it in
the shape it's supposed to be."

Aunt Sự's home exuded such harmonious living. On the other
hand, all the adults at Mỹ-Hướng were at war with one another. Aunt
Huỳnh had isolated herself from us. If she spoke, it was to indicate
that we had left the light on late into the morning or to tell Mom,
"Thank you for the custard apple you brought back from the market
for me. But it upsets my stomach and is a waste of your money."

My parent's marriage, too, took a nosedive. For over twenty-
eight years, they had clung to each another in a symbiotic
relationship. Their opposite personalities and complementary
strengths worked like a pair of oars to propel their marriage. Mom
was practical but easily anxious; Dad was gifted with a good dose of
creativity, but his bloated ego kept him stagnant. Mom worked at
obtaining results. Dad put himself at the wheel to explore

possibilities. Mom's eyes focused on the road, while Dad's vision pierced beyond the present.

In 1980, the couple's marriage was, for the first time, truly tested; their oars, in a flowing river, worked in tandem, but in the turbulent whitewater—dodging boulders, confronting drops, swallowed by swift rapids—the pair began to have trouble with their coordination. They lost patience with each other. Their oars collided in midair when they instinctively shifted sides, and then when they overcorrected, their motion almost capsized the troubled boat. Mom could hardly repress her disdain for Dad's overconfidence even after the latest failure. She kept repeating herself, "You could have doomed this family with that kind of oversight."

"Do you think I did not measure the risk?"

"You told me the trip was well planned."

"It was."

"Was it? You loaded us on a riverboat to cross the ocean. Have you got no sense?"

"It was just bad luck. I relied on Captain Nam's judgment."

"Bad luck? You are plain foolish. Just jump headfirst at any opportunity without thinking."

"Fine. Let's stay here and rot."

"At least we live," Mom concluded, lines deepening on her face. She looked oppressed, exhausted. Dad's demeanor was no better. His hair had turned almost completely white and was unkempt. His untrimmed chin hairs did not grow any thicker, only longer. He had lost most of his body mass and stooped slightly. It was hell on earth to see them like this, wasting away, bickering at each other at the slightest provocation.

Dad learned to tune out Mom's daily complaints. Her verbal bullets bounced off him like the rubber kind, unable to pierce through. However, with time, we children noticed Dad's deliberate deafness was not faked but the manifestation of hearing loss. He regularly misheard us. We had the habit of relying on Dad's impressive knowledge of French vocabulary to find out the meaning of words we encountered when reading, instead of taking the time to consult our dictionary. We knew we had his full attention when we interrupted him with our vocabulary questions—Dad enjoyed helping us improving our knowledge and engaged himself fully. Yet, the words always came to him distorted.

One such day, I asked him, "Dad, what does *grenier* mean?"

His reply shocked me. "Rainy day? It's rainy today? Are you certain?"

It seemed that Dad did not realize his hearing had worsened. Perhaps, as always, he tried to downplay the seriousness of his symptoms. He might have thought that his willful tuning out had worked wonders in helping him avoid unnecessary quarrels with his wife, lately a tiresome, hissing cat. It was during this same period that I enjoyed Dad's companionship the most. I felt that, although not openly challenging Mom, he discreetly protected me from her abusive critiques. He praised me constantly. When I exercised in front of a mirror, he was the only one to notice my agility. We enjoyed the solitude of book reading and shared the same ecstasy at finding new reading materials. I read to him the long letters I wrote to my friends and, in turn, received his appreciative remarks with an intense pleasure, his positive encouragement for my writing talent. He used to tell me, "You are another Madame de Sevigné." Madame de Sevigné was well known for her extensive collection of beautiful letters.

I remembered coiling happily in his arms, hugging tenderly his protruded stomach, weaving with him colorful tapestries, phantasmal visions of beauty and wealth. I used to insist, "Dad, tell me again how we would live in America."

"Wonderfully."

"How wonderfully? Will you build a library for me?"

"One full with books, from floor to ceiling."

"Will Mom let you do it?"

"Why not? She will be too busy decorating the house to notice."

"Dad! Do you think my sisters and brothers are doing well?"

"Hồng-Mỹ! We will conquer the West with our talents."

Our daydream was often shattered by the approaching footsteps of Mom. She was again angry with both of us, and her words were often spiteful, full of poison and detestable insinuations. She was very much like our Grandma, old-fashioned in regard to girls' comportment. Seeing her husband and grown daughter napping together threw her into a fit. Her words reflected her state of mind. "Don't you feel ashamed of yourself, Hồng-Mỹ? For God's sake, behave properly." She felt left out, I thought. She would never understand why I was closer to Dad and preferred his company. I wanted to tell Mom, "It's only make-believe, our daydreaming. It's unrealistic but gives us the courage to go on." I had a half a mind to give her my nasty tongue-lashing—break the boundary for once and viciously rebuke her. But my spirit was still cheerful from our imaginary trip to the West. I "rolled my tongue seven times," swallowed my pride, and walked away. Dad feigned sleep and was soon snoring loudly.

Mom's anxiety mounted when our parents discussed their grownup children's next phase, marriage. Sister Mai was well settled. But sister Marie and brother Khải had yet to find a suitable spouse. Sister Mary was cautious with her choice and, so far, had been responsible in most aspects of her life. But Mom's eldest son, Khải— what would become of him? He had been a good son, too good for a man his age.

Many times, Khải's name entered my parents' conversation. In our family, he held the special title of *Trưởng Nam*, meaning *First Boy*. Vietnamese families treated their First Boy with an enormous respect even at a tender age. He would be responsible for his mother and family when the father passed away. In 1972, when Khải graduated from high school, fortitude and circumstance combined had lent Dad a hand to realize his American dream through his First Boy. Normally, Khải would have followed his sisters to France—an obvious choice since most students of the upper class were fluent in French. However, that particular year, the South Vietnamese government began to restrict students' access to European countries in favor of the United States. It would be prohibitively expensive, nearly impossible for our parents, already burdened with two daughters in

Europe, to afford the dollar amount required for Khải's tuition and living expenses in America. But there was no other option. It was either the USA or nothing.

Faced with the obstacle of his son's education, Dad saw instead a golden opportunity. He immediately enlisted the help of his younger brother, Uncle Mục. Ignoring his sister-in-law's undisguised irritation, Dad picked up Uncle Mục daily from his home and brought him to the Department of Education for further inquiries and explorations. Together, the brothers visited Uncle Mục's many friends in the university circle and other professors and veterans in the teaching profession. They explored many options and venues, listened to conflicting advice, cajoled assistants, even resorted to bribery to put Khải's name onto the student list to the USA. I cannot tell you the absolute truth about Khải's stroke of luck, whether the enlistment of Uncle Mục had helped Dad to obtain special recommendations for Khải, or whether the tricks were learned through the effective counseling of the professionals, who knew the education system well. I never knew whether it was through bribery that Dad had obtained the required paperwork for his son, or whether Khải's exceptional grades had earned him the full scholarship sponsored by Esso. My cousin Hiền-Minh, Uncle Mục's daughter, insisted that without her father's help, Khải would have languished in Vietnam. The accolades were therefore attributed to their brotherly love and mutual support. Dad assured me it was his position at Esso that had earned Khải the special scholarship to Harvey Mudd College in California to study electrical engineering. Of course, Khải had a pristine grade record, but then so did many other boys who were not among the selected scholarship recipients.

Good fortune continued to smile at Khải. He obtained a job with Westinghouse in Philadelphia, Pennsylvania, as soon as he finished his undergrad studies. He moved east, bought a house, and took over Mai's charge of the family back home. Thence began a weekly correspondence between the First Boy and his family, through a system of communication in which each letter was numbered, beginning with Letter Number One. This helped track missing letters, which we believed the government confiscated for spying. Being the First Boy, well employed, and still single, Khải was definitely in a better position to shoulder the family in the place of Mai. Thus, Mom could finally relax a little.

Dad's vision of our future in which the older children would help the younger ones, inspired by the famous character Frank Gilbreth of *Cheaper by the Dozen,* helped our family navigate through this difficult juncture of our life. Inwardly, Dad understood that this system would work for only a short time. In the longer run, he had to take his family out of the quicksand that day by day pulled down his family members, one at a time, into the constricting jaws of death. Time was running out. The typhoon season would return in a few months. Then, it would be impossible to navigate the Pacific Ocean.

Through Khải's many letters, we learned about his life in America. Dad was quite proud of his son's faithful reports, which read like a travel guidebook, with detailed news and weather excerpts. Khải traveled extensively throughout America, and a pad of lined paper seemed to be his most intimate companion. He wrote from each hotel, while flying, in between meals, at rest stops. The thorough letters depicted the many cities he visited, the mileage he covered between them, the altitude at which the plane flew, the size of each lake, and the height of each passing mountain. He wrote like an engineer, in exact words, presenting only the facts, omitting the dimension of his own soul. He was never sad, nor joyful, nor lonely, a constant applicant at his job, recording, taking careful notes.

Often, Mom would come to Dad with a statement, question-like, but we could already detect that all she needed from her husband was a confirmation, not an answer.

"Khải wrote often about some Mrs. Schwab?"

Dad was nonchalant. "She was his sponsor and landlady for a long time."

"He thinks too much about her. I don't like it."

Dad did not answer. But his next statement confirmed her anxiety. "I'll write to him. I'll remind him again about his duty to us, to his younger brothers and sisters. Our constant demand for assistance will keep him focused on the family."

Whatever had bothered Mom was now occupying Dad's thought. He became moody, almost unpredictable. Once, at the lunch table, Patrick's monkeying around seemed to irritate Dad. He told Patrick sternly, "Sit down and eat." Since Dad was usually a rather carefree person, Patrick did not pay too much attention to this command but continued to fool around with Michelle, stepping on her foot under the table and, since it did not seem to bother her, pulling the plate of fish away when Michelle tried to serve herself. Consequently, a large morsel of fish dropped on the floor. Dad's eyes narrowed, and he roared, "Pick it up." Patrick's laugh froze in his throat. He looked at Dad to verify his father's seriousness. Dad stood up, menacingly. "Pick it up, I said." Patrick complied promptly. Dad's next words came in staccato: "Put it in your mouth. Now." All of us held our breath while poor Patrick, shaken, but not completely convinced of Dad's new temper, slowly bent down and scooped up the bit of fish, unsure about what to do with it. He quickly nibbled it down when Dad's hand rose high above his head. "I said eat it. Eat, you . . . monstrous child." At this last roar, Dad dropped heavily on his seat, drained.

Multiple problems assailed our parents all at once. We were quite all right financially, with sufficient money and gold to pay for a boat passage to Thailand, which was all that mattered at the moment. Money, Dad often told us, would always be there as long as we were well educated. It was the loss of precious time that made Dad cringe when he looked at the four of us, innocent and wild, like galloping beasts. Our parents worried about Khải and his late affection for the Schwabs, although it was not clear if he had fallen in love with the mother or the daughter. Either was horrid. Both Daniel and Madeleine had failed their first session's examination and likely would have to repeat the third year of pharmacy school. To top it all off, Aunt Huỳnh had indicated that she would like to know when our family would vacate the house.

Aunt Huỳnh was our constant thorny issue. One would think that, being childless, she would love to have the company of children.

But no, our youthful restlessness bothered her greatly. She isolated herself most of the time in her living quarters, refused to eat with us, and repeatedly shunned our attempts to include her in our daily activities. At first, Dad paid little attention to his sister-in-law's antagonistic behavior. But in time, he grew to dislike her for her constant harassment of his family—her complaints about his children's boisterousness, his wife's messy housekeeping, his indecent walking around the house in boxer shorts.

It was time to hasten our next departure, despite the odds against us.

30.

Via Cambodia

Dad decided that we could travel by land to Thailand through Cambodia. The city of Tây-Ninh was fifty-five miles away, half a day's bus ride. From then on, it would only be a long trek across the borders, with assistance along the way.

Indeed, we arrived at the town square on a late August afternoon, when the slanting sunrays were still beaming through the sky. We were a conspicuous group of pale-skinned city dwellers in black outfits, shuffling around as lost and out of place as chickens by a duck pond. My instinct told me to act natural, but I did not see how I could blend in on such alien stage. We were definitely making a spectacle of ourselves, obviously at a loss for our next move. All we could do was to keep silent and wait for some signs, enduring the hot sun and the curious stares of the few motorists still lingering about with their empty rickshaws, waiting to see what we would do, perhaps waiting for us to use their service.

Everything seemed wrong to me, suddenly a Gulliver in a strange setting. I was afraid to look around for it might indicate that I was bewildered. I wanted to hide away my bundle of belongings. It was so small when I left home with it and now it seemed to have grown so bulky, like the gleaming Samsonite suitcases accompanying the Westerners when they descend on the town. I did not dare to flex my fingers, numbed from tightly clenching my bundle, for fear someone might notice how delicate and pale they were—the hand of a city girl with no business in this part of the country.

I anticipated the worst and admitted to myself that whatever was awaiting us could not be worse than what we had already experienced. But that made the apprehension even more unbearable, knowing beforehand the steps leading to another capture. I was distracted in the reliving of my previous jail time by the loud arrival of a motorcycle. Stepping down from the idling vehicle was a tall, dark man. He flashed his rows of straight teeth benignly, and I thought I was mistaken that he smiled at us. But he did and extended his right arm to pull Dad into an embrace, exclaiming, "Brother Khoa! Welcome!"

The exchange of warm and happy greetings dissipated my apprehension, but nonetheless appeared theatrical in our situation. I did not feel less like a chicken by a duck pond. The only difference was that we had a duck among us, and his familiarity with the locals was to us reassuring.

We followed his motorcycle on a hired, motored rickshaw through long, dusty streets to an isolated thatched house. The man's long shadow led us into the dark home, through a small entrance, and into a dirt-floored kitchen recognizable by the primitive clay stoves located in a corner, cold without their fire. From this small cookery, we fumbled deeper into the shadowy interior, which seemed uninhabited, for the scant light that filtered through the thick but imperfect thatched wall revealed no furniture. The place was as cold as a tomb, more deserted than a storage room without the comforting presence of inanimate objects to keep people company in their loneliest hours.

It turned out that two or three men and women, including one girl about Michelle's age, were already waiting inside. They sat so quietly in the dark, silent like mice, and started to stir only after they were sure who we were. We noticed their humble presence only after adjusting ourselves to the darkness and eerie quiet of the empty space. The hours passed and blended us into that space where neither action nor sound was detectable. We were one with the darkness and silence that seemed to annihilate us. Our waiting was itself the waiting hours, ticking, ticking by to eternity.

Night folded in quickly, draping its thick blanket over us. Soon it was pitch-black, in the thickness of which I could not see my own hands and had to hold them together to reassure myself that I still existed. With the night, its creatures arose along with the sounds they made. I became one myself, for my ears began detecting movements around me. Then other sounds became distinguishable. I heard the muffled voices of the adults, indistinct and breathy. Their clothes ruffled with each delicate movement. Someone dragged his feet on the dirt floor, moving slightly about. Now and then, over the low, two-tone croaking of frogs and the incessant chirping concert of crickets, a motorcycle roared past, like an arrow piercing the thick of night, leaving us in heightened suspense. And now and then a lone dog barked, starting a chorus of high and low barking and yelping.

Time had ceased.

Suddenly, there were movements outside. Could it be the long-awaited guide? I craned my neck, peering intensely into the darkness. The clicking sound of metal against metal was unmistakable. We froze. There were many people closing in. They cocked their triggers. I yanked my arm away from Dad's anxious grasp and stooped down on the floor, looking for a crevice, a corner, somewhere to hide. Or should I run?

"Freeze, or we shoot," was the command.

Someone burst out of the house, bolting hard and fast away. Dad pulled me upright. Softly, he said, "Don't. It's useless." They poured in with blinding torches, ordering in loud voices, "You are surrounded. Surrender or we'll shoot. You, kneel. You, kneel. Hands behind your back."

They surrounded all the men, handcuffed them, and led them in single file into the back of a closed truck. Then they grouped all the women and children together. We were loaded onto a separate truck and driven off into the night.

After about an hour, the vehicles stopped and we were ordered outside. They first led us women into a sort of storage room. I knew what to expect: the stripping of clothes, the minute search for precious stones, gold, jewelry, anything valuable. When they were satisfied, they led us, four women and three girls, marching in a long line, to the front of a high guard tower.

"Repeat after me," the young guard who accompanied us said. "Permission requested to enter the women's ward."

We performed like wooden puppets and were guided into a dirt-floor room with a high bamboo platform. There, we collapsed—cold, hungry, filthy. Although segregated, men and women were housed inside the same large, thatched structure. Two raised-wall panels separated the small women's ward, in which lived about a dozen women. The numerous men occupied an area three times larger. I could see their feet through the bottom of the raised walls.

A deep gong woke us at dawn. Through the opening of a small entrance between the two wards, I saw Dad sitting on a platform not far from us, his left foot now locked to a long metal bar with four other men. Not far from him, on a different platform, was Mr Sương, our guide.

Bound together to a rod, the men made their bathroom or shower trips as one giant caterpillar with ten legs and ten arms. A steely look on his face, Dad struggled to keep his movement in sync with his group. As he filed past, Mom gazed at him, lovingly, but I avoided his eye, sparing him the humiliation. Patrick was housed in a separate unit with Tenth Uncle, not too far from us. They were not in chains. We passed one another on our way to take baths or use the toilets. "The toilets," for lack of a better word, were bamboo planks raised like a scaffold. Four or five prisoners shared the platform at a time, squatting above the maggot-filled excavation, around six feet deep.

One huge faucet, looking almost like a fire hydrant, served the whole camp. Each morning, the women were let out before the men. We crouched around the running faucet to brush our teeth. Then, using a large can, we took turns filling the fifty-gallon drum inside the common bathroom to take a bath. We worked quickly so everyone could have her turn. The men were allowed only one draw of water each, and about five minutes time. They hurriedly showered in the open with their boxer shorts on before being called back in.

We returned to our cell, refreshed but starved. Breakfast was being prepared in the kitchen across from us. I inhaled the perfumed smell of the rice steam, ravenous. The cook called the three little girls out to give them the discarded boiled rice broth, which when mixed with a little sugar tasted like milk. The cooked rice was spooned into a small bowl, packed tightly, and the packed rice was thrown into a large basket for mass distribution. That was our meal ration, one pack of rice and some crude sea salt crystals.

As we became accustomed to the pace of life at Bào Cỏ Camp, we devised ways to help Dad. We could see that, clumsy and handicapped with his shackles, he needed assistance in the too-short bathtime alloted to each prisoner. Michelle, still looking like a young boy and allowed to roam around, ran over to bring Dad water for his washing. Mom yielded her portion of rice to Dad at each meal, and we women divided the three remaining portions among the four of us. Dad did not eat much either. But he used his extra rice to obtain help and services from other prisoners. At night, they taught him how to ready his foot cuff for inspection, keeping it loose enough so that he could wiggle his foot out of the chained bar at night.

Initially, we were all kept inside and forced to remain seated in silence. I learned to use the long seating hours for meditation and prayers. I also learned to nap seated. We spent part of our days killing the bedbugs that lived in the platform's bamboo slats. The pungent smell of crushed bedbugs was distinct. We soon called the other women by name. Madam Four traveled alone. She had sad, sad eyes. She could sit for hours, collapsed into herself like a sock doll that had lost most of its stuffing material.

Caboo was a Vietnamese-Cambodian girl about thirteen, traveling with her mom and her mom's lover, our guide. Caboo, a cheerful kid with tanned skin and bright eyes, spoke fluent

Cambodian. Anne and Michelle soon learned to sing a Cambodian song with Caboo.

Oh Sroaii chang tee
Nating own oil
Bat meen sa kha

My sisters sang without understanding. But the song made us feel good. Caboo was to us like a dew-filled flower in the desert.

One local girl was imprisoned for stealing from the government office where she worked. She never spoke a word. One day, they took her out for a whole day. And as months passed, her belly swelled up, her cheeks became flustered and filled.

"She looks pregnant," Hường whispered to Mom.

Hường was tall and shapely. She had a beautiful angular face, perfect straight teeth, and large eyes. She spoke with a melodious voice and seemed to have an easy way around the camp with all the men, guards and prisoners alike. She was not only good-looking but also smart and sharp. She could carry on an interesting conversation with one person while eavesdropping on another without missing a single word. She was fully alert, saying hello to each guard, to each prisoner by name; she knew how to flatter and stroke each person's ego. She lived in the same room with us, but it was as if she could see through the walls: she could tell us exactly who was sitting where and what happened on the men's side. I could see she had my mother's admiration. Mom asked her questions like, "Miss Hường, in your opinion, when are we going to be let out of this place?"

Hường wrinkled her cute nose, dispensing her wisdom: "Aunt Khoa, ah! You worry too much. There is time to scurry like rats, and time to relax and let God take care of us. Use this time to pacify yourself. Let me read your palm. See this line? It leads outward. You will live in strange lands. You will not stay here for long."

I followed their soft voices with interest. I was also attracted to this intelligent lady and her beauty. After her palm-reading session, Mom relaxed a little. Periodically, she would grasp the stick broom and pretend to clean the floor, using this opportunity to glimpse Dad through the rectangular opening. She would clear her throat loudly to let him know she was there, and he could furtively communicate to her how he felt, what he needed, soothing her with his smile and his well-being.

Since it was crowded and hot on the platform, Mom told us to sleep with our heads and feet alternating. I chose to sleep with my head toward the wall to take advantage of the fresh air from a small barred window. One night, I had the sensation of being observed and woke to see a pair of eyes glinting from outside. The eyes quickly disappeared as I lifted my head in alarm. In the morning, I told Hường about it. She relayed to me in low voice, "Men . . . could be anyone . . . the cook, a guard . . . . They are craving the touch of a woman. It happened to me, too. That's why I sleep head in. They tried to fondle me once."

My eyes almost popped out of my head. I could only dimly understand what Hường said about the hunger of the flesh, about what drives men, about how men view women. No, a woman's pretty face or feminine manners are not what men are after. It is something else. She laughed mockingly. "Enough said. You will learn as you grow up." I thought long about this revelation and puzzled over it all the years to follow. It was not the way I had comprehended love through reading literature and poetry. It was not about eyes capturing eyes and longing hearts but something very base, the lurking of animals looking for meat. I told Mom we needed to switch places, and I would sleep head in. She could have all the fresh air she wanted. I left Mom with no alternative, although I knew full well she preferred to keep her head warm. She could sacrifice her health, I thought, but I would not be used as an object of lust.

Hunger gnawed at us constantly. We could hardly wait for the morning for a cup of the sweet rice drink. Sometimes, a miracle happened. The cook slipped one drizzling morning while carrying out his big basket of rice and dropped a few packs onto the muddy floor. Our six pairs of eyes were glued on those mud-stained rice balls, waiting. Would he pick them up? Would he let them go to waste? The cook decided to let go of the lost portions. Michelle darted out as soon as she was able to and quickly picked up the extra portions of food. I felt so ashamed, but I was too hungry to refuse her offer. We wiped the mud off and ate heartily, glad to have a snug belly.

As the weeks passed, we joined the other prisoners outside to work, clearing the weeds, picking up debris, etc. One morning, Mom and we girls were called out to receive visitors. There, through laughter and tears, we met Aunt Trọng and Aunt Sự, ladened with supplies for us. We quickly exchanged news and were reassured that everybody was fine back home. Aunt Huỳnh still had her house. That night, we spread out the newly received plastic sheets to protect us from the bedbugs and slept blissfully. Somehow, knowing that someone out there was caring for us kept our spirits up. Mom nurtured Dad with bits of sugar and salty pork. I was glad for my pack of sanitary napkins. I had been using my own underwear as pads, folding them into strips and washing them after each use.

Soon, they transferred us to a larger camp with more than a thousand prisoners. We lived in a two-story structure, enjoying the novelty of climbing to the upper bunks. A large proportion of the prisoners here were Cambodians, captured while fleeing the Khmer Rouge into Vietnam. We listened to the horrific tales of mass killings. Many women, and many young girls my age who were among us in the camp, had dug their own graves and were shoveled in live. By the grace of God, they survived the ordeal and crawled back out, scraping their way south.

Mom paled when she heard their stories.

"I didn't know," she stammered softly. "We could have been there. Oh God! A massacre."

31.

The Octagonal Oven

Shortly before Christmas 1980, about three months after our capture in Tây-Ninh, our family was transferred to Chí-Hòa, Hồ Chí Minh City's massive prison—widely known as Hỏa Lò Bát Giác, the Octagonal Oven. We were crammed into the back of a military truck and its tailgate was latched with a sonorous *clang,* reducing us to mere human cargo inside an induced darkness, the projection of our own hopelessness.

What sort of place is awaiting us? What are they going to do to us? For how long? Those were the questions in my mind while, hands clutching the barred gates, I struggled for space and a rising claustrophobia. For the moment our family was together and that was all that mattered. I hung on to that precious brightness and was grateful for it. It was my gatekeeper, raising its shield where anxiety attacked, preserving me.

A sense of foreboding weighed down upon all the jail mates. Our collective silence was crushing. We kept our brooding to ourselves and buckled down to our changing fates. The transfer of prisoners back to Hồ Chí Minh City was what we feared most after our recent capture but thought we could have avoided it. This time, we had the experience and adeptness of wild animals that had been once trapped, that knew the ways of the hunters but had to risk the hunt again to keep alive. We had given our interrogators false information about ourselves: where we lived, whether it was our first time breaking the laws, our motivations, our ages—all the best possible answers in the hope of a shorter jail stay. Having learned that seniors would be released promptly, Mom and Dad declared themselves to be fifty-five and sixty years old. They looked aged. Dad's hair was now dominantly silver, and Mom's worries etched deep lines on her forehead. People said a woman's age showed on her hands. The backs of Mom's hands were shriveled like Grandma's, her nails yellowed and cracked. We children reduced our ages by two years. This precaution was mostly to keep me safely underage so that, if asked why I tried to escape, I could say I was following my parents.

But this time, we were out of luck. This time, the local authorities in our native city had our civic details. This time, we would be dead fish, hooked and soon clubbed.

The ride to the most notorious prison in Saigon ended too soon. My legs began to hurt from the hour-long standing, but I would rather go on standing. My heart began to pound when the gate that separated us from the prison ground was unlatched with the same *clang*, but this time, the sound made my blood curl. I could not stop myself from visualizing the axe coming down and a head rolling, rolling like a ball, with its eyes still wide open, beads of perspiration dampening the forehead.

I was not yet ready to face the next phase of our ordeal; the Octagonal Oven was the most secure, forbidding prison of the Southland. It was here that many generations of political prisoners had been brought to die under different regimes. It was a bloody place, a death trap, a place of no return.

It was hard to remember in detail what I first saw, or heard, once we stepped out of the stuffy truck. I hadn't enough time to formulate my thoughts and be mentally prepared for the adversities ahead of me.

I was high-strung, watchful, and sickened with apprehension about the upcoming series of interrogations. What would I tell them? Would I be tortured? As I was internally debating what to say, my preoccupied mind registered the high, thick concrete wall, topped with barbed wire. From the highly secured parking lot, we were led from one area to the next, passing through long, damp, and dark corridors. Each corridor was enclosed between two heavy metal gates, rusted with time, which the guard opened with a key from his large bundle. Each gate was closed behind us with a sinister clank that followed us down the passageway and reverberated between the walls. Each was carefully locked as we moved deeper inside. In the corridors, the ceiling was arched high and filled with cobwebs. The floor was inlaid with heavy masonry stones. Our footsteps echoed back and forth, simultaneously amplifying and multiplying to create an illusion of an invisible foot army. Perhaps many had gone through these passages before us and had perished; their ghosts might still be around, mourning. Finally, we arrived in front of a similar corridor, this one filled with people. The stone-faced guard unlocked this gate, too, but stayed behind while he let us in, deaf to the inquiries of little children, blind to the lives unfolding inside, perhaps hurrying a little to hasten away from the emanating stench.

We were left surrounded by a train of people, stretching far into the open tunnel. Stepping over bodies and bags, we moved down to the other end of this final corridor to compose ourselves, and there to claim our spot by a steel barrel and a small plastic bucket. Once here, we understood why the other prisoners had huddled far away. The barrel served as a large dumpster and the bucket a makeshift toilet, screened simply with a torn bamboo mat, loosely covered by a sheet of plastic; the flies swarmed up from it thick like black beads, still wet with the content of the oozing mass.

We had no choice but to carve out a place for us to settle down, not too far from the offensive buckets. As always, people started to inquire about us, the usual questions. Where were we apprehended and how long had we been held, etc. A woman, in the process of taking her trash down to our end, stopped short and exclaimed, "But it is Madame the Pharmacist." Mom looked away uncomfortably, but there was no escaping this recognition. The woman was sincerely happy to see Mom. Murmuring, the two reacquainted neighbors exchanged information, each trying to extract more data from the other and divulge little of her own.

"I thought your family had settled in the West. You left a long time ago."

"No, not really," Mom fibbed. "We just moved into our sister-in-law's house to take care of her."

"So, when did you leave? Which route?"

"Uh . . . a few weeks ago."

Sensing Mom's reservation, the lady squeezed Mom's hand and said, "Don't you worry. We are in this together."

Mom gave her a smile that looked like a grimace. Her reply was polite and distant: "I thank you for your kindness."

The conversation veered toward the next subject, more relevant to us. Mom asked, "Are we going to be here for long?"

"No, a few weeks only." I was encouraged for a moment, but my gift was taken brusquely by the interlocutor's next phrase: "This is only a temporary holding place until they finish interrogating you. Then you'll be transferred into a real cell. But hurry to get ready for the bath time."

The minute the gate swung open, the women and children poured out like chickens held too long in a pen. Towels on their shoulders, soap and toothbrush in their plastic cups, jugs to carry back water, they chattered as they hurried toward their goal, their moods lightened as if anticipating a street gala. I, too, pushed forward, sensing in the air the importance of our early arrival.

I could not believe my eyes when we reached the bathing area. The scenery was beyond imagination, even for me, who thought she had experienced enough. I had never seen so many naked women in one area. It was shocking! So many breasts exposed and not one person was concerned to be caught this way in public. In between two concrete walls—one was the back wall of another female ward, very high, with barred windows on top, with a multitude of shower heads spilling forth sprays of fresh water, and the opposite lower wall, erected to keep the bathers shielded from the adjacent central courtyard—the women, heads tilted back, offered themselves with delight to the cool jet of water, scrubbing themselves frantically, trampling the clothes at their feet, simultaneously rinsing off soap from their hair and body and washing their clothes. Another line of inmates was already waiting with soap and shed clothes, brushing their teeth busily. People with some conscience vacated their bathing area as soon as they could, while those still lingering were hurried off by the next person in line. Everyone was frantically occupied, too absorbed to notice my horrid stare.

Here, time was of the essence. I quickly realized that when the bathing time was up, the prison guards would not give anyone a minute more. Whether your mouth was still foaming with toothpaste or your body half-washed, the inmate would be marched back to her ward.

Mom was already stripped down to her underwear, but I was still trying to figure out how to disrobe without showing myself. As I hesitated, I heard many voices and the spraying sound of multiple showerheads behind the tall wall. It seemed that behind that concrete wall were other women, also taking part in the cleansing rituals. I hurriedly took off my blouse, turning to the low wall as I exposed myself. My sister Anne, her breasts budding like all fourteen-year-olds, would not be influenced. She took her shower with clothes on, scrubbing underneath the fabric of her clothes and then over it, and thus, rinsing the soap off her covered body and washing her laundry in one act.

An older woman walked around with her sagging breasts, obviously admiring each person and commenting, "Beautiful melons you've got there!"

She must be "cuckoo" in her head, I thought, moving away from her.

Michelle pulled on my arm. "Did you look beyond the wall?"

I looked. My God! I understood, then, why this prison was dubbed the Octagonal Oven. Open in front of me was the central court, a sort of Roman arena, spacious and deserted. Our shower was in one aisle of the ground floor of a massive octagonal building encircling the central court. There were a number of floors. I tried to count the levels but somehow couldn't, confused by the façade of air-holed bricks that made the structure into one giant birdcage, with iron pales. Hanging thick on the cage were bats, perhaps monkeys. No—I rubbed my eyes. They couldn't be human. They were. Thousands upon thousands of skin-clad skeletons with shaved heads in place of skulls, whitish and ghostly, were hanging on the iron bars. Eight to ten floors of silent, unmoving corpses laid out to dry in the sun.

I cowered. "What are they? Why are they there?"

A woman answered me, taking no heed of the offensive tableau, "Male prisoners. They're there sunbathing and why not, feasting their eyes."

I imagined Dad and Patrick clinging on that cage. No! It was impossible. Did they not have their dignity? "You have no choice when it comes to life," someone explained. "It's survival. People don't only need water and food; sunlight is as important, or your skin breaks down. With men, watching nude bodies is as vital. It keeps them alive."

My stomach formed a tight knot. I felt nauseous. I could not bear to look at the zoo enclosure and its human display. Suddenly, I needed to wash this dirty feeling off: rub myself with soap, get rid of the grime on my clothes. Scrub away the stubborn stains.

It was about time: The line had formed for the return trip.

Within three days, we were through with the interrogations. Excluding Anne and Michelle, each grown individual in our group was taken up by turn. I was surprised to face a young administrator in civilian clothes instead of a uniformed man. This person was clean-shaven, modern looking. He was sensibly dressed in a well-pressed shirt tucked inside his trousers. Like a scholar. He addressed me politely in a pleasant, soft tone, calling me *em*, the equivalent of "little miss," and other than very innocuous questions, let me go about my confession.

I had been bullied for answers, stripped and searched by brutal hands. This time, I was treated almost civilly. He was the teacher, I the student called up to answer for my bad behavior. Suddenly, I gave up pretending. I remembered who I was, and the golden rule: honesty always pays. Across the table I saw his gentle countenance. And I lifted my false cloak, revealing to him who I was and which background I came from, wishing with all my heart he'd see me as I was, a good and honest girl. I told him plainly and frankly that, yes, I had lied about my age and was actually two years older, eighteen instead of sixteen.

"I believe you. You are a brave girl." He nodded gently. "Anything else you wish to share, little miss?"

My eyes widened, seeking the mercy in his soul, trying to connect. "Nothing else!"

I left with a strong conviction of his humanity, imagining his perplexed gaze as I walked out of his office.

A few weeks after, we were moved into a permanent cell, facing a yard. There were five such holding cells side by side, each full of women. They were identical concrete boxes with one metal door containing a small window. My cell was the size of a classroom, with a concrete floor, thick wall, and high ceiling. There was a single barred opening in one of the walls, through which a bit of sky was showing.

Inside my cell were some thirty women, a few of them with shaved heads and ghostly pale skin. All were hungry for the news from the outside world. They posed naïve questions such as, "What month of the year are we in?" or "What currency is being used?"

We were relieved to finally face these inmates. Not one of them matched the violent descriptions we had heard from the people in the corridors. Perhaps, like us, they had been ignorant of their new environment and were projecting their fear onto phantom creatures.

Somehow, we managed to find a small space for the four of us, which was fortunately not too close to the little shower room and far enough from the toilet stall raised on a concrete platform. We rolled out our plastic sheet on the concrete floor, an act equivalent to a dog's spraying his urine, in order to stake out our corner.

As the days stretched on with their prison routines, we blended in, grateful for the simple things that life brought with each rising sun. We were not so different from the majority of women in that cell. Originally from different walks of life, with the exception of a few real criminals, we were committed to this prison for the same crime—illegal border crossing. Our goal for the time being was simple: to survive and go home.

We also knew that home, eventually, was only a rest station. Most of these woman inmates would again abandon the safety of their home to seek freedom beyond their country's borders.

"My husband was waiting for us. He left a year ago," a woman confessed to Mom, smoothing the hair of her little girl, a younger version of herself.

We were no different from the houseflies that hurled perpetually toward the burning lamp. I used to watch them, fascinated by their suicidal dashing toward the light source, watching their sizzled bodies dropping on the floor. Not one stayed alive.

I met many types of women, all courageous and self-sustaining, each fighting for preservation in her own way, each a personality shining through despite her effort to remain anonymous.

One particular criminal stood apart in my memory. Sister Huệ had a smooth shaved head, no eyebrows, and the sun-starved look of a long-term captive. She had been inside the Octagonal Oven for over five years, serving her time for murder. Her right wrist was shackled to her left ankle, but she moved gracefully, showing off her slender calf with each small stride, jingling her metal fastener more like an adornment. Her dark eyes were always shining and penetrating, betraying the independent and rebellious spirit of their owner. Hearsay was that this beautiful nymph used to be a notorious gang leader on the streets, and her uncontained furor over some lost territories had resulted in the killing of a fellow gang member. The months that I spent alongside this hippie-looking queen, with her life-embracing smile and large, serene eyes, did not help to convince me of her hideous crime. Such a fanciful tale seemed more to enliven the imaginations of the forsaken women who languished in this overpopulated dungeon, whose minds had ceased to properly register the passage of the seasons and the boundaries between reality and induced awareness.

A few weeks' stay had smoothed our daily navigation of the new environment. Except for an hour of sunbathing daily in the yard in front of our compound, we were locked inside. The meals were delivered to our door three times a day and, infrequently, gift packages came for the inmates from their families. We were back to square one, new inmates without any outside connection. We would have to wait until our relatives found out for themselves that we were no longer at the other jail.

The short time spent outdoors became the more precious for my mother. She had discovered—or believed so—that Dad and Patrick were located on the upper floor opposite us.

"Look carefully," she instructed us girls one day, not pointing to the object faraway but fixing her eyes in that direction. Our eyes followed her gaze to the other side of the courtyard, scanning upward.

"See Dad's boxers hanging there to dry? Only he has those multicolored shorts."

I did not see anything like that. How could she see so far across, and with those iron pales limiting the view? She was so excited, almost happy, as if she was the tethered string and those boxers up there were her kite, lifting her up above towns and mountains and seas. From then on, my mother had her morning ritual; Dad's boxers were her daily news broadcast. When they were there, all was fine. When she could not locate them she went berserk, wondering, obsessing.

For me, it was another event that brought me solace. A Chinese inmate, a middle-aged woman large and jovial like Buddha, befriended me with food gifts, sometimes a bean cake, other times a sugary drink. I believed she favored my Chinese demeanor. Maybe I reminded her of a daughter sent abroad with whom she had failed to rejoin.

As I began to feel comfortable with my jail mates, even with sister Huệ, as I dismissed my uneasy feelings about the Octagonal Oven, an event shattered my false sense of safety. A howl woke us up one night—strident, piercing, woeful—the cry of a wounded animal. We listened to determine the nature of this shriek, wild yet human-like, the sound of somebody in deep pain, then all was silent again. In the morning, the mysterious sound became the topic of conversation in every group. As they socialized on different mats, a terrifying rumor spread. It was indeed a woman's agonizing cry for help. Such occurrence was not rare at Chí-Hòa, a place of unimaginable deeds.

Sister Huệ laughed deviously as she relayed a tale from her own experience.

"Love spat," she said. "Someone pays for her dilly-dallying."

In her words, it was, after all, only a crime of passion. I listened in. The other women gathered around Huệ, who sat with her top off, her breasts peeking out through her hand gestures. She was like a queen with her circle of attendants, a tale-weaving Scheherazade. She painted in my mind another foggy world within the thick walls of our prison, the underworld of female inmates, where the smoke of time had transformed friendly affection into passion. In this strange new world, the women possessed one another, forming pairs, tying knots. These couples were like husbands and wives, "slept" with each other, meaning . . . . Oh! I was so hot with curiosity. What did she mean by this word, "Sharing bed?"

Huệ's lips were moist and red. She looked possessed—a mischievous smile dawning.

"I had a lover once. Someone took her from me." A dark mood rose and steeled her face. There was now a new meanness, visibly vicious. She bared her teeth like a wolf.

"She cheated on me. Like that bitch last night." Her fist closed. It held up a corner of her blanket. "I slashed her throat."

In my ears sounded that animal howl, silenced by a sharp piece of metal. I backed away from the nymph with the chains around her wrist and ankle. She still did not look monstrous enough for me to hate her, but she had intimidated me with her mysterious transformation.

The cheater always paid; her cry smothered by a thick blanket. Most acts of vengeance went undetected until it was too late to rescue the victim. Some were murdered, others disfigured for life, unable to even identify the perpetrator. Huệ's shining eyes revealed to me a much darker side of her personality. Haunted by this vision of being muffled and raped or murdered inside a blanket, I was thankful to have family with me.

Day after day, we woke pondering our fates. None of us had an exact idea of when she would be "pardoned" to go home, or where she would be sent next or for how long. Through that window, on many sleepless nights, I saw a different darkness gather outside, separate from the darkness inside the cell.

In the daytime, through that opening, I could hear the sounds of the kitchen staff working their shift, moving their huge pots around, banging on these vessels with utensils. The aroma of steamed rice and boiled vegetables reminded me of Chị Ba's kitchen.

Beyond that window was an open sky, stars at night and birds and free people in the day; beyond it was life—its sweet pace lengthened, spanning the weeks, the months, the years to come without us.

I fought my nighttime phobia, learning to dissociate from my paralyzing fear by swimming into a place of sunshine, traveling with my mind back to Tân Sa Châu, my old home, where safety and love resided. This practice extinguished all thought of fire or calamity, calming me, easing me through another night. I learned to call up that sacred place of happiness in my most desperate moments.

Right before New Year 1981, Anne and Michelle were summoned away. We were told they were being released to the care of a relative who had come for them. Who came for them? We soon found out. That same afternoon Mom and I received a bag of food and basic supplies, with this note in Patrick's handwriting: "The three of us send our love. Patrick, Anne, and Michelle."

Once again, I was alone with my mother, alone under her sole protection. At the same time, I was the only one left now to protect her. There would be no one else to compete with me for her attention, but by the same token, there would be no one else to distract my mother's mind. The hardships that we endured in the last few years had changed many aspects of our lives and had lowered our expectations, making us humbler, more realistic. However, the forced alteration did not smooth the ill-matching seams of our basic characters.

Mom was, at her core, an indomitable mother, rigid like an oak. Her large, embracing umbrella extended to shade the whole family. She stood upright, shielding us from the storms of life, withstanding the barbarous foes, rooting her courage firmly in the ground of love, extracting the necessary nutrients from the scorched soil to yield for her family a cooling canopy. In my yearning for independence, her embrace, her vigilant protection, intending to protect us from harm, felt stifling at the same time. Her canopy was too large, and the view underneath it limited.

Mom's femininity was not soft, nor tender, but resilient, yielding only to the demands of her own family. Uptight and conventional, she would not allow her daughter to befriend her maid's daughter, fearing she would acquire the unpolished habits of the servile class. But also a daring and practical social being, she would wear her husband's briefs if that meant comfort or parade around town in the ridiculous large-pocketed shirts that she had sewn herself for the convenience of ample storage. She was too pragmatic to believe in her fellows' goodwill.

At one point, in their desperation to save us, our parents had thought of sending us ahead of them, one after another, with an escape group, as chances arose. The opportunity came for me when my sister Madeleine wrote from France about a Swiss fellow, who had agreed to help me get out of Vietnam through a *mariage blanc*. Mom was at first elated, but she finally opposed it. In her bleak vision of this philanthropist's proposal, she saw only her daughter in an enslaving and exploitative marriage with a total stranger, a fate worse than living a slow death. No, she said to Dad, we would either survive or perish this ordeal together but would not separate.

I, however, was a hopeless romantic and idealistic, a pine arching away from the familiar slopes of the alpine heights. Although I was as inflexible as my mother and as obsessive in pursuing what I valued, our objects of devotion had been oddly different from the start. The umbrella that my mother held high above my head was to me an obstruction to the expanse of life that I aspired to be exposed to, whether it rained or shined. Where my mother disdained, I explored. Where she found quality, I dismissed with contempt. She cautioned me not to be naïve. I labeled her with cynicism. The fact that my choice caused my mother discomfort convinced me that it was worth my investigation.

In terms of career and marriage, we were butting heads. She boiled my blood talking about "choosing among social equals" and "following where money leads."

Through my adolescent years, Mom and I were pulling on opposite ends of a rope, two cats similar in our feline outlook but one bearing the soul of a tiger, longing for the freedom of her own forest. Confined together, we struggled to live together harmoniously. Here I was, suddenly, the protector of my protector. Mom relied on me for security, an anchor to her familiar seabed. At night, she slept with her feet wrapped around me. For heat, for space, or for physical love, I could not say.

But her nightly clinging feet irritated me. I felt trapped under her new emotional demand, which I could not translate. I had grown up unaccustomed to physical forms of intimacy with my mother. Her embrace was to me a torture that I could not reject for fear of hurting her feelings. I was extremely uncomfortable with my proximity to her. In my knowledge of Mom, I sensed her changing, a letting down of a barrier that was her essence, a barrier that made her the mother I feared but had grown used to. The gradual loss of her proud aloofness caused me to shrink from her attempts to reveal to me her truest feelings regarding our relationship. Her newly acquired vulnerability was to me strange and unnerving. I was unable to respond to her distress call. All I felt was the humility of her new weakness. I raged silently at her breakdown. Her nightmarish cries woke me up, trembling and concerned. I fiercely wanted to protect her, to prevent her from further degrading herself by deserting her last fortress, her dignity, even at a time when we all subsisted like caged animals, waiting impatiently for mealtime, fighting for a bigger or better morsel.

I wanted Mom to be that same upright oak, although it had been hacked at. I wanted to be that same pine, growing on some terrain distant from her. The awkwardness of this sudden intimacy and emotional dependence, where I was forced to be the oak and my mother, shamefully, a vine to the pine, confounded my long-held view of our relationship, making it as suffocating as the four walls of the prison. I lived on guard—to be responsive to my mother's needs, but at the same time to shake off her panicked grip on me. I took care of her dutifully but never tenderly.

The day my mother was released from the prison was a great relief for both of us. A guard came to open the cell door in the late morning after we had all come back from the precious daily hour of sunbathing. Only Mom's name was called and, for a moment, we both were suspended in fear. Our companion, Hường, the inmate transferred with us from Bào Cỏ Camp, was summoned in the same way, her name called and she was led out without any explanation, only to be sent to solitary confinement in a steel box for a crime we did not understand.

But that minute of horror passed quickly when the order came clearly, "Pack up to go home."

Mom did not even pack up. She left everything for me. She did not utter a word, did not even question why I was not being discharged with her. It was as though we had understood all along that this day would come, that I would be the one paying time for the rest of the family, the one being sacrificed. She left with a large smile, hastily, stumbling on her feet, without a word, without saying goodbye, without counseling me.

I grew suddenly—an upright pine, her clinging vine severed from me and with it, my life's shade—alone for the first time in eighteen years to fend for myself on my own strength.

With my mother safely home, I felt somehow liberated, free to act upon my instinct. The consequences of my actions would now reflect solely upon myself, independent from the rest of the family.

Most of us "escapees," who were not pardoned for the New Year, knew we would not be home for a long time and had mentally prepared ourselves to be sent into forced labor.

In the meantime, the earth had turned a full cycle around its sun, and the moon many times around its earth. The cosmic dance of the universe had not stopped to ponder the fates of this tiny population of women inmates, nor had it slackened the pace of time, although the leaps and bounds of the weeks had long ceased to make a difference. We braced for the upcoming events of our life journey, turning to our faith for strength, to our families for the will to survive, to our hope for a better future as reward. Meanwhile, the bad spirits of the previous years had to be swept off to welcome Luck, Health, Success, and myriad other Good Spirits that would come with the Year of the Rooster.

The preparation for the New Year gave us a festive diversion. We used our idle time to elaborate and work on our fanciful ideas about the upcoming celebration. There was never a question about whether celebrating was a deluding act. How to assemble a sumptuous meal was what intrigued us. We agreed that we would celebrate like one big family, with everyone sharing what she had and everyone working. But how would we find meat, noodles, vegetables enough for all? Where would we find the necessary tools to work with? How could we bake without flour, spice without condiments, chop, dice, mince without knives?

Ah! Only in dire circumstances does the human spirit triumph over its indifferent environment. From dust we came, to dust we return, but not without some valiant resistance to remain. All we had was the time in our hands, and our goodwill. But time is all that God ever grants that speck of dirt to rule over its garden. And it's up to that dust, in that allotted time, to accomplish and leave its monuments.

Between the four walls of our confinement, with the minimum subsistence —rice, salt, water, and some sunlight, we created our New Year's feast. First, we sent word through the prison's underground system that we wanted to borrow knives and sewing needles. Inside the high-secured Chí Hòa, these rare commodities were always available for purchase or loan.

Metallic or glass objects were routinely smuggled in through the checkpoints by various means: hidden inside other objects, or through underhanded dealings with corrupt guards. Any simple piece of metal or glass, even ceramic or heavy plastic, could be made into a useful tool. Wood handles could be easily attached to these simple blades and turned into full-sized knives by a skilled craftsman. When found in the routine raids, the objects were confiscated and destroyed, their owners sent to confinement or hard labor. But the need for knives prevailed; the business of knife smuggling was necessary to supply poor or drug-craved inmates with cash and the inmates with sharp tools.

The Octagonal Oven transformed me. Nothing was impossible in order to survive. Even inside this place, the business of living went on, requiring money, tools, fire, and love. I became an avid student of the penal system, learning by doing.

We set to work.

With needles (made of bamboo sticks) and twine, we sewed together the torn plastic bags that were once used for food storage into larger mats and used these to mash our rations of rice. These, in turn, were sweetened and shaped into squared rice cakes or transformed into other rice-based dishes or soup. The few people with privilege to work outside the cell would return with herbs and vegetables, planted once by other prisoners and now proliferating. Curiously, we discovered among these leaves some type of wild grass jellies that, when pulped and mixed with a small amount of toothpaste and sugary water, produced an excellent cool jelly drink. Meat dishes sent in by our relatives were pooled and shared.

We temporarily rise above our pettiness. Inspired and urged by some mysterious call, we cast aside our differences, insecurities, and animal competitiveness, for the sake of our race: to celebrate not only the arrival of a brand-new moon but also our unity as beings, our temporal camaraderie in bondage, our grace in abject misery.

The same drive that had elevated our ancestors above the other animals propelled us forward. With the same ingenuity, we conquered our environment and coerced rocks to ignite fire in our hearts, convinced the blunt objects around us that they were spears, hammers, axes.

The Octagonal Oven was feverish with its yearly theatre production, a singing folk opera of Southern style called *cải lương*. We were left guessing and anticipating, our excitement mounting with the approach of New Year's Eve. When it finally arrived, the guards let us out into the central courtyard. We sat on the cold floor, encircling an imaginary stage where the big show would take place. This was the only time in my life I witnessed an assembly of this magnitude. It involved the whole prison, totaling almost ten thousand people forming a massive wall, rising from the central court to the roof level of the Octagonal Oven. We did not look human—more like ghosts, the wrecked souls of a gigantic ship, traveling an ethereal sea. In the gathering darkness, I could only distinguish the whites of the prisoners' eyes, flashing moth-like with the tilts of heads and reflecting the shine of the new moon. Their voices, at times, were as hushed and indistinct as the whisper of leaves; at other times rising in notes of acclamation, or deep like the sound of a gong, piercing and pulsing through the cool evening air.

When the actors and actresses appeared in their elaborate costumes, magically transformed, the animated stage was a vision. Look at the sparkling crown the haughty queen bore. Was it once just wild vines, broken twigs, and field flowers? How gracious were her movements. How colorful and exquisite was her costume. But look closely. Was it not just newspaper dyed simply, painted red with Mercurochrome, pasted green with leaf extracts, and stained with the juice from wood bits?

We cried out when our queen swooned into the arms of her strong hero, a bare-chested peasant with a simple dark garment, whose shoulder was symbolically wrapped with the checkered kerchief of the proletarian class.

It was love that triumphed over all, tragic love that transported us, prison staff and prisoners now the same passionate beings, into another place infused with pain as real as ours, with love buried and now uncovered, courage deserted and momentarily regained. Love reached into the crevices of our emotional chambers, bringing tears to adolescent eyes and hardening the jaw of the lost male souls clinging like apes in that hellish tower.

The Octagonal Oven faded away to that shining jewel in the central court. We forgot our own breath in front of the vision created to again taste the struggles of a normal life with its normal struggles. When the heroine finally collapsed, her heart perforated by the shining sword of her noble king, thirsty for blood and power, we all seemed to collapse with her, our hearts bearing intense hatred for that ignoble member of the royal class. When she was carried lifeless from the stage, the magic was suddenly dispersed like dust and our shackled life resumed, with its burdens.

We retraced the steps back to the four walls of our cell, crying silently for home. When the midnight fireworks burst outside, I woke from my sleep to the illuminated sky, framed by the plastered work of men, searching among my mates for the trace of a queen.

Slaves, arise! Catch your magic while the Spirits are exchanging thrones! The doors of heaven are ajar! In the name of the Father, the Son, and the Holy Spirit, watch upon my soul.

32.

Dufong Island

This was it! The uncertainty was now a fact confirmed. My fear, vague and formless until this minute, had taken shape. I had arrived to this place to meet my fate, to regain my life or to die. And it would be a long time before our meeting would conclude—a very long time.

My instincts were on alert. I scanned the new territory like a trapped rabbit, registering—recognizing and learning—sorting out the predators by their colors and shapes, by the sounds they emitted. In the air was an earthy smell and laced to it, the scent of the wilderness, of tree bark, leaves, grass. The sky stretched like an ocean until the far horizon came up to it; still in my eyes the sky was immense, and I so small and defenseless.

In front of me was the wooden entrance to the camp, gateless, with a large sign: "Welcome to the Polytechnic School of Industrial and Agriculture Đồng-Phú." The name had such a fanciful ring to it that it soothed the agony in the pale prisoners' hearts, who just arrived by the truckload. Typical tactic! Who could they fool? But did I not breathe a little easier at the flowing letters, captured by the word "Welcome?" I had to force myself to reconcile with the reality, that this—despite the gateless entrance, despite the blue sky, despite the idyllic greenery around me—was but an imitative Russian gulag, a re-education camp, a place for punishment and reform.

There! It was done. I had steeled myself. I was ready to take my first step into Đồng-Phú, going where I had to go, fighting when I had to put up resistance. I would not think too much ahead, but step by step would come to meet my destiny and see for myself what was reserved for me.

No one expected to depart from this place quickly, unless to be carried out in a coffin. I had no misgiving about my current fate. But, being young and hopeful, I was determined to face my new situation with strength, if not with courage, "a hero born of difficulties."

I had no option.

* * *

"You're well?" she asked, adding a teasing scold. "Hey, do not mess with my old gate. It keeps me safely inside at night so you don't have to hunt me down."

Her impertinence did not bother the young guard. He laughed. "That kind of talk will bring you trouble with someone else." Then, pointing to me, he changed the subject. "You have a new camp resident."

She chattered on. "I got three new last week. We have no more room in here. Why don't you bring her to Fifteen?"

"Fifteen is a zoo," he said impatiently, turning back on his heels. "I'll stop by tomorrow with some yams. They found a new patch of yams where we're clearing. Huge roots. Sweet as sugar."

With him gone, she turned her attention to me.

"I am the head of this unit, Phượng. Follow me in."

There was no feeling in her eyes, only appraisal. I followed her into a long barrack with a dirt floor, and my nose was immediately assailed by the acrid smell of cooking smoke. Lining the whole length of the middle passage were clay stoves, on which soot-blackened pots sat above charcoal fires, holding the upcoming hot meals of the day. Lining the walls on opposite sides were rows of bunk platforms with bamboo mats rolled up against the walls.

The women stopped what they were doing to eye me openly. Bags hung from all the beams. Small windows interrupted the thatched walls, a few of them decorated with blue curtains. Flip-flops littered the dirt floor. Phượng gave me a brief introduction to the camp's rules and schedule. Her voice was clear, authoritative, and matter-of-fact. She did not ask about my health as she had with the male guard, as if to establish a boundary between us. We stopped in front of an empty space, where there was no sleeping mat, no bag dangling from the beam, no slippers on the floor. She tapped the knotty surface of my future bedstead and said, "Here's your place. Roll out your mat here if you have one. Do you have one?"

"I have a plastic sheet," I told her.

"That'll do until your family brings you one. It's not too cold here until the monsoon season."

Before leaving, she reminded my bunkmates about the evening's assembly, and turned to me as the thought occurred to her. "Friday night is assembly night, right after the evening meal at five."

Then she walked back to her sleeping area by the entrance. As our group leader, she was to keep watch of the residents' movements in and out of the unit. She had the responsibility of reporting to the guard for the daily roster call and work assignments.

That evening, like every Friday evening, the camp residents marched out to an open space in the center of the camp and sat down for the camp assembly, unit by unit. There was the sound of an acoustic guitar, plucked expertly by a man in camp uniform. He began to sing, and I was surprised to hear the whole camp joining in the refrain:

> *Đồng-Phú, my loving place, dear one!*
> *Today I promise to learn, and labor . . .*
> *So that I can see*
> *where stands the truth, where roams freedom.*

Đồng-Phú even had its own anthem. Its composer was a camp resident who had since left, but his legacy went on—a prisoner's contribution to the place of his captivity.

"Where stands the truth?" Did he know?

* * *

I was glad to be given two sets of uniforms. They were too large, made of coarse cotton, cheaply dyed dark blue. No buttons on the blouses. No elastic on the pants waist. They came with only strings in the places where we needed to fasten to keep ourselves covered.

"Why do I get this ugly thing and you the well-tailored clothes?" I asked my bunkmate.

Bình was quick to reveal her bubbly personality. "That's the secret of Dufong Island."

I was learning something new every day, but this was intriguing.

"Dufong Island? Where is it?"

"Right here. This is the name we call this place, Dufong Island . . . . Like Malaysia's Pulau Bidong, or Indonesia's Kuku Island."

"Stop speaking in tongues. Island? What island? Are we on an island?" I was very confused by all the foreign names Bình mentioned. She took pleasure in my confusion.

"Well, all lucky boat people land on some sort of island. Unlucky ones like us land on Dufong Island. You see, if you take out the letters "ph" in *Phú* and replace it with its phonetic equivalence, *f*, the rearranged anagram of the original name will be Dufong. Amazing, no?"

So proud of my people! Dufong Island, a foreign name with an exotic flair was how we survived our predicament. No! They did not fool us into thinking that this is a place of education and reformation. We created the magic ourselves.

* * *

With time, I came to know all forty women in my unit, with ages ranging from eighteen to fifty. It did not take long to learn about one another when we all shared a long platform. Soon, I knew whom to talk to for a pair of curtains, cut out from the extra camp uniform that the ladies accumulated each passing year. Some women furnished their corner with small cupboards. Their male admirers had made the furniture for them from bamboo canes.

I could not help but to observe the unfolding lives of the people around me. I listened to their conversations and watched their interactions. I wished I could keep a diary to write down my thoughts—a foolish wish that I discarded quickly. I was particularly impressed by a group of three sisters. There was a charisma to each sister, a leadership quality in their voice and posture that distinguished them from the rest of the ladies. I was attracted by their topics of conversation, especially when they picked each other's brain.

The oldest sister, Minh-Nguyệt, would ask, "What is in quinine that makes it widely used here?"

The youngest, Minh-Thu, would offer her cognitive process, always beginning her sentence with an interesting phrase: "Let's reason it out."

"Let's reason it out. Quinine is an alkaloid found in nature from the bark of a certain tree and is also manufactured to treat malaria. But it possesses other useful properties. Phương-Nam, help me out here. Why is it also used for pain?"

Phương-Nam, the middle sister, softly elaborated: "As far as I understand, it may have an analgesic property. Also, anti-inflammatory. It's almost a magic pill on the Hồ Chí Minh Trail."

Here, the oldest sister cut in to conclude, "But it also destroys your red blood cells."

The three sisters were articulate, and their intelligence kept me tuned in.

The youngest sister, Minh-Thu, interested me most. She loved to recite poetry and knew many Vietnamese verses. Some of these verses I did not know; many I had learned or read but had forgotten until they were resurrected by her in the quiet nights of Dufong:

> I love him as a comb loves its mirror
> Like loving our parents and our own lives.
> How the moon loves its sky's stars
> How I love you among the earth's multitude.

Where were these sisters from? My curiosity was piqued.

In time, as we talked on, we discovered that our families knew one another. Their father was my parents' old friend, Mr. Nguyễn

Trung Quang. Their mother operated a pharmacy uptown and used to be Mom's classmate. Their brother, Thạch, and sister, Minh-Phước, used to come to our house to tutor us in math and French for pocket money. This chancy revelation thrilled me at first. I had lived so long in anonymity that I forgot how it was to be known.

"Yeah! Our brother told us about you," one sister said. "How you had refused to let him peek into your notebook."

"They live in France now, Thạch and Minh-Phước."

I was tongue-tied. The talk brought back so many memories: the mosquito-filled nights sitting at the large, egg-shaped dining table learning modern math and playing my enticing game with Thạch, just a few years older than I. I believed I was cute then. But now, what did these acquaintances from the past see in me? I no longer wished to be recognized. What image did I present of myself, so badly clothed, so out of shape? Unpolished. A complete degradation. I had gained so much weight that I resembled more a pig covered in rags than the girl who once had been privately tutored by their handsome brother.

As to the three sisters, if our common history at all affected them, they surely did not show it in their emotions or in the way they treated me. They continued to relate to me as to anyone else, with a friendly reservation and an aloofness, as if to say, we trust you no more than the rest of the world outside our circle. I understood their detachment and retreated readily to my inner sanctum, keeping our prior connection a thing of the past, undisturbed and never to be mentioned again. After all, we were in a shark-filled sea, each trying to survive on her own terms, each focusing on protecting her identity and true mission. If we had met outside in better circumstances, we would have surely formed a tighter bond.

My life had taken such turns. And to cross these sisters' path here was, to me, an incredible coincidence. I had no thought of improving myself until I met these bright girls, still hanging onto their knowledge, still dignified in every fiber. I was ashamed to let myself go to pieces like this, to gorge myself for solace. All was not yet lost.

Then there was Sister Nhường, a sentimental Catholic nun, who reminded me of my grandmother each time she called out, "Jesus Christ! Oh, dear God!"

Sister Nhường cried easily, blushed easily, and laughed easily. It was hard to believe her, with her passionate personality, as a veiled member of the church, yet she was a nun in all other aspects. She stood apart in my memory because she was the only person in our unit who had no other relations outside the camp to take care of her. Her subsistence depended entirely on our charity. Perhaps because of this, perhaps because she was used to a submissive life, she was an effacing, humble person. But she laughed all the time, thankful for our friendship, full of gratitude for each helping hand, each good moment.

There was Châu, of Mường ethnicity. She was illiterate but performed folk dances charmingly. Her body was plumpish, yet pliable. Her exotic face kept us all in a trance when she put on her colorful sarong and moved about gracefully, swaying like a bird in the *baba-boom* beatings of our collective hand claps and stick strikes.

These were moments that have stayed with me forever, moments that taught me that we humans could thrive and find happiness even in the darkest time. We could reinvent life and suit it to our imaginations, to make life into an art. Châu's dance was, indeed, the dance of life on the brink of destruction.

The bodies could be confined, but the spirits found their ways to roam free. They found music in the hollow wood of a flute, in the vibration of human voices, in the rustling leaves, in the howling of wolves. In the bird song was our gaiety. In the colorful threads of embroidery, we gathered our thoughts, kept them still and subdued. With Minh-Thu's recitation of Thế Lữ's "Nhớ rừng," I felt free.

> *Sucking on my loathing inside my cage*
> *I prostrate to the sound of flying time*
> *Despising those people whose arrogance made ignorant*
> *Babe's eyes, dare mocking at the king of jungle.*

All convinced me that as long as the mind was not affected, in it was a person's salvation. In it was the ultimate refuge. In it shone our sanction. If it aspired for beauty, it could create heaven from thin air, a reasoning creature from dust, like God.

On my nineteenth birthday, someone from the male ward sent me a hand-carved lantern. It had a candle in the middle that, when lit, turned a small merry-go-round that depicted the traditional scene of a homecoming scholar on horseback, followed by his young wife in a horse-drawn carriage, with the whole village trailing behind on foot. I had seen this type of lantern before, but to hold a miniature handicraft version of it on the day I turned nineteen, on Dufong Island, was more than joy. I wept.

"Come on, why are you sobbing?" said Ánh, admiring my gift. "Such a piece of art. Who sent it?"

"I have no idea," I said to her.

But she was teasing. "Come on! Tell me the truth. What a clever actress. I did not know you have an admirer. Who is it?"

I shook my head in disbelief. I had not a clue. But the gesture made me feel very special on my birthday. The handwritten note said simply, "Happy birthday, Hồng-Mỹ."

I shared the joy of that scholar coming home in all his glory.

* * *

To preserve my sanity I floated through the endless months at Dufong in a daze. I remember very little of how I managed to keep going, when each day began the same before first light.

A sound sleeper, I had to be roused by my bunkmate, Ánh. In that pre-dawn hour, there was always much to be frantic about. We had but one hour to prepare ourselves before heading out to the field. The line to the pit toilets was long, as was the wait for our turns at the wellhead. The darkness made walking to these places dangerous. No one wanted to fall into the shallow pit filled with human waste and maggots, nor plummet to the bottom of the well. We proceeded slowly and cautiously.

The well mouth was slightly raised above the muddy ground

around it. Bamboo slats had been laid on top of the mud to prevent accidental slipping, but with time, these too almost disappeared under the thick layer of soil deposited by the heavy foot traffic.

The well was full and clear in the early morning but turned murky and brackish with each succession of buckets. After a time, the water was only good for rinsing our feet. Needless to say, there was a race to get to the well before the crowd poured out.

People crouched wherever they could to brush their teeth, raising their faces and gargling freely to the sky, then spitting loudly onto the ground. There was no remnant of civility where we lived.

Breakfast was leftover rice. When it was my turn to pick out working tools for our unit, I would head out with an assistant to the tool shack, a boxy place manned by a few men young enough for us to address as "big brother." The tools were thrown in a heap onto the dirt floor: crescent axes, pickaxes, mattocks, hoes, blades, and rakes. I pulled out the good tools from the pile, the axes and blades with sturdy handles, blades free of dints and nicks and, if possible, sharp. The good tools were rare, and were always quickly selected on a first-come/first-served basis. I finished my task fast to make room for other people to get their tools.

I remember one time, as I was absorbed in selecting the best tools for my team, a man said suddenly, "Woman! Get out of here before your scent drives me crazy."

Not fully understanding him, I turned around. "You said?"

His mood darkened. Morose and mean, he shouted, "Be done and get out! Else, don't blame me." Even with my arms full of blades, I left quickly, frightened.

In early dawn, the whole camp gathered in front of the flagpole, queuing by unit—a loud army in blue. Each person had some sort of tool, axes in hands and rakes on shoulders. The women's faces were wrapped in thick cotton scarves, leaving only their eyes, noses, and mouths visible under their conical hats.

One by one, each unit departed, starting with the males, escorted by an armed guard. Only the sick and elderly stayed back in the camp. These people would work under a big roof, making baskets and sorting the grains.

The sun rose as we marched to the field. Often, the muddy trail disappeared into dense thickets, and the green, leafy branches took hold of our hats, grasped our tools, caught our legs, and poked our faces. The birds sang the morning's glory, perhaps mocking our attempt to invade their territory. Regardless, the guard marched us on. We chopped down the branches as we passed through them, our blades coated with the sticky sap.

"Go on, go on," shouted the young guard as he pushed us from behind with his long, easy strides, his feet well booted. "We don't have all day."

From deep inside the wood, the sound of crashing lumber all around kept us guessing about our destination. The tired and weak were now lagging far behind, dragging their tools. The stronger ones among us slowed their steps to let these people catch up, and the strongest, who had been accustomed to physical labor, even traced back to help, relieving the burdening rake from one, for another exchanging the heavy mattock with a lighter ax.

Sweat began to run down my back. I tore open my scarf mask with my gloved hands, marching without a thought in order to keep up with the line. I mentally blocked the tiredness in my legs and let them drag on their own accord to bear me along. *One-two, one-two, one-two.*

An hour or two later, the sky opened up. The trees had been cleared previously by a group of men; the cut logs piled in neat rows. We were allowed a ten-minute rest to drink water that we carried with us in small canteens. Then our morning work began.

Phượng would call out, "Oy! Sisters! Line up and spread out."

Moving in rows, we duck-walked slowly through the grass field, cutting down the green, sharp blades on our path with the crescent axes. Standing up frequently to stretch out my legs, I could see the progression of my team by the white tips of their hats in the tall grass. Where we had been, the curtain of grass was drawn aside to reveal the forest floor beneath, covered by a green grass carpet.

"Sit down, Hồng-Mỹ. Who are you spying on across the field?"

Bình would tease me. She was the youngest in her family, the only one caught after the rocks had punctured their boat when they pushed it out from a marsh. Like most Chinese, she spoke a funny Vietnamese.

"No! No one," I replied, "Just resting my back a little. Are we lagging behind?" I returned to my work. It was easier to work in tandem with another person than toiling alone.

"We work fast today. It helps to have a sharp ax."

"Your mom come up last week? Or your sister?" I asked.

"My ma. My sister . . . ." She did not finish her sentence. I did not want to intrude, knowing that was her way to keep the information to herself.

I said, instead, "After a week or two, this field will be ready for seeding."

With our worn backs hunched, we moved slowly forward on our bent legs, drenched with sweat, looking up now and then to judge the distance ahead that needed clearing. Then, gathering ourselves, we continued to work, wiping away all thoughts, absorbed in our task. Tortured by the pain in our backs and knees and the burning sun overhead, we longed for the break call. A week, then two; then months soon turned into a year. How the time fled. My thoughts wandered. On this patch of newly cleared wood, I would one day see a field of beans. Or rice.

From a distance, the guard looked on, bored and impatient. He was also waiting. A shrill whistle reverberated throughout the wood.

"Break time," he shouted, almost too gladly.

Poor guy. He was himself our prisoner, standing there gazing at us all day under the sun. It must be warping his soul. We stood, staggering under our own weight, dizzied with our rising blood. We swarmed toward the large jug of drinking water brought out to us by the kitchen staff to fill our empty canteens. The sweet water poured down our throats, soothing our parched tongues. We uncovered our faces and fanned ourselves with the cone hats, cheeks flushed, our faces caked with dried sweat.

Then the ten-minute reprieve was over. We were again pushed

into the field; again our backs bent like convicts on a galley, swallowed by the waves of grassy blades.

We spent our lunch hour in various shady corners, sitting on fallen logs, on rocks, on tree stumps. The men were sitting not far away, and the teams tossed teases back and forth, enlivening the atmosphere with hearty laughter.

In Dufong, males outnumbered females. Out of sixteen housing units, only five were reserved for the women. The country's sons, once its future, were now its captured foes. But male they still were, strong and yearning. Like the croaking calls of bullfrogs, their calls for a female reverberated in the wood.

"*Em ơi!* Beautiful, will one of you come sit with me on this simple rock?" one man shouted.

Even the guards joined in the hooting. One guard proposed, "I'll give you, lady, an extra half-hour break if you come sit by this handsome lad here."

"Why should I when I have my own rock?" Bình's voice rose with the breeze. A bird chirped at her in reply. The voice of a man cut the ensuing silence, "Beautiful, even the male bird thinks you are not wise, you see. My rock is better, because I am next to you."

"*Wahaha.*" The male team slapped their thighs in collective glee.

"Charmless, *dô diên*," protested my friend in her throat, blood rising on her face.

I was amused by her retort, so typical of a girl. Bình still behaved like a schoolgirl, like myself not so long ago.

But it was over with me, a thing of the past. I was transformed into a prisoner and had learned to live in a cage, without emotion.

Here, they nicknamed me "Imperialist America," the same pejorative our new government called the United States, all because of my robust shape. The months of craving and using food as a source of solace had taken a toll on my body. I had morphed into a heavyset field girl, clumsy and awkward.

The working day, however long, would end. The long trek home began when the sun was but a shadow on the horizon. Again, the road would fill with prisoners accompanied by vanilla-uniformed guards. There must have been something in the darkening wood, in the disappearing sun, that affected the souls of these guards, for they were no longer marching us but walking home with us, allowing husbands and wives to pair up and mothers and sons to join rank; the men helped carry the heavy tools, the women the empty water jugs—we walked home like families of farmers after a day in the fields.

The long road also brought together bachelors and eligible maids in open courtship. The thick wood was a rolling stage, and I a moving audience. My feet had a life of their own. Food. I was thinking only about dinner: the chunks of salted pork Mom had lugged up for me every two weeks stored in various plastic bottles, the hot bowl of rice, some sweet afterward. Food was my way to keep my thoughts occupied, to look forward to a new day, to calm a rising terror.

Then came the night.

Boong, boong, boong. The first night shift began about nine o'clock. There were five guard shifts per night, each lasting an hour and a half. Following the gong's sounds, the camp generator was switched off, and with it, the two electric bulbs in our ward.

Tonight's last watch was mine. *Sigh.* I went to bed promptly, and as soon as the previous watcher shook me awake, I crawled out into the cold air. Wrapped in my blanket, I sat down by the dying fire, not too far from the rickety bamboo gate blocking the entrance. When assigned the earlier shifts, I would have my embroidery in hands to keep me awake and occupied. This pre-dawn shift took a heavier toll on me because I could not crawl back to bed afterward, but had to get ready to go out into the fields. Trash duty began at dawn, so it was upon me to keep track of the three inmates crossing the field with the garbage. The fog was so dense it seemed to drown the land out of sight. Unable to see them well, I strained my ears to the sound of their retreating footsteps, then the heavy barrel being inverted on the ground. Where were they? I prayed that they would not choose to disappear during my shift, for then I could be charged as their conspirator. People did choose this early time between light and darkness to evaporate into thin air. They would take out the trash, then vanish with it.

The thought of escaping crossed my mind a few times. But I was a coward. I went cold every time I imagined myself disappearing into the forest.

"She never found her way out," someone told me about the last escapee. "They found her clothes in the jungle. Some beastly thing ate her."

I knew I would not have the courage to attempt an escape.

I thought about Dad, running like a rabbit at gunpoint. I thought of all the rumors about escaped inmates being attacked by tigers, about women being raped by the guards, dragged back to camp with hands and feet bound, and being accused by her fellow prisoners of offering her body in exchange for freedom.

But I often gazed toward the edge of the wood and wondered.

On the weekend, we were free. Weekends were festive periods in Dufong. It was time to receive visitation from relatives who arrived in the morning with bags full of life-giving supplies, from basics like sugar, stew meats, dried meats, pickles, and salted eggs, to luxuries like soaps, additional clothing, feminine napkins, and medicines. Without these additional resources, a prisoner's health would quickly deteriorate from malnutrition and illness.

One day, a skin-wrapped skeleton stepped out from the men's bunkhouse to meet me.

"Hồng-Mỹ, remember me?" he said.

"Are you Mr. Sương?"

"I am," he said sadly. "Hard to believe it's me, isn't it?"

He was right. Our former escape guide, previously robust and handsome, was now gaunt and yellow. He had deteriorated beyond recognition. He asked for food.

"Yes, of course, yes," I said, shocked.

I had taken my food supply for granted, but I saw now the importance of nutrition. I understood why Mom came up every other week to bring me more food, although I had told her I had enough to last me a long time. Mom also brought me cash and letters from friends that I smuggled in through the checkpoints. Money was useful in case I needed to buy extra meat; wild boar killed by the locals living in the periphery of the camp. All this brought me not only material comfort but also the services of many people wanting to earn cash to buy food and medicine.

Mom reminded me often, "Take your quinine regularly."

The rainy season soon followed the hot weather. With the rain, all the roads around Dufong turned muddy and impassable. The trucks that brought up the visitors and their weekly supplies had to stop and unload where the paved road ended. While many families stopped visiting, my mother never failed to return, laden with food totes, covered in sweat and mud.

The weekends came and went and were always too short. During the monsoon season, we sat morose, surrounded by our wet laundry draped across the window like a curtain and hung from beam to beam on cotton rope. The soaked thatch roof gave out a moldy odor. In no time, it started to leak, so we placed pots. Then as the pots were needed for cooking, we replaced them with an assortment of plastic containers. Everything was damp, including our floor. We dragged our flip-flops, heavy with wet mud, praying that they would last until our relatives could bring replacements.

Each Monday morning, we had trouble walking on the slippery roads full of large puddles. Foamy yellow bubbles had grown overnight to indicate the return of the bull frogs, which croaked all night long, unseen. The lines of inmates and guards advanced painfully on the muddy path, stopping now and then to wait for the clearing crew to line the flooded areas with chopped branches, cut as needed along the road.

I was thankful for the pair of knee-high plastic boots Mom had brought me; but even then, the splashing mud soiled the upper sides of my pants legs, ruining my laundering effort. We took a long time to reach our destination, only to discover that the vegetation had all grown back; the woods were thick and rich with multiple sounds: water dripping from the leaves, insects and birds singing, our own footsteps on soaked moss. There was no choice but to redo the work that nature had undone.

The air was cooler. But now we watched anxiously at the dark clouds rolling overhead, hoping the wind would blow them away. Our left hands, although gloved, were quickly soaked by the wet grass. Saturated with rainwater, the grass blades resisted our dull blades. We sheared in vain. Our right hands soon pained.

One afternoon, three gunshots in the distance startled us as we were laboring in the field. We looked up, puzzled. The guard awoke from his reveries to shout for us to resume our work. After the break for lunch, the sky darkened, and the dragonflies came out hovering. We worked hurriedly to finish our assignment, but the imminent storm finally gained on us and the guard gave way to the inclement weather. He signaled for us to gather for the march home. On the road, we learned about the first jailbreak of the season. Three men had escaped in the woods and vanished.

"Lucky for them Six Run is not around this week," someone commented.

It was true. Six Run was a high-ranking officer in charge of the camp. He was lean and mean, notorious for his ability to run like lightning when tracking down escaped prisoners. He was proud of his nickname and of his job. Women admired his chivalry, his readiness in helping the sick and weak on the roads. He was a fascinating character. The rumors painted him as some sort of demi-God of the camp, one who is just but who punishes hard, caring for the wounded but brutal and merciless with lawbreakers. His reputation was soon confirmed, as jailbreaking increased with each new success.

When the first woman failed to return after her early-morning garbage duty, her disappearance created a rippling agitation in the women's camp. Word of mouth traveled quickly that she had been aided by one of the guards, to whom she had given her body inside a storage room. Livid with rage, Six Run took off immediately in early dawn, before we headed out to the woods. By lunchtime, word was received that Six Run had returned with the prisoner. She was brought inside the guard quarter for interrogations that night, and we heard her howl.

Afterward, she was taken to the infirmary for a whole week. She was released into Unit Five, but she kept the experience to herself. No one ever knew what really had happened with her. Had she been assisted in her escape? Did she give herself for this service? How was she captured and how did she survive the ordeal with Six Run?

Other, more minor incidents remain in my memory. I learned to check for small tree stumps before lowering myself in the grass to urinate. The pain was unbearable the first time I made the mistake and too embarrassing to be shared with others in the group. When I finally told Ánh, she only laughed. "You're lucky it wasn't longer, or sharper." I winced at that image in my mind.

The labor camp was a place of danger. Snakes loved to nestle inside the lower roofbeams. Scorpions lurked in every bush and under stones. Malaria visited camp residents often, and diarrhea attacked routinely.

We faced each new day as it came. We had no way to avoid illnesses, predict an accident, or stay away from poisonous bites. The protection had to come from above. Who would know, looking at our newly constructed workhouse, with its soaring beams and 30-foot roof, that one afternoon the wind would bring the walls down, crashing onto the unsuspecting workers inside? I was in that workhouse when the wind began to whip up, blowing dust and turning chairs on their sides. The bamboo that supported the roof cringed. I remember looking up at the tall poles, concerned but unsuspecting. As I stood to grasp a broom, the groaning of wood turned deafening. Then everything swayed. The whole roof came crashing down in a rain of splinters as I ran for my life. When everything was again still, I was facedown on the floor. There was an eerie silence, then crying sounds and moans.

I opened my eyes to the blue of sky. Behind me, lying in one heap, was the workhouse, its thatch grasping my feet. I had outrun it. I pushed myself up in the soft drizzle, trembling violently. From under the thatch, heads poked up. One by one people stumbled out frantically, disoriented and terrified. From all camp corners, people ran toward the collapsed house to help extract limp bodies from the wreck. I staggered dumbly away, shaking like a leaf. The accident caused no deaths, only few broken bones. I was unscathed but traumatized. In the ensuing months I ran out of my unit every time the wind kicked up.

Then the dry season returned. One weekend brought me a nice surprise in Phượng's excited voice: "Some crazy guy is down the road, singing French." I knew without a doubt who that crazy guy was. Sure enough, from very far down the road, my ears could pick out *Frère Jacques! Frère Jacques! Dormez-vous?* The wind carried the unmistakable voice of my dear father, who had until that day refused to come see me suffer. Trailing behind him were two men carrying a long pole between them, with many bags of supplies. Oh! Father! He would never learn to suffer. I guessed that he had hired these prisoner-laborers cheaply on the spot. The capitalist in him had not died, more than six years after the communists had returned the country to the Stone Age.

* * *

I was buried alive for fifteen months. Fifteen months in a full life is a blink of the eye. But in my case, "One day of imprisonment is eternity." In that eternity, the irreversible damage to my sense of security had been complete, my innocence taken. I no longer trusted so easily. God, order, truth . . . these things are not long lasting. The foundations of my former life—whether of faith, social structures, or humanity—had crumbled to pieces.

My last night on Dufong came unexpectedly. I was preparing for bed when Phượng, coming back from her nightly meeting with the staff, hollered for me. I worried immediately: Did I break any rules? Had they found out about the letters and the money that I hid in my bags?

Phượng assembled my whole unit as usual. Everyone sat on their bunks with their feet dangling out as usual. She talked about the assignment for the next day's work and then she wrapped up the meeting without once inquiring about me. I began to suspect that I had misheard her, when she stepped toward me, her eyes shining with excitement.

"You are going home tomorrow, girl!" she said, her voice betraying her emotion.

It was as if I was lifted up to the clouds of heaven. I floated peacefully away, and there, looking down, I saw the women of my unit preparing their beds, bringing down the corners of their mosquito nets, shaking off their blankets. I heard the sound of Phượng singing softly. On the floor, here and there the cooking fires crackled, lids dancing wildly over the bubbling pots of soup. The steam rose up and misted my face. No! They were my tears of joy. I looked around to register my last night at Dufong, readying myself for the journey home to a new beginning and folding up the painful chapters of my misadventure.

Goodbye, everyone! May courage sustain you until your return home.

Goodbye, hardship!

I am free.

I am going home.

I was given the choice the next morning to either stay and wait until the end of the week for a truck ride or depart immediately walking. I opted to leave that morning in the company of three other women, two of them in their fifties.

We set out on foot, carrying our bags on our shoulders. The long road was still muddy from the last rain, but we happily plodded on. We could not avoid the large potholes filled with water. We stepped into mud to our knees and kept our pace, heading toward the next camp reserved for the officers working around Dufong. We ate lunch there and, following the given direction, headed out to the closest bus stop. We walked and walked. I felt a little itchy on my calf and reached down to scratch, only to realize that my feet were covered with leeches. I froze. "Where did they come from?" I asked the ladies. "From the swamp. You can't see them until they swell full of your blood. Just scrape them off with something flat, or let them be until they fall off on their own." That was what I decided to do. I ignored my feet, fearing that if I looked down once more I would panic and faint. We walked and walked. We finally boarded a small van as the day waned, leaving behind a bad dream. It took us straight to the city in less than two hours.

I arrived late at night to Trương Minh Giảng Market. It was the first week of December 1981, close to the first anniversary of my Grandmother's death. I arrived at Aunt Sự's door and knocked, then glued my face to the glass door to look inside. At the dining table, my aunt and Mom sat, conversing. It was as if time had stood still since I last saw them together that way, speaking soft words that did not reach me. They looked out while the old maid peered outside and asked, "Who knocks at this odd hour?"

I told her my name, which she could not hear with her deaf ear. But my mom jumped from her seat. "Hồng-Mỹ! It's Hồng-Mỹ. Open quickly. She's home."

From Aunt Sự's house, we both flew to Aunt Huỳnh's home, where Dad and the kids, having just finished dinner, might have been looking up at the sky full of shining stars. Had they just mentioned my name and wished that I would be home in time for Christmas?

We rang the bell and shook the metal slats. Michelle ran down, alarmed by the ruckus. Then Anne appeared, so tall and pretty. Then Patrick behind her. Oh, was it him? He was square shouldered, as tall as Dad, who wore only white boxer shorts. They stopped at the top of the stairs, looking down as I walked up. We embraced there, with the dangling lightbulb shining on my face.

My ordeal was over.

I was home.

33.

The Theft

After a time, all losses are the same.
One more thing lost is one thing less to lose;
And we go stripped at last the way we came.

(from "After a Time" by Catherine Davis, 1961)

Mỹ-Hướng was no longer the same. Stepping in from the back entrance, we no longer had the option to run up either left or right. Only a single stairway, the one on the left, rose in the dark, since the light socket was without a bulb.

On the half-landing, in a low-ceilinged, hatch-box sort of room, with a miniature meshed-screen window spying day and night into the opposite neighbor's home, now lived a woman, a Catholic ex-nun whom we nicknamed Angel.

Like ourselves, forced over and over again to cope with the impoverished circumstances of our lives, Angel's room had been repurposed many times over the span of a few years to suit the need of those inhabiting it. We had first used this tiny room as a kitchen, where Chị Bảy, our former cook, rehired to prepare our meals, labored over the clay stoves and thus solved the nagging cooking problem between Mom and me. Later, for a short time, Anne's chickens followed her in single file here nightly to happily settle down. The kitchen-turned-coop would soon be quiet, with now and then a soft, guttural sound of fowl contentment. Now, in place of their nest,

Angel's large bed stood, topped with a bamboo mat. In place of the stoves was Angel's Singer sewing machine. The needle would skip busily through her length of fabric when she sat down to treadle, leaving in its path a neat trail of ants, or chick footprints, sometimes black, sometimes white.

Where the dining area used to be, in the center of the second floor, a dividing wall stood guard. In the shadowy haze of late December evenings, the impassive gray face met me, refusing to let me back into the familiar quarter I had left less than two years ago. My aunt's home had further shrunk, the other half sold to another family. Our family now shared one bedroom, previously my uncle's library, at the end of a long and narrow hallway.

We spent most of our daytime studying on the terrace, up another floor, off one of the rooms crudey added in my uncle's time, whose purpose and use was unknown and didn't make any sense to me; his home was already so spacious, with so many empty rooms for just the two of them. Sandwiched on the open terrace thus, with doors banging at its opposite walls, our little study was battered by the sun, wind, and rain like a lighthouse. My younger siblings flew in and out of this lighthouse like birds, coming in with a book under their arms and leaving it promptly on their small desks, as if these volumes were twigs with which to build their nest.

Dad looked at this scenario differently. Chagrined to see his flock breezing in and out, he said, disappointedly tapping the unopened books on their desks, "These books are all you get to build your future," referring to their carefree attitude about learning.

Each day Dad climbed up into the lighthouse as its faithful keeper. He rearranged the little makeshift desks that he and Patrick had bought cheaply from the market, propping a carton box under one for Anne to keep her notebooks, leaning a shelf on another to add more writing space for Michelle. When the weather turned windy, to keep the balcony side's door from banging, he tied a string to its wiggling handle and fastened it to a nail in the wall.

Patrick had painted the wall of the hallway linking our study to the terrace a limpid blue and transformed this narrow space into a minuscule dining area, again furnishing it simply with a set of folding table and chairs, the kind used by food vendors at every street corner. At night, a sixty-watt bulb with its soft yellow light threw the symmetrical shape of a woven lampshade made from an inverted trash basket onto the blue wall.

Mỹ-Hương was no longer the same house. We had lost the space, but the simple setting of our new home was a product of art, the love child of creative minds, from the plain low table in the tiny but airy study, with carton boxes as drawers and shelves, to the makeshift kitchen, tucked like a dollhouse under the awning of the balcony, guarded by an old, wooden cabinet wearing its meshed door like a shield. We still had what we most desired: the blue sky and the open space beyond our walls.

From our lighthouse we could almost dream of freedom, each rooftop a departing ship, each terrace floor a landing pad awaiting an airplane.

On the terrace was a potted garden alive with Aunt Huỳnh's beloved plants and herbs: roses, dwarf kumquats and lemons, mint, green onions, bright red chilies, night jasmine, and orchids. Our daily laundry flapped on the clotheslines, underwear like SOS flags and shirts and pants like half-dressed scarecrows, limpless and headless but fighting with such strong spirit they scared the birds away from the potted fruits. Underneath the defeated army and plant guardians, our hammocks were suspended, two giant webs awaiting their human cocoons.

For the first few mornings at home I found myself waking as if in a dream, walking upstairs to the terrace alone, standing on top of this world, admiring the routine setup of the market below. Everything amazed me: each sound a novelty, each object remarkable. I was fascinated by the varied pace of city life, the clothing my siblings wore: their jeans, their white blouses, and their colorful day pajamas. I was baffled by everyone's activities—the church choir practice, the weekly guitar and drum lessons, the constant movements on the stairs to bring up the bicycles, bring down the bicycles, and the calling of my siblings' new friends. I woke early by habit; not knowing what to do with my time, I washed the dirty dishes piled on the concrete floor under a faucet, taking pleasure in the water jetting out conveniently at a turn of a knob.

Slowly, my life normalized. I felt strange the first few days in my city clothes; my trousers hugged so tight to my waist and the pant legs squeezed my thighs like a glove on fingers. I climbed into a pair of high heels as if they were stilts. Sporting these modern contraptions, I mounted a bike and had the impression that I was a clown on a high-seat unicycle.

I did not forget the incredulous look in Patrick's eyes the night we first reunited. Little Michelle was less diplomatic. She blurted out what her brother only thought: "But Hồng-Mỹ, you are *fat*," then quickly covered her mouth. She had spoken the truth too fast and too soon. I avoided the bathroom mirror, although it reflected only my face. From the first day after I returned home, I imposed on myself a vegetable diet, living off papaya and tofu. I buried myself in the books and, with my dad's encouragement and guidance, started an independent crash-course to study English and math.

I remember my first party, on a late December night, to celebrate Michelle's 14th birthday, a week after my return. For the occasion, the kids set up a few tables and chairs on the terrace and hung paper lanterns. Patrick covered the tables with a white bedsheet and placed a few vases of flowers around. The flowers were cut from my aunt's garden with her reluctant approval. At seven, when the sky turned crimson and the air cooled, our two lady guests showed up, Phương-Dung, Patrick's belle, and our cousin Yến-Dung.

Hiding in the kitchen, I looked out shyly and awkwardly. What should I do? I felt alienated and lonely, old and betrayed by my siblings' joy of life, their ease of movement, their social skills and normalcy. I wanted to return to my books and leave them to enjoy their party, not burden them with the introduction of a strange-looking sister, ugly with her massive thighs and her baffled air. However, they looked around for me, and Michelle led me out by my hand and all the company looked up, their eyes shining with happiness.

Michelle introduced me to their new friend. "Here is my sister Hồng-Mỹ, returning from faraway just in time to celebrate my teenage years." I guessed they had talked about me before, for the girls' eyes softened with understanding of my sudden presence in the family. I sat with them for a while, but since I refused to eat, they finally agreed to let me retire early.

My first excursions into the city were to pay homage to old jail mates. Some had not yet returned, but I spoke to their families. I went to Như's house to look for her.

"She is not home," the woman I assumed to be her mother said, not elaborating. I wanted to find out if my friend was still locked up inside the Octagonal Oven or had come home while I was at Dufong.

"Are you Như's mom?" I asked, finally. I had decided that I would get her to talk at any cost. The shy girl in me had grown into a braver ex-convict. I could be blunt when I wanted to.

"Yes, I am. But I have nothing to say to you, nor would she," was all that she said. Her firm lips and apathetic eyes told me not to intrude.

I saw her pain. The sea pirates had attacked Như's little boat, and her innocence was taken by not one or two, but a dozen Thai men. I only vaguely understood what they had done, how they had robbed my friend of her sacred gift for her future husband, but I knew what it was to be brutalized, stripped naked, and forced down. I could see terror carved in the lines on Như's mother's face, could see it in her eyes.

The mother had been there when the attack happened. She must have seen the blades slashing the men's throats, one by one, and their blood-dripping bodies pushed into the sea. She must have heard them beg to be spared, the lusty sneer of dark bodies hurling on tiny frames, the smell of virginal blood and slaughter and the stench of sweat and human fluids. Như's mother was there, on her knees in front of her daughter, tearing off her own blouse and offering herself instead. But they took her and her daughter side by side, one after another, until they knew no more.

Như had slept with both eyes open. Her mother had been

released, leaving Như in the care of other women. Như's will to live had left her. So, we took turns bathing her, washing her hair, and forcing food into her mouth. When I met her, she was a baby in a woman's body. She spoke in a childish language and laughed easily at our jokes. She laughed with her eyes wide, and terror still in them. She never, never spoke of herself. What I learned about her, I learned from the soft murmurs of other women. Our friendship was born from my protection and care for her. When I left, she simply said "Bye" to me. I was the one who wanted to cling on, so I promised her, "I'll keep in touch."

"I'd like to keep in touch with Như." I repeated my thought out loud to her mother, almost begging. Without a word, the woman left me and retreated back into her home. I mounted my bike and left.

I had no right to intrude.

My visits with other friends were better received. The people who had been released long before me did not believe I could have ballooned out that much. Everyone teased me about my weight, which seemed more pronounced in my city clothes.

I spent most of my time learning the English language from a series called "English for Today." Everyone called it "English for to Go," because whoever learned it did so with the sole intent of leaving the country. I taught myself, reading English like I had read French, stumbling along the way on the confusing *i* that sounded like an *e* in French, *j* pronounced like the French *g*, and stumped by such monstrous words as "Seattle" that somehow was not *Sit-though* but became *See-a-though*. I aspired to do well and, since I was my own teacher, I allowed myself to cut corners and progressed very fast. Soon, I began to greet Patrick each morning with, "Good morning, how are you?"

"Fine," he would retort, even in the days that he was sick, for that was the only English he knew. I still remember my first English rhymes. They were silly, endearing lines:

Oh, Timothy Tim has ten pink toes
And ten pink toes has Timothy Tim.

Not having the distraction of friends, I caught up with my siblings' English in no time, and started to reaffirm my authority over them with strict demands on their study schedule. Dad, as always, beamed with pride over my performance.

Steadily, I returned to my normal self. But I wanted more. I was craving a different kind of nourishment, starved for the intellectual stimulation that I had not had for more than six years. The self-reliant women who I met in the jails and forced-labor camp had given me the inspiration to thrive under all situations. No wall could possibly imprison a determined mind. I signed up to study classical guitar with my siblings' teacher, while they pursued modern music. The differences between the two schools of study were many, from the way I had to sit, placing the guitar on my left thigh and plucking the strings note by note, to the methods I followed that leaned heavily on scales and arpeggios. Before each new song, I had to bring a score sheet home and copy it into my manuscript book, note by note. Soon, I was playing "Never on Sunday" and "Johnny Guitar." I did not know the lyrics to these English titles but it was enough that I plucked the notes and hummed the melody lines instead of singing the words. It was enough that music flowed again from my fingers. I regained my dignity and confidence with each new lesson.

Angel tailored many new outfits for me from the colorful fabrics brother Khải sent home from Pennsylvania, USA. I visited a hair salon to have my hair cut short and permed for the first time. I acquired the vain habits of grownup ladies, and after the perm, I progressed to manicure and pedicure. Each morning, I spent some time in front of a mirror plucking my eyebrows and applying makeup. The steady low-calorie diet had a marvelous effect on my adjusting body, giving it a slender look, with one detrimental effect from the papaya: My skin began to turn slightly yellowish-orange. I supplemented papaya with watermelon and began to consume some fish.

In March 1982, after my twentieth birthday, my friend Thanh-Thủy, my last close friend from school, came to say goodbye. She was leaving for Paris. She came with my diary in her hand, which I had given to her as a farewell gift. In this book were the last shreds of my beautiful childhood, now destroyed, now elapsed. She handed the notebook to me and a whiff of perfume escaped from its pages, bringing back the bossy little girl of thirteen dreaming about her upcoming birthday, the Esso Man with his upturned hand saluting the world, Grandma and her rosary, and Tân Sa Châu, my childhood home.

My friend said regretfully, "I am not a writer. So here is your book with not much added to it. In fact, I did not write at all."

I was not surprised to hear her confession. Each of us was born into life with a separate mission. She was gifted with a loyal heart, an unselfish devotion to her family and friends. I gave her all my sisters' addresses in Europe.

"Call them often if you want my news," I told her. Then I used this opportunity to share with Thanh-Thủy our good news.

"This is between us only, Thủy. I think we'll soon follow you."

"We are the last witnesses of a changed time," my friend answered. "Don't forget it, you, the writer."

"Me? The writer? Where do you get that?" I pretended disbelief. We both knew I was the one who wrote her essays before each exam, which she learned by heart to reproduce in class.

"Keep in touch. Go now," she said, her eyes liquefied.

"Go! Send my regards to your family." I slammed shut the rolling gate.

I was the last of our mutinous group to remain in Hồ Chí Minh City. But this time, I was not desperate.

* * *

A few months before my sudden release from the forced-labor camp, on the verge of a breakdown from her distress for me and the stress of her biweekly bus travel to visit and supply me with food, my mother had gladly accepted to tag along with my aunt to a dinner party. "Come," Aunt Sự had urged. "Wipe away your tears and let your troubles be forgotten for a couple of hours. You need a distraction."

She was well rewarded with a sumptous meal and a good time

among lady friends which she had not had in years. It was over in a flash, and soon, people were head-bowing and saying "Thank you" at the door.

"Remember us," someone had shouted into the room before leaving.

My aunt explained to my mother, "Her flight is tomorrow," then turning to the guest of honor waiting for her turn to say goodbye to the host, she said, "Have a safe travel. We might never meet again," her voice cracking mid-sentence.

"Surely, you will not have this kind of food anymore," the host said, tearfully. "Remember this farewell meal."

They held hands and bowed. And the lucky lady left.

Leaving her sister-in-law behind with their small talk after "*Cám ơn*" and "*Chào bác nhé*," the usual thank yous and goodbyes, Mom hurried after her target.

"May I?" she shouted to gain the lady's attention.

Still in her celebratory mood, her new friend retraced her steps and told Mom, "I may as well dawdle and go directly to Mass."

Mom didn't waste time diving right into her subject. This time, her practical directness was lifesaving. She lowered her voice, "Did anybody help you?"

"You mean, do I have a connection?"

"Yes, yes," Mom's voice trembled. "Do you know anybody who can help us with the same type of paperwork?"

"I do." The answer took her breath away. "He has been reliable and has helped many people before me."

"Please," Mom could hardly contain her excitement. "Give me his name and address. I will be indebted to you forever."

Never a good storyteller, Mom nonetheless spared us no details of her serendipitous exchange at the farewell dinner. In due course, my parents began to apply for exit visas to Belgium as they tried multiple ways to secure my freedom, to no avail. Desperate, my mother approached any stranger who might be able to intervene for my release. When she happened to find such a person, a retired officer from Sông Bé, the area where I was detained who knew almost everyone there, she wooed him with tokens of appreciation. She called him "my adoptive brother" as she poured him tea and offered him snacks. She smiled prettily under my father's very eyes. She would be Kiều herself, if her life's tale would require this next chapter, if my freedom would dictate a sacrifice of that magnitude. My reserved mother, my oak, the pouncing cat with sharp claws in my childhood years, had learned the art of enticement.

My homecoming did not stop the man's visits. He had never claimed to be my savior, but Mom swore it was all possible because of him and continued to dote on him. I had to say, the man was manly: large shoulders, towering figure, tan, with the large steps of soldiers.

Meanwhile, sister Mai had already secured all the necessary entry visas to Belgium, and the UNHCR (United Nations Haut Commissariat of Refugees) had promised her plane tickets. Our application for family reunification had been submitted and was going through the maze of bureaucracy and inflated roadblocks that demanded the exchange of cash. The new connection that Mom had established was there to smooth out the wrinkles in the lengthy process. Aunt Huỳnh had said to Mom, "It is believed that witnessing the midnight blooming of orchids will fulfill one's most fervent wish. Be with me when these bloom."

Finally, it was time to pay the person who would hand-deliver our applications for the necessary signatures and approval stampings. The payment in gold, slowly accumulated for this day, was hidden in a box inside our bedroom, whose door was locked during the day, while we gathered in our lighthouse for our daily lessons.

Unbeknownst to us, someone else also had the key to our bedroom, someone Aunt Huỳnh had trusted with her bundle of keys when she was away at church. That someone entered our bedroom one day and took all the gold bars from underneath the pile of fabrics, soap bars, and medicines.

Sobbing hysterically, our mother recounted the minutes after she entered our bedroom in the dark. She flipped the light switch as usual, and the box was placed by the wall with our sleeping mats piled on it, as usual. She went to touch her gold bars, an obsessive habit, to know that she would have them when the time came. She opened the box, searching through the items for the cold touch of her gold bars. They were gone. Hysterical, she dived into the box and lifted the fabrics out one by one, shaking each furiously. Then, seized by an unreasonable last hope, she turned the box over. Nothing. She immediately looked around, thinking, perhaps, she had moved the gold somewhere else.

"I am losing my mind," she told Dad. "I'm having a nightmare while fully awake."

No! It could not be. Nothing was different. It was as if the gold bars had never existed and their memory in her head was the product of a deranged mind. She looked around, doubting herself, trying to pierce the mystery that now shrouded the atmosphere she breathed, trying to find the inexplicable cause for her loss. She fell backward, then getting back on her feet, tried hard to scream out to us. But her voice was lost. She dashed out along the dark corridors toward the terrace, trying to breathe the warm vapor of the noodle factory, her heart racing, her vocal cords constricted, her lips parched.

"Anh Khoa! Anh Khoa! The gold is gone. Gone!"

That was when we heard her. I had never seen my mother in the state she was that day, and for a moment I feared she had gone berserk like her cousin. Things like this ran in the family. Tears were streaming down, choking her moaning, her unintelligible words. "Gone, nothing left. What are we going to do? What are we going to do?"

I took her by both her shoulders, "Mom! What happened, Mom?"

"She must have woken from a bad dream," Patrick murmured, thinking about his own experience and the nightmares he often had when he was younger.

But Mom raged at him, "Ill-trained one! Who are you to tell me my state? I am not crazy." Then she turned to Dad, her mouth quivering. "It's gone, our gold."

It was a shocking discovery to all of us. Dad walked Mom back to our bedroom, and together our family inspected every item in that box, searching through all the corners, opening all the cupboards, just to make sure nobody had rearranged the bedroom and moved the gold to some other place. Methodically, eliminating all speculations, Dad queried the details of each household member's whereabouts throughout the day. Who was last to leave the bedroom? Was it properly locked? Were any of the windows to the outside left open?

Did anyone notice any of the windows to the noodle factory below forced in? How was the box when Mom found it? Was it obvious that someone had fumbled through the room to search for valuables and chanced upon our treasure? "No" was the answer to all of Dad's questions.

Dad questioned my aunt next about her visitors and acquaintances that day. The little girl who lived next door had easy access to Aunt Huỳnh's room on the second floor through a communicating door linking the two properties, per Aunt Huỳnh's arrangement to obtain the girl's help with small chores. The girl was about twelve, a solitary and timid figure who admired our sisters Anne and Michelle and silently sought their friendship through unrequested favors, like washing our dishes during our absence and lending us novels to read. She never spoke a word to any of us. We ignored her furtive presence and her good deeds but accepted her books when she brought them over. Although my aunt had complained about losing small items to her, we could not see in her the adept thief we sought. First, she would not have known what we had in the bottom of that box. Second, even if she had accessed our room, we presumed she would, being a small kid, remove the valuables that were in plain sight first, the fabrics and other things lying on top of the gold. She would have to fumble through the room first, not going directly to the box as if she had intimate knowledge of its contents.

While Dad proceeded with his meticulous approach to solving the crime, Mom sunk into a depression. She had no one to confide in, except Angel. So good to our family, cheerful and effective, she had been helping whenever she could, and often accompanied Dad, who always preferred the company of a female assistant, on errands. She knew we were getting ready to leave Vietnam and had recently visited the emigration office on Nguyễn Du with Dad to apply for our exit visas. My parents often talked about her as a benevolent addition to our household, and had promised to help her emigrate once we were safely settled abroad. She had been with Mom to the markets to buy and sell. She came to pray with us sometimes and participate in our family conversation after dinner. In the absence of a resolution, Mom was compelled to share our painful loss with Angel, seeking to unburden herself and elicit some feminine understanding.

Angel wrapped Mom in her arms, and Mom broke again into tears as she told her of the consequences of this loss. Our prospects of leaving Vietnam would end, since it would be impossible to re-initiate the lengthy emigration appeal process, including setting aside enough money for the cost, in time to save Patrick. My brother, being almost eighteen, would be drafted into military service. We simply could not afford to wait. It seemed the devils were against us. Angel's tears welled up in her pockmarked face. She knew our long suffering. She knew our ill fates.

"What if I lend you money," she inquired, gently. "Would it help, Mrs. Khoa?"

"What can you do? It's not a small sum," Mom murmured, touched by her willingness to sacrifice, knowing the situation of Angel's own poor family with numerous members.

"No, really! I can arrange for it. I have friends."

"Miss, you are too good. But I don't need small money. We need gold. Bars of gold."

"Three bars? Four?"

Mom looked up, suddenly alert. "More!"

"How many more?"

"A lot more. Twice as much."

"I can only help you with four more bars." Angel stood and pulled Mom up, reaffirming her proposition without hesitation. "I will bring them to you next week. Let me arrange it."

That night, Mom talked with Dad in her low voice for a long time. By bits and pieces, we understood that Angel's extraordinary proposal had awakened an old suspicion in Mom. Months ago, three of our bikes were stolen from downstairs. At the time, we blamed the theft on the noodle factory workers. We should not have left our bikes there to tempt the destitute. After that incident, we took pains to bring our bikes upstairs to our bedroom. We kept our valuables in a big carton box next to our sleeping area. In the box were yards of imported fabrics that we sold intermittently to raise cash as we needed. Returning from visiting Angel's parents' crowded home one evening, Patrick pulled Mom aside to share with her something that had puzzled him. "I saw clothes in the same fabric color and design as ours. Could it be coincidence?" My parents had dismissed his suggestions as mere associations. Fabrics do look alike when not being compared side by side; patterns with square shapes can resemble one another more or less but are not identical. However, to find any similar pattern or color in Saigon would have been very rare, since all the fabrics sold in the market came from private sources in small quantities.

Now, those minor and unrelated incidents formed a definite pattern in Mom's mind. The missing pieces of a complex puzzle fell in place as if by magic. Aunt Huỳnh had also confirmed that her bunch of keys to all the rooms in the house was sometimes trusted to Angel. Mom needed time to ponder. But Dad insisted on a bold move. "Tomorrow, tell her we need eight gold bars. Let's see what she comes up with."

The next day, Mom brazenly suggested to Angel, "Is it possible that we could have eight bars immediately? The payment cannot be delayed."

Angel's eyes widened. "Eight? It's difficult, but not impossible. Give me until tomorrow."

All eight gold bars were placed into Mom's hand within a week's time. There was no other explanation as to how a poor nun could so easily produce these gold bars except to surmise that she was returning them to the owner from whom they had been taken. We did not understand this Dr. Jekyll and Mr. Hyde character, her dark motives and stirred conscience. Dad believed that the higher angels had finally listened to our supplication for a miracle and intervened for us, allowing her turn of heart.

The heavenly stars and planets had finally aligned in our favor. We would now await the night-blooming orchid to flower and fulfill our ultimate wish.

34.

The Flight List

It was Dad's idea to keep a family diary beginning June 16, 1982, to record our last days in Vietnam. He had wanted us to practice our English writing on these pages.

Our emigration document had left Hanoi around April 21, 1982, with the much-prayed-for approval stamp to release us from our long "penitentiary" in Vietnam. These documents were en route to the Interior Affairs office on Nguyễn Trãi Boulevard, Hồ Chí Minh City. We continued to pray for the swift and safe arrival of our paperwork, keeping our hope alive but in check, ready for any last-minute derailment. Dad kept a meticulous list of all the bureaucratic hurdles, and one by one checked them off until the final step, in which we would be placed on a confirmed Flight List. Our exit permits were signed on May 30th. We were hoping to be listed on July 8, 1982.

In the meanwhile, we tried to live as normally as we could, adhering to our busy schedules. Each Monday, Dad and Angel visited the emigration office to scan its walls for the awaited Flight List. Mom and I went downtown daily to purchase the special lacquered paintings with mother-of-pearl and sea-shell inlays which were well appreciated by the West, along with embroidered silk fabrics and blouses, and, per Dad's request, a traditional *đàn tranh*, a seventeen-string zither. The reason for all these last-minute purchases was clear and simple: Since gold could not be taken out of the country, we had to convert our soon-useless money into valuable goods—coveted Vietnamese products that could be brought with us. If nothing went wrong, these exotic items would be gifts to our family abroad to show our appreciation for the years they provided for us. But if we found ourselves penniless in foreign lands, turned away by our family—"a remote possibility nevertheless worth preparing for," as Dad said— these would-be presents could be easily sold and converted to cash for immediate survival. After seven years of continuous training, it was only natural that we had mastered "disaster preparedness."

During this period, Michelle and Patrick continued to play tennis twice a week and had drum lessons every Monday, Wednesday, and Friday from nine-thirty to eleven o'clock in the morning. Here is what Michelle wrote on June 6th about her class:

It's noon. I just returned from my drum lesson. It took place inside a large room with four red walls, studded with dozens of large nails. On each of these nails hung three, sometimes four, string instruments. They were mostly guitars, with the exception of two mandolins. All of them were beaten up, badly scratched and engraved with crude drawings of nude women. Words like "I love you" scaled the bare walls like some grotesque folk art. In the farthest corner of this room stood two sets of drums, old, neglected, with their heads punctured and their shells covered with graffiti. The dozen students looked no better, scrubby and bedraggled, contrasting sharply with the one teacher, a Jack-of-all-trades with well-oiled hair, all decked out in white, calf-length, five-inch heeled boots, shirt neatly tucked in, its white fabric now a shade of tarnished vanilla.

Dad's entry on June 18th was a mix of hope and acceptance.

We continued to wait for the orchid cactus to bloom. The first bud opened one week before the return of Hồng-Mỹ. It has been raining almost continuously. The termite-infested door shook with each strong wind, dumping as much cold liquid onto us through the cracks

*and holes with each push and grope as if we were fighting the
elements standing in the streets. The wind knocked off everything in
its path, from papers to books, sending me flying left then right to
retrieve them. Even our tiny bamboo furniture was not spared, lying
on their sides like prostrating dogs. Could it be to blow away all our
misfortunes? We both, Hồng-Mỹ and myself, like two true monk
poets, sat mute in the turbulent rain to appreciate its wide range of
sound and to wonder about the safety of Mr. Parrot, our parakeet,
who had finally left his cage for the open sky. Perhaps, through John
Masefield's verses, the open skies are beckoning us to follow Mr.
Parrot:*

> *My road calls me, lures me*
> *West, east, south, and north;*
> *Most roads lead men homewards,*
> *My road leads me forth.*

Patrick neatly penned:

*The last days are passing fast, yet Dad insisted that we continue our
studies. At the mentioning of "vacation," Dad would frown and a
worried look shadowed his face. He wanted us to be well prepared for
entrance into good schools. "Children," he often reminded us, "we
have lost seven years, but that is not an excuse for any of you to not
succeed in life. All we need is will—the will to become great, to be at
the top, to achieve our goals."*

On June 23th, Dad spelled out his reasons for the importance of
our continued perseverance in education.

*How to reconcile conflicting interests? Daddy wants his kids to spend
most of their time in studies. Mom wants them to accompany her on
her business trips. Not that she needs their assistance, only their
companionship. The kids like to go out with their mom. It's
understandable that kids prefer pleasure to serious work, but their*

future lies in their studies. I incessantly remind Mom of this, but she does not seem to be convinced that a college education is necessary to earn a living. It is possible that Mom has preferences for simplicity and poverty, as preached Jesus. There is, however, a difference. Jesus can make miracles, while we cannot. Jesus can transform water into wine, while we cannot fly a rocket without proper training.

His entry on June 24th depicted the excitement of the unfolding events. We were scheduled to appear at the Emigration Office to have our fingerprints taken. The Flight List was officially posted. We would be on Air France Flight Number 175, departing from Saigon at three in the afternoon on July 15, 1982.

Dad quoted Tennyson's thought:

> *Who can say*
> *Why To-day*
> *To-morrow will be yesterday?*
> *Who can tell*
> *Why to smell*
> *The violet, recalls the dewy prime*
> *Of youth and buried time?*
>
> *(from "Song")*

On July 7th, we picked up our plane tickets from the Air Vietnam Office on Nguyễn Huệ Street. We were only given tickets to Bangkok and were left still in the dark about the rest of our trip to our final destination in Belgium. Among the formalities to finalize our departure were clearance with the Customs and Tax Office and release from the Real Estate Office. The final navigation through the bureaucracy was sheer torture, described by Dad with his usual humor: "Are people without any possessions free of material burden? Not in Vietnam. I had been dragging my feet from one office to the next to prove to the government that I no longer own any property on this land. The Real Estate Office needed a certification from our current landlord that she was indeed the owner of the property we lived in. I did not know what to tell Auntie Huỳnh. Should I insist that she prove the actual ownership of a property she has been living in for the last thirty years and that she had the charity to let us share? I think she would boot me mercilessly."

On July 9th, Dad debated in the diary about whether to bring his parents' ashes with us.

Our studies at home were officially suspended for many reasons. Both parents were extremely busy with many preparations to fulfill the government requirements before our departure. I was busy packing for the whole family. Patrick needed time to sell off the remaining goods that we still held.

On July 10th, Dad's wish to send Uncle Linh a final package was fulfilled. Uncle Linh was still held in a concentration camp after seven years, without a date of release. Dad's writings in our family diary were full of reminiscences. In it, as if to bring our whole past with us, he pasted in old photographs of family members, of Grandpa and Grandma and their eleven children, of our family of nine in various episodes of our lives from 1966 to the present. "All mingled inside my mind," he wrote in the diary's pages, "the past, the present, and the anxiety for our future. It was rumored that we could be detained in a concentration camp once inside Bangkok. What is to become of us? All this euphoria acted like a strong wine on my tired mind and body, the shadows piercing through the blinding rays of our recent happiness."

On July 12th, a government-authorized rental van brought our luggage to Tân Sơn Nhất Airport for a final inspection and weigh-in. Each passenger was allowed 25 kg, a lifetime in one bag. That night, Dad met with Angel and told her point-blank, "There might be a possibility that we cannot return the gold you lent us."

She was pale as a sheet and took in the hinted accusation with the restrained posture of a martyr. "I had no choice but to do what I did."

Dad let the silence speak for him.

Angel's voice rasped on, "Help me to get out."

"We'll see," said Dad, in a voice that indicated no sympathy. He had placed a blind faith in her, and her treachery was to him an unforgivable blow. Before he turned away, he said to her, "Miss, do you believe in good and evil?"

I guessed in her silence that the answer would be painful. She said instead, "I believe your family once loved me. And I sense that love exists no longer."

Dad's voice was like steel. "God has mercy. He will help those who are good and true." Then he said goodbye to her. I could not bear to see her tears, for I had seen her cry those same tears for Mom when she first learned of the theft, and yet, it turned out she was the accursed thief, crying only "crocodile tears." A thought occurred to me, then, about the meaning of the word "truth" in the refrain of Dufong's anthem, "Where stands the truth?" Perhaps this was the prisoner-composer's true intention, calling for the truth to answer for itself.

That was our last night at Mỹ-Hưởng.

On July 13th, we moved into Aunt Sự's home to avoid a possible confrontation with Angel and Aunt Huỳnh. Until the last minute we kept a low profile, hiding our happiness from envious hands like a coveted crown. The Lês gathered to celebrate our freedom and bid us farewell. It was a subdued celebration. Once a large and joyous clan with over sixty members, it had been decimated to a couple of men and a dozen women and children. Present were Aunt Linh and her three children (her second son had escaped on a boat), Uncle and Aunt Sự and their four children (three had landed safely in Thailand), and Aunt Trọng with only two of her five children.

On the last page of our diary, Dad's farewell was directed to Tân Sa Châu, our childhood home of fifteen years, to Mom's pharmacy, to Saigon the bygone city and all its streets where we had traveled—then by car and now on foot and bicycle. Goodbye to all our schools, to Cercle Sportif Saigonnais, to Trương Minh Giảng Market, to Bến Thành Center, to our city cathedral, to our whole past.

Farewell, beautiful country of my childhood.

The coach is at the door at last;
The eager children, mounting fast
And kissing hands, in chorus sing:
Good-bye, good-bye, to everything!
. . .
Crack goes the whip, and off we go;
The trees and houses smaller grow;
Last, round the woody turn we swing:
Good-bye, good-bye, to everything!

(From "Farewell to the Farm" by Robert Louis Stevenson)

A day after the celebration of the Bastille, we boarded the air-conditioned Boeing 747 operated by Air France airline. I wore a bright yellow tunic, intricately embroidered, over soft black slacks—a sunflower blooming.

As soon as we sat down in our respective seats, as soon as the plane doors were closed, we began to relax; our fear of last-minute catastrophes dissipated as the plane lifted into the air. The lilted greeting words of the French air hostess floated like a song as I looked out my cabin window to see white clouds, like cotton poufs to swaddle me, a newborn. *"Bienvenue à Air France, Mesdames et Messieurs!"*

For seven long years, we had been mere puppets behind a Red Curtain, jerked to dance in a multiple-act tragedy by an invisible stage manager, our lives suspended by mere strings.

How do I describe that moment of sublime joy, except to say that we were finally cut loose, human once again, on our own feet, stepping outside the Red Curtain into the sun, finally able to reveal to the world who we truly were?

The long drama in which we were reluctant players had finally ended.

Epilogue

We lost everything with Saigon: our birthplace and the burial grounds of our ancestors, a lifestyle rooted in North Vietnam and transformed by the Southern culture, and all the landmarks of our youth. What memories that remained have grown old with us. We are the last of a generation to preserve South Vietnam's history and prevent it from being written over into a version that would eradicate our place in the world, making our heroes into losers. We are the last witnesses still carrying our old scars, thriving yet not entirely free of suffering.

When I sat down to write this memoir, the hovering specter of my past slowly took shape, revealing its prior form. I thought I was able to forget and dismiss the painful loss, but as the words poured out, my loss reappeared in its original torture, and I suffered all over again, cried all over again, and all over again lost my home, my school, my childhood dreams, my youth, Grandma and Uncle Huỳnh, and the trust in everlasting loyalty between family members. I realized I am a casualty—not of war but of peace. The emigrated Vietnamese like me are victims of the world's treaties, conveniently formed to safeguard and enrich a few countries, and conveniently abandoned once our mutual alliance was exhausted.

Unless I took my time to reassemble the fragments of my

generation's history, tell the story until now untold, my deliverance would be a waste, my reclamation an unfinished labor.

Unlike the destruction of Pompeii, the death of my beloved city did not obliterate all lives. Saigon still lingers in a ghostly life. Her identity was simply carved away. Saigon goes on under an assumed name, wearing her new garments, pretending to have new ideals, and obeying her new bosses. Slowly, time has smoothed the phenomenal losses and pain, replacing the mountains of grief with valleys of vague memories, a past that was perhaps only imagined. The ghosts have given birth to new lives. The city lives on in bondage.

When I sat down to write this book, I strained to recollect the events of the past. I had no desire to recapture those seven years of our life, to retrace my steps behind the Red Curtain and look for the child that I once was. But as a writer, I had the responsibility to tell my story. I had to go back in time to a place I'd rather forget. The young girl had to speak up for herself and for many others, to relay what we had experienced with the loss of our country.

She had to tell the world what had happened after the last helicopter left Saigon, after the curtain had come down. How her family and she—the young girl who no longer dared to dream—had survived the collapse of the only world they had known, to face the Red Regime, the loss of freedom that came with it, the deprivation of basic rights, and how they had clawed their way out.

Vietnamese are now all over the world, speaking different languages, singing different national anthems. By no fault of their own they were dispersed, all the while holding on to their identities. Inside each heart is home.

I had to write my story, for I believe it belongs in the latest chapters of my people's history. And although my life has taken a new direction and my future is here, in America, how can I ever deny it, deep down I am a Vietnamese robbed of my birthplace. My country still writhes under a dictatorship, suffering silently behind the Red Curtain.

Acknowledgments

This book is a tribute to my parents. They valiantly fought the communist regime with everything they had, down to their last cents and breaths, with bleeding fists and hearts, to bring our family to freedom and back together.

I wrote this memoir on stolen time—in between cooking, after homeschool lessons with my son, over long summer nights— wherever and whenever I could. Some paragraphs were written in my head as I commuted. I worked in solitude, learning as I wrote. I forged ahead with few words of encouragement. Writing, after all, is a demanding yet uncompensated job. And who am I? A first-generation immigrant with little English, a third language borrowed late in life.

I was doubtful of my writing ability. Despite the odds, just like my parents, I forged on. The burning desire to pass down our legacy to my children was my driving force. I thank God for granting me this passion to write and my family for allowing me to pursue this long-thought as a hopeless project.

I especially thank the devotion of my very first two editors. Christina Pineda volunteered countless hours to correct my first draft. Her devotion gave me the confidence to join a critique group. Libby Grande infused professionalism into my writing and elevated me to the rank of committed writers.

I would have given up my difficult literary journey without the support and camaraderie of the Writers' Club of Whittier. Until the realization of this book, I had thought it would be better for all involved that this past, so successfully blocked from my consciousness, be left untold. Turns out, this has been my most gratifying experience.

Without Los Nietos Press, especially my publisher Frank Kearns, my memoir would still linger in megabytes, and my story would be buried untold.

I owe the final, meticulous editing of Behind the Red Curtain to my editor, Beverly Voigt, who kept my voice intact but helped me polish the manuscript to near perfection.

Now that my memory of the past events was safeguarded from the corruption of time, I found in my memoir a reward, an incomparable solace, knowing that the lost years were also the pages of my life. I am proud to have achieved two goals: to leave a family record for my children and, most importantly to debut my writing career. With this book, I am freed from my bondage to practicality.

My retreat into the past brought forward, incidentally, another wish: the wish to contribute my survivor's witness. This book is about my personal loss, which reflects the collective loss the Vietnamese diaspora have suffered. It is a tribute to all who have lost their place of birth, family, faith, courage—a whole lifespan—by their forced emigration.

About the Author

Born and raised in Saigon, Vietnam, Hồng-Mỹ Basrai (née Lê) is fluent in Vietnamese and French. Hồng-Mỹ's love for literature and languages was evident from a very young age. Transplanted at age twenty-two to Southern California, she picked up English and improvised with the borrowed language to make it her own. She holds a Chemical Engineering degree and some degrees of self-taught English. Hồng-Mỹ's writings can be found in Eastlit Literary Journal, 2011 Writing from Inlandia Anthology, East Jasmine Review, Invisible Memoirs "Lionhearted". She is a member of the Writers Club of Whittier.

Also by Los Nietos Press

*Dutch Girl from Jakarta: from Indonesian Concentration Camp
    to Freedom,* Maria Zeeman (2020)

Star Chasing, Thomas R. Thomas (2019)

*Dancing in the Santa Ana Winds: Poems y Cuentos
    New and Selected,* liz gonzález (2018)

California Trees, Kit Courter (2018)

Wingless, Linda Singer (2017)

Sharing Stories: Global Voices Coming Together,
    Various Authors (2016)

The Beatle Bump, Clifton Snider (2016)

Yearlings, Frank Kearns (2015)

So Cali, Trista Dominqu (2015)

Persons of Interest, Lorine Parks (2015)

ABOUT
LOS NIETOS PRESS

Los Nietos Press is dedicated to the countless generations of people whose lives and labor created the world community that today spreads over the coastal floodplain known simply as Los Angeles.

We take our name from the Los Nietos Spanish land grant that was south and east of the downtown area. Our purpose is to serve local writers so they may share their words with many, in the form of tangible books that can be held and read and passed on. This written art form is one way we realize our common bonds and help each other discover what is meaningful in life.

LOS NIETOS PRESS
www.LosNietosPress.com
LosNietosPress@Gmail.com